Confessional Identity in East-Central Europe

This book is dedicated to
the memory of Pompiliu Teodor

Confessional Identity in East-Central Europe

Edited by

MARIA CRĂCIUN, OVIDIU GHITTA and
GRAEME MURDOCK

Ashgate

Published by
Ashgate Publishing Limited
Gower House
Croft Road
Aldershot
Hants GU11 3HR
England

Ashgate Publishing Company
131 Main Street
Burlington
Vermont 05401–5600
USA

Ashgate website: http://www.ashgate.com

British Library Cataloguing in Publication Data

Confessional identity in East-Central Europe. - (St Andrews Studies in Reformation History)
1. Theology, Doctrinal – History – Modern period, 1500-
2. Europe, Central – Church history 3. Europe, Eastern – Church history
I. Crăciun, Maria II. Ghitta, Ovidiu III. Murdock, Graeme
280'.0943

Library of Congress Control Number: 2001095453

ISBN 0 7546 0320 2

This book is printed on acid free paper.

Typeset in Sabon by Bournemouth Colour Press, Parkstone and printed in Great Britain by MPG Books Ltd., Bodmin, Cornwall.

Contents

St Andrews Studies in Reformation History

List of figures

Notes on contributors

Joachim Bahlcke of the Centre for the History and Culture of East Central Europe in Leipzig, is associate lecturer at the Humboldt University of Berlin and at the University of Leipzig. His publications include *Regionalismus und Staatsintegration im Widerstreit. Die Länder der Böhmischen Krone im ersten Jahrhundert der Habsburgerherrschaft 1526–1619* (1994), *Schlesien und die Schlesier* (1996/2000), and he was co-editor of *Ständefreiheit und Staatsgestaltung in Ostmitteleuropa* (1996), *Handbuch der historischen Stätten Böhmen und Mähren* (1998), *Konfessionalisierung in Ostmitteleuropa* (1999), and *L. Petry-Breslau und seine ersten Oberherren aus dem Hause Habsburg* (2000).

Maria Crăciun is a senior lecturer in the Department of History at the Babeş-Bolyai University of Cluj, Romania. She has written *Protestantism şi ortodoxie in Moldova secolului al XVI-lea* (1996). Her recent publications include several articles on the development of piety in Transylvania and Moldavia prior to and during the Reformation. Together with Ovidiu Ghitta she has edited *Ethnicity and Religion in Central and Eastern Europe* (1995) and *Church and Society in Central and Eastern Europe* (1998).

Carmen Florea is a doctoral student in the Department of History at the Babeş-Bolyai University of Cluj, Romania. Her thesis deals with the cult of saints in late medieval Transylania. Her current research interests include urban patterns of religious devotion, and she has also worked on funeral orations in eighteenth-century Transylvania.

Thomas Fudge is a senior lecturer in the Department of History at the University of Canterbury, Christchurch in New Zealand. He has written *The Magnificent Ride: The First Reformation in Hussite Bohemia* (1998), several articles on late medieval and Reformation history (mainly on Hussites), as well as two books on American religious history. He is currently working on a documentary history of the Hussite Crusades, and a separate volume on the social implications of heresy in the period 1100–1700.

Csilla Gábor teaches in the department of Hungarian literature at the Babeş-Bolyai University of Cluj, Romania. She obtained her doctoral degree at the Lajos Kossuth University, Debrecen in Hungary in 1999. She is currently engaged in research into Catholic devotional literature of the seventeenth century.

Ovidiu Ghitta is a lecturer in the Department of History at the Babeş-Bolyai University of Cluj, Romania. He has published several articles on the history of the Uniate Church in Hungary and Transylvania, and is currently completing his doctoral thesis on the institutional development of the Uniate Church in Hungary during the eighteenth century. Together with Maria Crăciun he has edited *Ethnicity and Religion in Central and Eastern Europe* (1995) and *Church and Society in Central and Eastern Europe* (1998).

Judith Kalik teaches in the Department of Russian and Slavonic Studies at the Hebrew University of Jerusalem. Her doctoral thesis on 'The Catholic Church and the Jews in the Polish-Lithuanian Commonwealth during the seventeenth and eighteenth centuries' was completed in 1998, and she has published a number of articles in this field.

Graeme Murdock is lecturer in modern history at the University of Birmingham. His recent publications include *Calvinism on the Frontier, 1600–1660. International Calvinism and the Reformed Church of Hungary and Transylvania* (2000), 'The importance of being Josiah: an image of Calvinist identity', *Sixteenth Century Journal* (1998), 'Dressed to repress?: Protestant clergy dress and the regulation of morality in early modern Europe', *Fashion Theory. The Journal of Dress, Body and Culture*, 4 (2000) and 'Magyar Judah: Constructing a new Canaan in eastern Europe' in Robert Swanson (ed.), *The Holy Land, Holy Lands, and Christian History. Studies in Church History*, 36 (2000).

Pompiliu Teodor was Professor in the Department of History at the Babeş-Bolyai University of Cluj, Romania. He published a number of books on the Romanian Enlightenment, and on the history of the Uniate Church in Transylvania. In addition he published several articles relating to historiographical questions.

Krista Zach has taught at the Department of South-East European History at the University of Munich, and is now director of the Institute of German Culture and History of South-Eastern Europe at Munich. She has worked on the history of churches, minority communities, and on agrarian history. Her publications include *Orthodoxe Kirche und rumänisches Volksbewußtsein (15.–18. Jh.)* (1977), *Die bosnische Franziskanermission des 17. Jahrhunderts in Niederungarn* (1979), and *Konfession – Nation – Ethnikum im Donaukarpatenraum* (2001).

Preface

This project began with the idea for a conference on the significance of printed religious texts in east-central Europe during the early modern period. We were delighted by the enthusiastic response of those who participated in the conference, held at the University of Cluj in the summer of 1999. This encouraged us to try to develop further some of the ideas which had been discussed at Cluj. We felt that only a collection of articles by a range of scholars could hope to provide satisfactory treatment of this area, since printed literature was produced in such a wide variety of languages for different churches across the territories of east-central Europe. Much attention has rightly, and perhaps inevitably, focused on Transylvania in this book, but we regret that coverage of the Czech lands is not now as extensive as we originally had hoped.

Completing this project has involved maintaining long-distance contacts between a widely dispersed group of authors. Everyone has responded to the occasional problems that have arisen with patience and good humour. We are very grateful to all involved. For too long contact between western and eastern Europe was stifled by political division, and remains afflicted by cultural differences and mutual suspicion. In producing a book on sixteenth-century religious and cultural history, when east-central Europe played a key role in the Continent's affairs, is seems entirely appropriate that it be a work of true cooperation between western and eastern Europeans.

Maria Crăciun, Ovidiu Ghitta and Graeme Murdock
2002

Note on place-names

Many towns and villages in east-central Europe have several names which are used by the different linguistic communities of the region. The names by which towns and counties were mostly known in the early modern period are sometimes now less widely known than their modern equivalents. We wish to do justice to this variety of place-names in the region, without overwhelming the reader. Thus, names will appear here in their modern form, so that Romanian names are given for all towns in the current territory of Romania, Hungarian names for all towns in Hungary and so on. However, where it seems most necessary, when place-names are first mentioned alternative names will also be given.

CHAPTER ONE

Religious reform, printed books and confessional identity

Maria Crăciun, Ovidiu Ghitta and Graeme Murdock

The lands of east-central Europe played an integral part in the process of religious reform during the early modern period, but the significance of this region has been largely neglected by historians. However, since the collapse of contemporary political barriers in Europe, the true breadth of the Continent has become more apparent, and the need to include the territories of east-central Europe within narratives about the Reformation, as within many other aspects of European history, has increasingly been recognized as a pressing one.[1] Religious reform affected east-central Europe from the Hussite movement of the fifteenth century, to the different strains of sixteenth-century Reformation thought, to various waves of reform within the Catholic Church, to the emergence of Greek Catholic churches up to the early eighteenth century. In the Polish-Lithuanian commonwealth, the lands of the Bohemian crown, and across the former Hungarian kingdom, a range of churches attempted to establish their distinct systems of belief during the early modern period and to shape the religious identity of local communities. An extraordinary multiplicity of religions found support in this region: Catholics, Utraquists, Bohemian Brethren, Lutherans, Anabaptists, Calvinists, anti-Trinitarians, Orthodox, Greek Catholics, Muslims and Jews. Each confessional group was concerned to legitimize their own position, proclaiming the historic orthodoxy of their doctrine, and attempting to distance themselves from those they identified as innovating radicals and heretics. Many of these religious groups failed to gain support from state authorities. However, political and social power was divided between monarchs and their estates across this region, and where churches or movements of reform could gain noble converts they were often also able to receive constitutional recognition, as part of estates' desire to balance their corporate rights against the pretensions of royal sovereignty.

---

[1] For example, see the comments of Andrew Pettegree, 'Reformation Europe re-formed', *History Today* 49 (1999), pp. 10–16.

The early modern confessional environment of east-central Europe was thus marked by a wide variety of religions, by the development of distinct institutional frameworks for each church, by attempts to gain social support for different religious ideas, especially from the large ranks of nobles and from urban communities, and by struggles to gain legal protection for churches. Each church faced challenges from established rivals, and the battle for confessional space often centred on clarifying points of difference between churches almost as much as positively defining what each church stood for. This volume discusses such efforts to establish confessional identity in east-central Europe, and assesses the degree to which religious ideas were successfully transmitted to the social elites and to the ordinary people of the region. Taking into consideration the political environment which shaped the development of different confessions, it seeks to examine how far urban and rural communities were acculturated to different religious experiences, looking at the creation and reception of religious discourse during this period. This introduction will establish a framework for the different case-studies pursued here, provide a guide to the progress of religious reform in east-central Europe, and focus on the particular issues which will be examined by authors in this volume.

The construction of different churches in the wake of reform movements across the Continent is in many ways comparable, involving the production of agreed statements on key points of doctrine, making alterations to systems of ritual and patterns of worship, developing institutions to bolster reform, and establishing political and social support for reform.[2] Across much of early modern Europe success for religious reformers was often dependent on gaining state support for their cause. Territorial authorities could offer rights freely to practise religion, support the establishment of colleges and schools, and back measures which aimed to improve standards of moral conduct. States crucially also offered churches the prospect of establishing confessional dominance within their territories. The benefits of allying with state power for any church were matched by benefits for territorial rulers of having their authority sacralized by a church and gaining support for projects of social discipline. Confessional loyalty was also of great political significance to early modern rulers, as a force which could be harnessed to the interests of the state. A model of confessionalization, according to which alliances were forged between secular and ecclesiastical elites to dominate early modern states, offers a top-down

---

2 Robert Wuthnow, *Communities of Discourse, Ideology and Social Structure in the Reformation, the Enlightenment and European Socialism* (Cambridge [MA]: Harvard University Press, 1989).

vision of the institutionalization of reform and the growing integration of territorial states in this period. The confessional identity of officially-sanctioned religions took on a particular form, dominated by social elites, although ordinary people did not become merely passive recipients of religious discourse.[3]

East-central European rulers identified the potential advantages to be gained from an alliance with a particular religion. However, in the territories of east-central Europe, where confessional uniformity seemed to be fractured beyond repair, a different sort of relationship was established between states and a variety of religions for much of this period. Moves towards legal acceptance of confessional difference and widespread social tolerance of a range of churches in this region reveal an alternative path towards state-building, which reflected the potentially disruptive and centrifugal, rather than centripetal, forces which could be unleashed by attempting to build a confessional state.[4]

While churches in some territories across the Continent gained exclusive rights to practise their religion, in east-central Europe churches were forced to acknowledge the existence of immediate competition from rivals. Intolerance of confessional diversity could come from courts, and attempts to achieve religious uniformity often equated loyalty to the ruler's religion with loyalty to the state. Most church hierarchies also regarded one another with suspicion and hostility. The triumph of confessionalism in any territory was therefore frequently marked by the violent rejection of alternative churches and fostered aggressive militancy towards perceived heresies.[5] Popular intolerance

---

3 Joel F. Harrington, Helmut Smith, 'Confessionalization, Community and State Building in Germany, 1555–1870', *Journal of Modern History* 69 (1997), pp. 77–101; Heinz Schilling, 'Confessionalization in the Empire: religion and societal change in Germany between 1550 and 1620' in Schilling, *Religion, Political Culture and the Emergence of Early Modern Society* (Leiden: Brill, 1992); Wolfgang Reinhard, 'État et église dans l'Empire entre réforme et absolutisme' in Jean-Philippe Genet, Bernard Vincent eds, *État et église dans la genèse de l'état moderne* (Madrid: Casa de Velazquez, 1986), pp. 175–86; Heinz Schilling, 'Between the Territorial State and Urban Liberty: Lutheranism and Calvinism in the County of Lippe' in Ronnie Po-chia Hsia ed., *The German People and the Reformation* (Ithaca [NY]: Cornell University Press, 1988), pp. 263–83.

4 Robert Evans, 'Introduction' in Evans, Trevor Thomas eds, *Crown, Church and Estates: Central European Politics in the sixteenth and seventeenth centuries* (London: Macmillan, 1991), pp. xvii–xxix.

5 Ernst Walter Zeeden, *Die Entstehung der Konfessionen grundlagen und Formen der Konfessionsbildung* (Munich: Oldenbourg, 1965); Ernst Walter Zeeden, *Konfessionsbildung: Studien zur Reformation, Gegenreformation und katholischen Reform* (Stuttgart: Klett-Cotta, 1985); Ronnie Po-chia Hsia, *Social Discipline in the Reformation: Central Europe 1550–1750* (London: Routledge, 1992), pp. 53–72, 77–8, 160–73.

was also expressed in some localities against those who would not conform to religious and social norms or who threatened community solidarity. However, leading churchmen and state officials were left in many areas to confront the practical problems caused by religious plurality, especially where the limits of monarchical power required rulers to acquiesce to the presence of religious groups which they could not eradicate. Tolerance of religious difference could therefore be, as in most parts of east-central Europe, a product of legal concessions permitting freedom of conscience and rights of worship to minority religious groups. Local traditions of mutual acceptance of religious difference could also emerge, allowing shared use of church buildings and peaceful coexistence between confessional groups in the same region, town, neighbourhood or even family.[6]

Whether churches could rely on state support or not, and whether they shared territory with confessional rivals or not, their success was partly reliant on the effective transmission of key ideas. All churches were concerned to gain popular conformity to their statements of belief, to establish strict standards of moral conduct, and to eliminate traditional forms of religiosity. The initiative in efforts to transmit systems of belief and behaviour across societies was largely taken by clergy, sometimes with the support of state officials. Efforts to enforce theological orthodoxy and social discipline were pursued in parallel by all the major confessions, although the institutional mechanisms and moral priorities of each church differed. State officials and clergy often worked together to achieve similar disciplinary goals, responding to offences against state laws and moral codes with a mixture of secular and ecclesiastical sanctions. Crucial to the success of programmes to establish confessions was the degree to which parish clergy had effectively been remodelled as a professional body of teachers, agents of social discipline, and reliable channels of information between the centre and their local community. The key role of parish clergy was widely recognized by ecclesiastical and state elites, and much time and energy was devoted to improving the education and professional skills of clergy. The process of gaining acceptance for reform required parish ministers to manage a delicate balance between the interests of their own church hierarchy, of noble patrons or local magistrates, and of their

---

6 Ole Peter Grell, 'Introduction', Robert Scribner, 'Preconditions of tolerance and intolerance in sixteenth-century Germany' in Grell, Scribner eds, *Tolerance and Intolerance in the European Reformation* (Cambridge: University Press, 1996), pp. 1–12, 32–48; Hans Hillerbrand, 'Religious dissent and toleration: Introductory reflections' in Béla Király ed., *Tolerance and Movements of Religious Dissent in Eastern Europe* (New York: Columbia University Press, 1975), pp. 1–10.

congregations. The emergence of the clergy as an order of competent preachers and orthodox teachers with exemplary standards of personal morality was a slow one, but all the churches made progress towards the provision of proficient clergy and reformed religious orders, subject to tight controls from their own superiors.[7]

Attempts by clergy to impose confessional discipline on ordinary people involved challenging popular religious traditions and entering the realm of individuals' private beliefs. One element of this interaction between elite and popular religion concerned adherence to traditional ways of relating to divine power. Some writers have identified a significant change in the early modern period from the communal piety and immanent sense of the sacred in the religiosity of late medieval communities to the emergence of text-based, individualistic and reflective forms of Protestantism and a disciplined, regulated Catholicism. Many Protestant and reformed Catholic clergy were confronted by persistent traditional beliefs and popular devotional practices which proved stubbornly difficult to change. New forms of sacraments and styles of worship with limited visual and sensual stimulation were introduced to communities accustomed to collective piety and the presence of the holy in things and places.[8] Where intrusions on folk traditions and community solidarity were most obviously imposed on ordinary people from above, they normally received a less than enthusiastic response. Levels of cooperation to the demands of churches varied to a significant degree, according to the effectiveness of church institutions, or the degree of state support, and in some areas pressure was also exerted by groups within local communities for conformity to new patterns of belief and behaviour.[9]

Communicating ideas about religion and reform in early modern

---

[7] Andrew Pettegree, 'The Clergy and the Reformation: from devilish priesthood to new professional elite' in Pettegree ed., *The Reformation of the Parishes* (Manchester: University Press, 1993), pp. 1–21; Hsia, *Social Discipline in the Reformation* (1992), pp. 39–52.

[8] Robert Scribner, 'Cosmic Order and Daily Life: Sacred and secular in pre-industrial German society' in Scribner, *Popular Culture and Popular Movements in Reformation Germany* (London: Hambledon Press, 1987), pp. 1–16; Robert Scribner, 'Popular Piety and modes of visual perception in late medieval and reformation Germany', *Journal of Religious History* 15 (1989), pp. 448–69.

[9] Robert Scribner, 'Introduction' in Scribner, Trevor Johnson eds, *Popular Religion in Germany and Central Europe 1400–1800* (London: Macmillan, 1996), pp. 1–15; Eamon Duffy, *The Stripping of the Altars. Traditional Religion in England, c. 1400– c. 1580* (New Haven [CT]: Yale University Press, 1992); Marc Forster, *The Counter-Reformation of the Villages. Religion and Reform in the bishopric of Speyer 1560–1720* (Ithaca [NY]: Cornell University Press, 1992); Christopher Haigh, 'The Continuity of Catholicism in the English Reformation', *Past and Present* 93 (1981), pp. 37–69.

societies could take place through individuals, such as preachers and teachers, through sermons, public debates and private discussions. Alongside oral forms of communication, visual images, including printed images, were also widely used by reformers to convey the essence of their ideas and to attack confessional opponents. However, some Protestant reformers had a profound suspicion about the emotional power which visual imagery could generate. Calvinist or Reformed churches insisted on the removal of religious images from public view by responsible magistrates, although ordinary men, and very often women and the young, sometimes preferred to take matters into their own hands. There was no simple dividing line between Protestants and Catholics on this issue, as some Catholics were critical of the traditional use of images both before and after the Reformation, while some Protestants defended the role of images in stimulating piety in worship, provided this could be done without encouraging superstition.[10]

All churches relied on personal contacts, oral forms of communication, and to some extent used visual images to convey their ideas. They also used written words, especially in printed books, to make their mark on the beliefs of early modern communities. The relationship between the printed word and religion, between books and systems of belief, was an extremely complex one. In particular, the timing of the printing revolution and Protestant Reformation has invited comment on the connection between technological advances in communication and religious reform in early modern Europe. Some historians have depicted Protestantism as a child of the printing revolution and, from Luther onwards, Protestant reformers seemed assured that the authority conveyed through printed texts was their natural ally in propagating true doctrine. For Luther, printing was 'God's highest and extremest act of grace, whereby the business of the Gospel is driven forward'. From England, John Foxe was later equally clear that 'The Lord began to work for His Church not with sword and target to subdue His exalted adversary, but with printing, writing and reading.'[11] Part of Protestantism's potential appeal was to offer every believer the opportunity, previously reserved to the Catholic priesthood, to interact directly with the written sources of Christian belief. However, there are also good reasons to be cautious of the confident claims made

---

[10] Scribner, 'Cosmic Order and Daily Life' (1987), pp. 1–16; Scribner, 'Popular piety and Modes of Visual Perception' (1989), pp. 448–69; Carlos Eire, *War against the idols: the reformation of worship from Erasmus to Calvin* (Cambridge: University Press, 1986).

[11] Quoted in Elizabeth Eisenstein, *The Printing Revolution in Early Modern Europe* (Cambridge: University Press, 1983), pp. 147–8.

by reformers about the impact of the printed word upon the spread of ideas across the Continent. As Robert Scribner commented for Germany, 'the role played by printing is undeniable, but over-concentration on the printed word may seriously distort our understanding of how Reformation ideas spread among the population at large.'[12] Natalie Zemon Davis has also argued that in France 'for most peasants, the religion of the book, the Psalms, and the consistory gave too little leeway to the traditional oral and ritual culture of the countryside, to its existing forms of social life and social control.'[13]

The social impact of religious ideas conveyed through the medium of printed literature was certainly limited to those with access to books. This was related to the speed with which centres of printing spread out across the Continent, to the uneven spread of books from such centres into the countryside, to the gap between spoken forms of language and the standard vernacular used in print, which especially affected many rural areas, and to the extent of state censorship. The social impact of printed literature was also partly related to the cost of books, but although individual ownership of many books remained the privilege of the elite, in towns some sort of popular market for cheap forms of the printed word seems to have been established in many areas by the early seventeenth century.[14] The significance of printing was also restricted to some degree by the numbers of those with some sort of literacy skills. There are great difficulties in finding ways of accurately assessing levels of reading skills in early modern societies, but it seems clear that although the ability to read and write was spreading, beyond the social elites only a limited proportion of the general population had recourse to good skills of reading and writing for much of this period.[15] Early

---

[12] Robert Scribner, *For the Sake of Simple Folk. Popular Propaganda for the German Reformation* (Cambridge: University Press, 1981), p. 1.

[13] Natalie Zemon Davis, 'Printing and the People' in *Society and Culture in Early Modern France: eight essays* (Cambridge: Polity Press, 1987), pp. 189–226.

[14] Roger Chartier, 'Publishing Strategies and what the people read, 1530–1660' in *The Cultural Uses of Print in Early Modern France* (Cambridge: Polity Press, 1989), pp. 145–82; Roger Chartier, 'Figures of the "Other". Peasant Reading in the Age of the Enlightenment' in *Cultural History. Between Practices and Representations*, tr. Lydia Cochrane (Cambridge: Polity Press, 1988), pp. 151–71; Jean-François Gilmont ed., *The Reformation and the book*, tr. Karin Maag (Aldershot: Ashgate, 1998).

[15] Emmanuel Le Roy Ladurie, *The Peasants of Languedoc*, tr. John Day (Urbana [IL]: University of Illinois Press, 1976), pp. 162–4; Robert Scribner, 'Heterodoxy, Literacy and print in the early German Reformation' in Peter Biller, Anne Hudson eds, *Heresy and Literacy, 1000–1530* (Cambridge: University Press, 1994), pp. 255–78; Roger Chartier, 'The Practical impact of writing' in Chartier ed., *A History of Private Life, vol. 3 Passions of the Renaissance*, tr. Arthur Goldhammer (Cambridge [MA]: Harvard University Press, 1989), pp. 111–60.

modern movements of religious reform supported the spread of literacy skills and often promoted efforts to increase access to some formal education, and it was hoped that elementary schools would provide an environment in which ordered, disciplined learning could mould pious, obedient subjects.

Literacy often interacted with oral communication in the spread and reception of ideas, rather than having an innate privilege over other forms of communication. For example, books were commonly read aloud, sustaining a non-literate, hearing public for print. Although the relationship between an individual and a text could be personal and silent, reading was often a public and communal event. Books were commonly deciphered as a collective activity, involving school classes, households and groups of friends. For many, interacting with books was experienced only via guides with proficient reading skills, and access to printed ideas about religion was commonly channelled through educated interpreters, most notably the clergy. Oral and written forms of communicating ideas about religion therefore existed alongside one another in different sorts of combinations and forms between the sixteenth and eighteenth centuries. The considerable and enduring oral residue in this developing literate culture had important consequences for the ways in which religious books were structured and used. It also meant that memory continued to be a crucial skill for many in the art of reading, as books, at least for those with limited or non-existent literacy skills, had to be committed to memory before they could be considered as 'read'. This repetition of the content of books until stored in the memory hardly used the potential of print to its full advantage, as it only provided 'readers' with an inflexible block of knowledge rather than a basis for further enquiry and learning.[16] Authors and printers also attempted to widen access to printed ideas through the frequent use of visual images in books. While such strategies again diluted the intimate connection between rates of literacy and the significance of printed literature, men rather than women and those who lived in towns rather than those who lived in the countryside, remained more likely to be included within the world of printed ideas.

The potentially disruptive impact of unstructured popular access to

---

16 Elizabeth Eisenstein, *The Printing Press as an Agent of Change. Communications and Cultural Transformations in the Early Modern Europe* (2 vols), (Cambridge: University Press, 1979); Steve Ozment, *The Reformation in the Cities. The appeal of Protestantism to sixteenth-century Germany and Switzerland* (New Haven [CT]: Yale University Press, 1975); Jack Goody, 'Introduction' to Goody ed., *Literacy in Traditional Societies* (Cambridge: University Press, 1968), pp. 13–16; see also István György Tóth, *Literacy and written culture in early modern central Europe* (Budapest: CEU Press, 2000).

religious texts quickly became widely appreciated, with fears of spreading heterodoxy, heresy, and challenges to clerical and magisterial authority. Early Protestant reformers, influenced by popular anti-clericalism, had initially believed that the Bible had a plain sense which was accessible to ordinary people and that the common man was the most effective critic of established religion and surest guide to finding truth. However, reformers soon learned that ordinary people could not be relied upon to derive true knowledge about salvation from reading the scriptures for themselves, and questioned the degree of access to the vernacular Bible which should properly be given to the laity. Many came to the view that the authority conveyed by printed words needed to be mediated by clergy and teachers to allow ordinary folk to recognize true from false religion. Thus, the most common Protestant experience of the Bible was at best with the aid of marginal glosses, or through sermons, school-room instruction and devotional literature.[17]

The form of printed religious literature which was most readily suited to this early modern audience, with mixed literacy skills and who were often deemed too unreliable to interact directly with the Bible, was the catechism.[18] Catechisms were often relatively short and therefore cheap to produce. They were intended to be used by groups, including those with limited literacy skills such as women and children, relied on oral dialogue between an authorized interpreter and an audience, and were intended to be committed to memory. Different sorts of catechisms were produced, from shortened versions to detailed descriptions of doctrine in a question-and-answer format. Catechisms were taught in schools, studied at congregational classes, read from the pulpit, became the basis of sermons and the subject of oral examinations, and were learned at home. Members of catechism classes might sometimes have had access to copies of the text, but even then books were mostly only being used as aids to memory. The words of frequently repeated phrases and the cadence of the language in these texts was therefore as much a part of the experience of being catechized as was understanding the doctrinal certainty transmitted by the answers to catechism questions.

Protestant reformers placed enormous store by the effectiveness of catechisms in instructing children in the fundamentals of their faith. Protestant catechisms of the early sixteenth century owed something to

---

17 Scribner, 'Heterodoxy, Literacy and Print' (1994), pp. 263–78.

18 Lucien Febvre suggested that such books of religious instruction were the first with 'a truly mass readership and a popular literature within everybody's reach'; Lucien Febvre, 'The Book and the Reformation' in Febvre, Henri-Jean Martin, *The Coming of the Book. The impact of printing, 1450–1800*, tr. David Gerard (London: Verso Press, 1998), pp. 287–318.

the manuals for confession or preparation for communion used in the pre-Reformation Church, but these had presented doctrine in a far less structured format and placed less emphasis on its moral implications. The contents of Protestant catechisms varied, but were mostly based around explanations of the Ten Commandments, the Apostles' Creed, the Lord's Prayer, and the sacraments of baptism and the Eucharist. The Lutherans led the way in moves to formalize and standardize instruction about basic doctrine through printed catechisms. Martin Luther's 1529 *Catechism* and *Shorter Catechism* became the standard texts used by Evangelical churches. By the end of the sixteenth century sixty editions of the *Shorter Catechism* had been produced in Latin and a further twenty editions in Low German. Luther wrote to John of Saxony on the effect of the catechisms:

> our tender young people, girls as well as boys, are now so well taught in catechism and scripture that my heart grows warm as I observe children praying more devoutly, believing more firmly, and discoursing more eloquently on God and Christ than, in the old days, all the learned monks and doctors.[19]

John Calvin was hardly less enthusiastic about the impact of catechisms, and in the dedication to the 1545 edition of his *Genevan Catechism* he wrote:

> I deem it of good example to testify to the world, that we who aim at the restitution of the Church, are everywhere faithfully exerting ourselves, in order that, at least, the use of the catechism which was abolished some centuries ago under the Papacy, may now resume its lost rights. For neither can this holy custom be sufficiently commended for its utility, not can the Papists be sufficiently condemned for the flagrant corruption, by which they not only set it aside, by converting it into puerile trifles, but also basely abused it to purposes of impure and impious superstition.[20]

Calvin introduced Sunday catechism classes to Geneva, and children were examined on their knowledge of the catechism before their first communion. Calvin's *Catechism* was long and rigorous, but for Calvin it proved itself to be a vital instrument through which to advance reform. In a speech to other Genevan ministers given shortly before his death in 1564, Calvin commented that he would never have returned to Geneva in 1541 if the council 'had not pledged me these two things;

---

[19] Gerald Strauss, *Luther's House of Learning. Indoctrination of the Young in the German Reformation* (Baltimore [MD]: Johns Hopkins University Press 1978), p. 156.

[20] From the dedication of the 1545 edition of the *Catechism of the Church of Geneva* in *Tracts and Treatises in Defence of the Reformed Faith by John Calvin*, ed. Henry Beveridge (3 vols), (Edinburgh: Oliver and Boyd, 1844–51), vol. 2 (1849), p. 36.

namely to keep the catechism and the discipline'.[21] The catechism which was most commonly adopted across the international Reformed community was the 1563 Heidelberg *Catechism*, compiled originally for use in the schools of the Palatinate. This catechism contained a combination of Calvinist, Zwinglian and some Lutheran ideas in 129 questions divided up into 52 sections for weekly lessons, which proved simpler to use than Calvin's own work.[22]

Meanwhile in England, home-grown catechisms were mostly preferred to Continental models. There was also a great deal of confidence about the results of catechizing in England, and in the late 1570s Lancelot Andrewes could preach at Cambridge that by 'our catechizing the papists have lost ground of us, and can never recover it again unless by a more exact course of catechizing than ours'. The use of catechisms in England grew particularly after 1570, and it has been estimated that by the early seventeenth century there were as many as one-and-a-quarter million copies of officially sanctioned and unofficial catechisms in circulation in England, which only had a population of around four million.[23]

The Catholic Church soon responded to the apparent success of catechisms in spreading ideas with their own versions which explained the Ten Commandments, the Apostles' Creed, the Lord's Prayer, the seven sacraments, and also generally included lists of sins and more prayers than Protestant catechisms. The *Catechism* drawn up by the Jesuit Peter Canisius was reprinted 130 times between 1555 and 1600, and was translated into many different languages. The Council of Trent required that children be instructed about the fundamentals of the church's teaching, which was taken in some dioceses to mean that priests needed to begin weekly catechism classes. However, the impact of catechizing varied greatly across Catholic Europe, spreading out from Germany to Italy, but only adopted more slowly in France.[24]

The enthusiasm which religious reformers on all sides showed for catechizing primarily resulted from the view that these books could play

---

[21] William Monter, *Calvin's Geneva* (London: Wiley, 1967), p. 97.

[22] 'The Heidelberg Catechism, 1563' in Arthur Cochrane ed., *Reformed Confessions of the 16th Century* (London: SCM Press, 1966), pp. 305–31.

[23] Ian Green, *The Christian's ABC. Catechisms and Catechizing in England c. 1530–1740* (Oxford: Clarendon, 1996), p. 1; Ian Green, '"For Children in yeeres and children in understanding": The Emergence of the English Catechism under Elizabeth and the early Stuarts', *Journal of Ecclesiastical History* 37 (1986), pp. 397–425; Diarmaid MacCulloch, *The Later Reformation in England, 1547–1603* (London: Macmillan, 1990), p. 167.

[24] John Bossy, 'The Counter Reformation and the People of Catholic Europe', *Past and Present* 47 (1970), pp. 51–70.

a crucial role in educating the mass of ordinary people in the fundamentals of their faith. However, it also marked a withdrawal to some extent from promoting Bibles as the best means by which to transmit true doctrine. German Bibles came to be largely reserved for parish churches and for the educated elite. Luther's experience of the challenge posed by Anabaptism in the 1520s meant that he favoured presenting ordinary people only with a summary of the knowledge required of a true Christian in a catechism, rather than encourage exploration of the Bible itself. Neither the structure of catechisms nor modes of catechizing offered much opportunity for orthodoxy to be questioned. Indeed, the introduction to Luther's 1529 *Shorter Catechism* suggested that 'one must steer and drive the common crowd to learn what counts as right and what counts as wrong in the land where they want to live and earn their daily bread.' By the end of the sixteenth century Evangelicals were also concerned about the proliferation of catechisms by different Lutheran writers in the middle decades of the century, and reverted to recognize Luther's catechisms alone.[25]

There are many reasons to question the practical effectiveness of all this activity to instil basic religious knowledge among ordinary people, taking first into consideration the unwillingness of many clergy to lead catechism classes and the widespread absenteeism of pupils. In France the 1578 national Reformed Church synod had to remind ministers to catechize more frequently 'by short, plain and familiar questions and answers, accommodating themselves to the weakness and capacity of their people'.[26] Jean Delumeau also found Catholic catechizing in seventeenth-century France 'slow to infiltrate religious habits, because it was unpopular with both clergy and laity'.[27]

Historians have also expressed doubts about the extent to which clergy managed to inculcate their beliefs and values through catechizing. Did children and others taught from long, formal catechisms only repeat in unison and commit to memory words which were barely understood, or was catechizing able to instil disciplined conformity to orthodox doctrine and to establish habits of moral behaviour? Gerald Strauss suggested that very little of the theological doctrine contained in catechisms was actually taken in by

---

25 Gerald Strauss, Richard Gawthorp, 'Protestantism and literacy in early modern Germany', *Past and Present* 104 (1984), pp. 31–55.

26 Alistair Duke, Gillian Lewis, Andrew Pettegree eds, *Calvinism in Europe, 1540–1610. A collection of documents* (Manchester: University Press, 1992), p. 114.

27 Jean Delumeau, *Catholicism between Luther and Voltaire: A New View of the Counter Reformation* (London: Burns and Oates, 1977), p. 199; see also Christopher Haigh, *Reformation and Resistance in Tudor Lancashire* (Cambridge: University Press, 1975), pp. 245–6.

parishioners' habitual repetition of words, and even less was applied by ordinary people to their daily behaviour. Strauss noted how catechism writers were often aware of the limitations of the form, but advertised new structures, or techniques of follow-up questions to check on learning, to overcome previously experienced problems of partial understanding of answers. Strauss supported his case by referring to the results of parish visitations in Lutheran Germany, which tested the knowledge and monitored the behaviour of congregations, and concluded that overwhelmingly parishioners did not know their catechisms and had only a 'nebulous grasp of the substance of their faith'.[28] John Bossy has also commented that 'Counter Reformation catechisms may not, all told, have done much more than superimpose a mental automatism on the behavioural automatisms of the code of external practice', but added that 'this is perhaps a condition of any educational process, rather than a particular failing of the Counter Reformation.'[29]

It is indeed difficult to know how to assess evidence about the achievements of catechizing. It has been suggested that in England shorter catechisms intended for study at home, which contained more homespun expressions of true and moral sayings, might have been better suited to their intended audience. Even so, Patrick Collinson has commented on the difficulty in trying to implant 'a religion consisting of patterns of printed words in heads which had little use for words of this kind and which must have found it very difficult to convert the words into authentic and meaningful experience'.[30] Other historians have found more positive results from visitation records of popular knowledge and behaviour. It has been argued that in the area around Strasbourg there was good attendance at catechism classes in the 1550s and that, thanks to well-trained pastors, Lutheran ideas were quickly grasped by the young in this area. Steve Ozment has even suggested that the impact of catechizing might have been the opposite to that intended, and that through 'their incessant ridicule of unscriptural, hypocritical and merely external religious practices, Protestant catechisms, so carefully designed to teach the child to obey, were at the same time

---

[28] Gerald Strauss, 'Reformation and Pedagogy: Educational Thought and Practice in the Lutheran Reformation' in Heiko Oberman, Charles Trinkhaus eds, *The Pursuit of Holiness in Late Medieval and Renaissance Religion. Studies in Medieval and Reformation Thought 10* (Leiden: Brill, 1974), pp. 272–93; Gerald Strauss, *Luther's House of Learning* (1978), pp. 151–75, 299.

[29] Bossy, 'The Counter Reformation and the People of Catholic Europe' (1970), p. 66.

[30] Patrick Collinson, *The Religion of Protestants: the Church in English Society, 1559–1625* (Oxford: Clarendon Press, 1982), pp. 232–4.

programming him to defy'.[31] This wide variety of interpretations about the impact of catechisms on popular religiosity is partly the result of difficulties in finding any reliable way of assessing what actually happened in the school-room or congregational class, and of measuring the quality of religious knowledge assimilated by ordinary people from catechisms. It also reflects divided opinion about the overall success of the Reformation or Counter-Reformation in altering systems of belief and influencing patterns of behaviour in early modern Europe.[32]

The impression made by printed literature, including catechisms, in spreading religious ideas in east-central Europe must in many ways be considered more limited than in territories to the west. Across east-central Europe centres of printing were more dispersed than in the west, education opportunities were more limited, especially in many rural areas, and literacy rates were lower than in most areas of western Europe. However, the impact of printed literature on the spread of religious ideas and on the construction of confessional identity in east-central Europe was also affected by the politics of the region, with the survival of a wide variety of religious groups and only relatively ineffective censorship imposed by states on the circulation of printed books.

Turning to establish the contours of this political, social and religious context for the impact of printed literature in east-central Europe, the major states of this region between the sixteenth and eighteenth centuries were the Polish-Lithuanian commonwealth, born of the 1569 Union of Lublin, and the Habsburg monarchy, forged by Ferdinand I in the wake of the Ottoman victory over the last Jagiellonian king of Hungary, Louis II. Habsburg rule ran over their hereditary lands in the Empire, the lands of the Bohemian crown which were also in the Empire, Royal Hungary, and the Transylvanian principality after the 1699 Karlowitz treaty. Royal Hungary stretched from the Adriatic coast through western and northern counties of the medieval Hungarian kingdom, while eastern Hungarian counties in the *Partium* came under the rule of the elected princes of Transylvania. One of the main features of the region was a diversity of ethnic and linguistic communities. The Polish-Lithuanian commonwealth included Poles, Lithuanians,

---

31 James Kittleson, 'Successes and Failures in the German Reformation: the Report from Strasbourg', *Archiv für Reformationsgeschichte* 73 (1982), pp. 153–75; Steve Ozment, *When Fathers Ruled. Family Life in Reformation Europe* (Cambridge [MA]: Harvard University Press, 1983), p. 176; Green, *The Christian's ABC. Catechisms and Catechizing in England* (1996), pp. 557–70.

32 Geoffrey Parker, 'Success and failure during the first century of the Reformation', *Past and Present* 136 (1992), pp. 43–82.

Ruthenians, Germans, Armenians and Jews, and while Bohemia was mostly divided between Czechs and Germans, in Hungary and Transylvania there were Hungarians, Germans and Romanians, and a number of Slav-speaking peoples including Slovaks, Croatians, Slovenes, Serbs and Ruthenians.[33]

Royal sovereignty in east-central Europe had long been balanced against the authority exerted by noble-dominated estates, with strong and historic traditions of local autonomy. For much of this period the rulers of Poland, Bohemia, Hungary and Transylvania were all elected by their diets (Sejm, Sněm, Országgyűlés). However, the Habsburgs turned Bohemia into a hereditary possession by the terms of the 'renewed' constitution of 1627, and the right of the Hungarian estates to elect their sovereigns ended in 1687. The three estates of the Transylvanian principality were the Hungarian nobility, Saxon towns and Szeklers, who had joined together in 1437 to defend their power against peasant revolt. Elsewhere in the region, diets involved clergy hierarchies, magnates, the lesser nobility and royal or privileged towns. The episcopacy, mostly drawn from the ranks of the nobility, sat alongside magnates in the upper chambers of diets. However, in Bohemia this prominent political role for the Catholic hierarchy was removed by the political impact of the Hussite movement until after the Battle of the White Mountain in 1620.

Magnates played a leading role in diets and participated in the institutions of central governments. Magnates and nobles also dominated local administration and county society across the region. Landowners were all-powerful in the countryside, dispensing justice, collecting taxes and holding rights of patronage over parish clergy. Noble economic power tightened during this period with increased demands made by lords on the peasantry for labour services. However, there were enormous differences between the economic wealth, social prestige and political power held by great magnates and petty gentry. There were large numbers of lesser nobles, forming up to five per cent of the population of Hungary and around two to three per cent of Polish

---

33 Robert Evans, *The Making of the Habsburg Monarchy, 1550–1700: an interpretation* (Oxford: Clarendon Press, 1979); Robert Kann, Zdeněk David, *The Peoples of the Eastern Habsburg Lands 1526–1918. A History of East Central Europe 6* (Seattle: University of Washington Press, 1984); Peter Sugar, *Southeastern Europe under Ottoman rule, 1354–1804. A History of East Central Europe 5* (Seattle: University of Washington Press, 1977); Orest Subtelny, *Domination of Eastern Europe. Native nobilities and foreign absolutism* (Kingston [ONT]: McGill University Press, 1986); Robert Kann, *A History of the Habsburg Empire, 1526–1918* (2nd edn), (Berkeley [CA]: University of California Press, 1980); Jean Bérenger, *A History of the Habsburg Empire, 1700–1918* (Harlow: Longman, 1997).

society. These more modest property owners were represented in estates, but were not a significant political force except in Hungary and Transylvania.[34]

Towns were also represented in diets, but were not powerful enough to act as a balance against the interests of the nobility. Hungarian towns only sent representatives to the lower chamber of the diet, and held very little influence with only one vote. In Bohemia the right of towns to participate in the diet was only settled in 1517, thanks to Hussite pressure. The vast territories of these east-central European states had relatively few towns, and their size and social significance was not comparable to many areas of western Europe. Towns across the region varied in function and status, with royal free towns and episcopal towns holding a wide range of liberties, whilst mining towns and small market towns were dominated by noble landowners. There were few towns with a population greater than 10,000, and some of the faster-growing settlements remained market towns with limited autonomy.[35]

There were around 600 towns in Poland by the end of the fifteenth century. However, urban development then stagnated and only six towns had more than 10,000 inhabitants in the sixteenth century, with most towns still entirely dependent upon local nobles. In Bohemia towns were mostly small, and Prague dominated the urban world with 50,000 inhabitants by 1600. In Hungary during the late middle ages there were 45 free royal towns, but only two towns had over 10,000 inhabitants, and there were around 800 other market settlements dependent on local landowners. Towns were mostly centres for the export of raw products from the surrounding countryside along trading routes to the west, and for the import of finished goods from the west. Some market towns gained a range of urban privileges, but smaller market settlements remained very closely integrated to the immediate surrounding economy, and their residents were often reliant on income gained from agricultural production. While artisans had only limited social

---

[34] Winfried Eberhard, 'The Political system and the intellectual traditions of the Bohemian *Ständestaat* from the thirteenth to the sixteenth century', Alfred Kohler, 'Ferdinand I and the Estates: Between confrontation and co-operation, 1521–1564', and László Makkai, 'The Crown and the diets of Hungary and Transylvania in the sixteenth century' in Evans, Thomas eds, *Crown, Church and Estates* (1991), pp. 23–47, 48–57, 80–91; Jean Bérenger, Daniel Tollet, 'La genèse de l'état moderne en Europe orientale: synthèse et bilan' in Jean-Philippe Genet ed., *L'État moderne, genèse: bilans et perspectives* (Paris: CNRS, 1990), p. 45.

[35] Vera Bacskai, 'Small towns in eastern central Europe' in Peter Clark ed., *Small towns in early modern Europe* (Cambridge: University Press, 1995), pp. 77–89; Paul Bairoch, Jean Babou, Pierre Chèvre eds, *The Population of European Cities from 800 to 1850* (Geneva: Droz, 1988).

significance, merchant elites in many larger towns were on the fringes of politics, commonly separated by linguistic difference from surrounding noble societies and peasant communities.[36]

The peasantry faced increased demands for labour services in many areas of east-central Europe during this period, and were entirely excluded from participation in the various diets. Attempts by peasant groups to rebel against the political and economic system were easily and often brutally contained by the various states. In Hungary symptoms of social unrest were certainly evident with a major revolt in 1514, and a mixture of peasant discontent and radical religion continued to unsettle the border regions of Hungary into the 1560s. Hajduck bands of displaced peasants and soldiers from Ottoman-occupied areas also posed a challenge to local order and stability in Hungary.[37]

Poland, Lithuania, Bohemia, Moravia, Hungary and Transylvania were all affected by waves of religious reform, which introduced confessional diversity into political institutions and societies already characterized by powerful noble interests and strong traditions of local autonomy.[38] The Latin Church had dominated the region at the beginning of the sixteenth century, but the Orthodox Church was a significant if legally unsanctioned presence in many areas, especially among Ruthenes, Serbs and Romanians. There was also a substantial Jewish community across the region, and particularly in Poland. East-central Europe's first wave of religious reform pre-dated the era of printed literature. Despite the execution of Jan Hus in 1415, strong support for making the sacrament of communion available in both kinds in Bohemia sustained an Utraquist Church. From the 1485 treaty of Kutná Hora (Kuttenberg), Bohemian kings were obliged to promise on their election to uphold the freedom of both Catholic and Utraquist churches, and by the early sixteenth century Utraquists dominated

---

36 Maria Bogucka, 'The towns of East Central Europe from the fourteenth to the seventeenth century' in Antoni Mączak, Henryck Samsonowicz, Peter Burke eds, *East-Central Europe in Transition from the fourteenth to the seventeenth centuries* (Cambridge: University Press, 1985), pp. 97–101; Jacek Wiesiolowski, 'Le réseau urbain en Grande Pologne au XIIIe-XVIe siecles', *Acta Poloniae Historica* (1981); Bacskai, 'Small towns in eastern central Europe' (1995), p. 80.

37 Imre Révész, 'Debrecen lelki válsága, 1561–1571' in *Értekezések a Történelmi Tudományok Köréből 25/6* (Budapest, 1936); István Rácz, *A hajdúk a xvii. században* (Debrecen, 1969).

38 Graeme Murdock, 'Eastern Europe' in Andrew Pettegree ed., *The Reformation World* (London: Routledge, 2000), pp. 190–210; Andrew Pettegree, Karin Maag, 'The Reformation in Eastern and Central Europe' in Maag ed., *The Reformation in Eastern and Central Europe* (Aldershot: Scolar, 1997), pp. 1–18.

Bohemian religion. There was also a more radical Hussite tradition upheld first by Táborites and then, from the 1450s, by the Unity of Brethren.[39]

During the early 1520s the cause of religious reform in east-central Europe received fresh impetus from events in Saxony. Lutheran preaching spread first to Germans in Silesia, Lusatia and Bohemia. Although Ferdinand initiated anti-Protestant measures in Bohemia, the position of reformers steadily strengthened in Bohemia from the middle decades of the sixteenth century.[40] In Moravia, the majority of nobles and parishes had also become Utraquist in the fifteenth century, and the Utraquist Church gained legal recognition from the diet there. Although the Catholic Church held on to more support at the beginning of the sixteenth century in Moravia than in Bohemia, particularly in Moravia's towns and in German-speaking areas, Evangelical ideas quickly gained support among Catholics and Utraquists alike. Some Moravian towns also provided refuge for German Anabaptists in the 1520s after the Peasants' war, and for Bohemian Brethren when exiled to Moravia in 1526 and again in 1547.[41]

Support for Lutheran reform elsewhere in the region emerged first in the German-speaking towns of Poland, Upper Hungary and Transylvania. This has several possible explanations, including linguistic and communication links with Germany, but was also affected by patterns of urban late medieval piety influenced by Mendicant orders. In the Polish-Lithuanian commonwealth, Lutheranism also took hold in parts of Pomerania, Royal and Ducal Prussia and Greater Poland, where by the end of the sixteenth century there were 142 Lutheran churches, 110 of which were German-speaking and only 32 Polish-speaking.

---

[39] Thomas Fudge, *The Magnificent Ride: The First Reformation in Hussite Bohemia* (Aldershot: Ashgate, 1998); Frederick Heymann, 'The Hussite-Utraquist Church in the fifteenth and sixteenth centuries', *Archiv für Reformationsgeschichte* 52 (1961), pp. 1–26; Frederick Heymann, 'The role of the Bohemian cities during and after the Hussite Revolution' in Király ed., *Tolerance and Movements of Religious Dissent in Eastern Europe* (1975), pp. 27–39.

[40] Jaroslav Pánek, 'The question of tolerance in Bohemia and Moravia in the age of the Reformation' in Grell, Scribner eds, *Tolerance and Intolerance in the European Reformation* (1996), pp. 262–81; Winfried Eberhard, 'Bohemia, Moravia and Austria' in Andrew Pettegree ed., *The Early Reformation in Europe* (Cambridge: University Press, 1992), pp. 23–48; František Kavka, 'Bohemia' in Robert Scribner, Roy Porter, Mikuláš Teich eds, *The Reformation in National Context* (Cambridge: University Press, 1994), pp. 131–54.

[41] Jarold Zeman, *The Anabaptists and the Czech Brethren in Moravia 1526–1628* (The Hague and Paris: Mouton, 1969); Domenico Caccamo, *Eretici Italiani in Moravia, Polonia, Transilvania (1558–1611). Studi e documenti* (Chicago: Newberry Library, 1970).

Large numbers of Polish nobles offered support to Protestant denominations, and their freedom to choose Protestant preachers for their parishes allowed Lutherans, Bohemian Brethren exiles and Calvinists to make gains from the 1550s. Anti-Trinitarians in Poland separated from Calvinists in the early 1560s, again with some noble support. Trinitarian Protestants united in the face of this radical challenge and under pressure from reviving Catholic institutions. Lutherans, Calvinists and Bohemian Brethren agreed to terms of mutual recognition and to hold common synods by the terms of the Union of Sandomierz in April 1570.[42]

From the 1540s German-speaking towns in Upper Hungary and Transylvania supported reform-minded clergy influenced by Luther. Although Evangelical preaching also made progress among the Hungarian nobility and in Hungarian-speaking towns, by the 1560s a Reformed Church, influenced by Calvin and Swiss reformers, had gained widespread support. By 1570 the vast majority of Hungarian nobles adhered to one of the Protestant churches, and while the royal towns and nobles of western Hungarian counties mostly remained Lutheran, magnates, gentry and the market towns of eastern counties mostly backed the Reformed Church. Transylvania's German-speaking towns remained loyal to the Lutheran Church, but Calvinism, or from the late 1560s anti-Trinitarianism, was adopted by many Hungarian nobles and in the Hungarian-speaking towns of the principality.[43]

During the middle decades of the sixteenth century noble support alone ensured the freedoms of Protestant churches across east-central Europe, as in many other environments across the Continent. While ruling dynasties remained loyal to the Catholic Church, despite initial sympathy for Lutheranism at the Hungarian and Polish courts, the protection afforded by magnates and gentry offered refuge to Protestant reformers both on their estates and in many towns. While in parts of

---

[42] Janusz Tazbir, *A State without Stakes. Polish religious toleration in the sixteenth and seventeenth centuries* (New York: Kosciuszko Foundation, 1973); Janusz Tazbir, 'Poland' in Scribner et al. eds, *The Reformation in National Context* (1994), pp. 168–80; Jerzy Kloczowski, *A History of Polish Christianity* (Cambridge: University Press, 2000), pp. 84–164.

[43] Katalin Péter, 'Hungary' in Scribner et al. eds, *The Reformation in National Context* (1994), pp. 155–67; David Daniel, 'Hungary' in Pettegree ed., *The Early Reformation in Europe* (1992), pp. 49–69; David Daniel, 'Calvinism in Hungary: the theological and ecclesiastical transition to the Reformed faith' in Alistair Duke, Gillian Lewis, Andrew Pettegree eds, *Calvinism in Europe 1540–1620* (Cambridge: University Press, 1994), pp. 201–30; Kálmán Benda, 'La réforme en Hongrie', *Bulletin de la Société de l'histoire du Protestantisme Français* 122 (1976), pp. 30–53; Earl Wilbur, *A History of Unitarianism in Transylvania, England and America* (Cambridge [MA]: Harvard University Press, 1952), pp. 99–126.

western Europe, one element of the appeal of religious Reformation was to provide a new bulwark to the communal values of cities and towns against pressure for territorial centralization, in east-central Europe nobles found in Protestantism an additional means of defending aristocratic privilege against royal encroachment. Identification with a particular church therefore reflected feudal, community and family ties, and the nobility could easily appeal to their rights to present local clergy to justify their support for reform.

By the end of the sixteenth century a number of Protestant churches had emerged from localized reform initiatives across east-central Europe, although nowhere did any single Protestant group prove strong enough to dominate the confessional landscape. The different religious communities of this region managed to coexist without major eruptions of communal violence, and there was a remarkable degree of practical religious toleration in many localities. Anti-reform measures had been passed, but could not be successfully implemented. Decrees against Protestants were issued in the Polish-Lithuanian commonwealth in 1520, 1523, 1534 and 1540. They stipulated severe punishment for the import of Lutheran writings, for the propagation of ideas in favour of reform, or for going to study in 'heretical' universities. In Royal Hungary, Ferdinand I also initially attempted to restrict the progress of refom. Some reform-minded preachers were arrested, and Nicolaus Olahus, from 1553 primate of Hungary, attempted to identify preachers who had not been ordained by Catholic bishops and to prohibit them from exercising their offices. However, political divisions within the Christian parts of the former Hungarian kingdom, solid noble support for different Protestant groups, disrupted Catholic institutional structures, and the continued Ottoman threat, blocked any serious efforts to enforce anti-reform legislation.[44]

Sovereigns were then compelled to grant some sort of freedoms to Protestant churches across the region. The Polish nobility were granted the right to abandon Catholicism by a 1555 decree which suspended the authority of ecclesiastical over lay courts. This effectively meant that lay courts were not compelled to punish religious dissidents indicted by ecclesiastical courts. This eventually allowed Protestant churches, schools and printing-presses to function undisturbed on the estates of sympathetic nobles. In 1557 and 1558 Sigismund II Augustus granted the towns of Royal Prussia, six royal towns in Greater Poland, and towns in Pomerania the right to choose Lutheran preachers, and in 1562

---

[44] Daniel, 'Hungary' (1992), pp. 54–9; Katalin Péter, 'Tolerance and Intolerance in sixteenth-century Hungary' in Grell, Scribner eds, *Tolerance and Intolerance in the European Reformation* (1996), pp. 249–61.

and 1563 anti-heresy laws were effectively annulled. The position of Trinitarian Protestants who agreed to the 1570 Consensus of Sandomierz was then protected by law under the Warsaw Confederation of 1573. This guaranteed noble freedoms in religious affairs, aiming to preserve peace 'among those who differ in religion and rite'. It has been suggested that the nature of the Polish-Lithuanian commonwealth, as constructed under Jagiellonian monarchs, offered a legal and ideological framework which was able to accommodate religious diversity among the nobility, as it had accommodated ethnic and linguistic diversity. Noble freedoms were certainly upheld in sixteenth-century Poland, but the lack of territorial institutionalization among Protestant churches rendered them vulnerable to noble reconversions to the Catholic Church.[45]

The Transylvanian court reacted to the spread of Protestantism among the estates first by attempting to bolster princely power through the appropriation of Catholic Church property in 1556. From the late 1550s Protestant churches were recognized by the diet, and in 1568 the diet instructed ministers to teach Christian religion according to their understanding of it. The diet extended legal status to four 'received religions'; the Roman Catholic, Lutheran, Reformed and anti-Trinitarian churches. Transylvania's Romanians meanwhile mostly remained loyal to Eastern Orthodoxy, although some gentry were attracted to a Romanian Calvinist Church from the 1560s. Romanians were not represented in the Transylvanian diet, but legal status for their Orthodox religion was granted as a concession by the ruling princes.[46]

In Bohemia a legal framework had been established which granted freedom of conscience and worship to both Catholics and Utraquists from 1485. In the latter half of the sixteenth century the court mostly concentrated on strengthening Catholic institutions, rather than attempting to challenge the position of Protestant groups directly. The

---

45 Tazbir, 'Poland' (1994), pp. 168–80; Jerzy Kloczowski, 'The Polish-Lithuanian Commonwealth' in John O'Malley ed., *Catholicism in Early Modern Europe: a guide to research* (St Louis [MO]: Centre for Reformation Research, 1988), pp. 83–112; Antoni Mączak, 'Confessions, Freedoms and the Unity of Poland Lithuania' in Evans, Thomas eds, *Crown Church and Estates* (1991), pp. 269–86; Janusz Małłek, 'The Reformation in Poland and Prussia in the sixteenth century: similarities and differences', Michael Müller, 'Late Reformation and Protestant confessionalization in the major towns of Royal Prussia' in Maag ed., *The Reformation in Eastern and Central Europe* (1997), pp. 182–91, 192–210.

46 Robert Evans, 'Calvinism in East Central Europe: Hungary and her neighbours' in Menna Prestwich ed., *International Calvinism, 1541–1715* (Oxford: Clarendon, 1985), pp. 167–96; Róbert Dán, Antal Pirnát eds, *Antitrinitarianism in the second half of the sixteenth century* (Budapest: Akadémiai kiadó, 1982).

response of the noble estates to royal efforts to coordinate Catholic recovery in Bohemia was to encourage Protestant clergy to reconcile their theological differences and draw up a unified confession. Protestant nobles managed to broker agreement between Lutherans, Utraquists and Bohemian Brethren to the 1575 *Confessio Bohemica*. Maximilian II's agreement was then secured in the diet for nobles to freely practise Protestant religion under this confession.[47]

In Royal Hungary Protestant noble anger at the inconclusive results of the 1590s Ottoman war, and at Rudolf II's attempts to reassert Habsburg sovereignty over all non-Ottoman Hungary for both his dynasty and the Catholic Church, led to outright rebellion in 1604. This revolt under István Bocskai aimed to defend aristocratic privileges and Protestant freedoms. The success of Bocskai's rebellion compelled Rudolf to agree to the 1606 Vienna peace which extended the free exercise of religion to the nobility, royal towns and military garrisons of Royal Hungary. The rights of both the Lutheran and Reformed churches to regulate freely their own affairs were also established. These rights were ratified by the Hungarian diet in 1608 during the battle between Rudolf and Matthias for control of the Habsburg monarchy. In 1609 the estates in Bohemia were also able to use this Habsburg crisis to gain Rudolf's agreement to the 'Letter of Majesty', which granted religious liberty to the nobles and to towns.[48]

Religious reform had spread quickly across east-central Europe during the sixteenth century. Protestants were successful in gaining support and constitutional recognition by the end of the sixteenth century, but these achievements were soon undermined during the early decades of the seventeenth century as Catholic recovery proved to be widespread and enduring. Protestant Churches were increasingly placed

---

[47] Joachim Bahlcke, 'Calvinism and estate liberation movements in Bohemia and Hungary (1570–1620)' in Maag ed., *The Reformation in Eastern and Central Europe* (1997), pp. 72–91; Gottfried Schramm, 'Armed conflict in east-central Europe: Protestant noble opposition and Catholic royalist factions, 1604–1620', Jaroslav Pánek, 'The Religious question and the political system of Bohemia before and after the Battle of the White Mountain' in Evans, Thomas eds, *Crown Church and Estates* (1991), pp. 129–48, 176–95; Karin MacHardy, 'The rise of absolutism and noble rebellion in early modern Habsburg Austria, 1570–1620', *Comparative Studies in Society and History* 34 (1992), pp. 407–38.

[48] László Makkai, 'István Bocskai's Insurrectionary Army' in János Bák, Béla Király eds, *From Hunyadi to Rákóczi. War and Society in Late Medieval and Early Modern Hungary* (New York: Brooklyn College Press, 1982), pp. 275–97; David Daniel, 'The Fifteen Years' War and the Protestant response to Habsburg absolutism in Hungary', *East Central Europe* 8 (1981), pp. 38–51; Kálmán Benda, 'Habsburg Absolutism and the resistance of the Hungarian Estates in the sixteenth and seventeenth centuries' in Evans, Thomas eds, *Crown Church and Estates* (1991), pp. 123–8.

on the defensive from the early seventeenth century, and the Orthodox Church, which had remained largely unaffected by Protestant ideas, was also in turn impacted by the resurgence of Catholicism in the region, marked above all by Greek Catholic unions with Rome.[49]

Although rulers had conceded legal rights to a range of religions, confessional uniformity was still perceived as a powerful instrument of social cohesion, and religious dissidence was increasingly identified with political disloyalty. In the Transylvanian principality, the Reformed Church became the dominant confession during the early decades of the seventeenth century under a series of Calvinist princes. These princes supported their co-religionists, developing local Reformed educational centres, making combined efforts with leading clergy to improve standards of moral discipline, and backing the Reformed Church against its confessional rivals, particularly the anti-Trinitarian (or Unitarian) Church. Reformed clergy in Transylvania soon identified their princes as godly protectors of true faith, and worked in tandem with princes to impose social discipline on their congregations. Despite the force of this Reformed confessionalism in Transylvania, the inclusive constitutional arrangements agreed in the principality during the 1560s remained in place. Thus, although the Reformed Church became the 'public' church of the principality, it continued to have to share the territory of Transylvania with the three other 'received' religions.[50]

Outside the Transylvanian principality, the Catholic cause was championed by the Habsburg and Polish courts. In Poland toleration of religious difference had been granted of necessity, but as Catholic, and especially Jesuit, mission efforts brought increasing numbers of the noble elite back into the Catholic fold, the need to tolerate minority faiths became less obvious. Although churches in towns under the rule of Protestant magnates were protected, elsewhere Protestant churches were closed down, as in Cracow in 1591, in Poznan in 1611 and Lublin in 1627. Meanwhile, in the Protestant towns of Royal Prussia, Catholics were unable to hold public processions or funerals, and were denied membership of guilds.[51] An increasingly intolerant religious culture came to dominate Polish public life. Beginning with anti-Trinitarians in 1638,

---

[49] Winfried Eberhard, 'Reformation and Counter-Reformation in East Central Europe' in James Tracey, Thomas Brady, Heiko Oberman eds, *Handbook of European History, 1400–1600: Late Middle Ages, Renaissance and Reformation, vol. 2. Visions, Programmes and Outcomes* (Leiden: Brill, 1995), pp. 551–84.

[50] Graeme Murdock, *Calvinism on the Frontier, 1600–1660. International Calvinism and the Reformed Church in Hungary and Transylvania* (Oxford: Clarendon Press, 2000); László Makkai, 'The Hungarian Puritans and the English Revolution', *Acta Historica* 5 (1958), pp. 13–45.

[51] Tazbir, 'Poland' (1994), p. 178.

the state withdrew freedoms granted to religious minorities. In 1668 the Polish diet prohibited repudiation of the Catholic faith, while from 1673 only Catholics could be ennobled, and by the end of the eighteenth century there was even consideration given to expelling Poland's Jewish community. A significant element of changing perceptions about confessional diversity were the growing connections made between membership of the Polish nobility and membership of the Catholic Church. German-speaking Lutheran burghers in Royal Prussia thus found themselves more and more excluded from the religious and political culture of the Polish state.[52]

In the Habsburg monarchy court-sponsored Catholicism was steadily, and sometimes violently, imposed by secular officials and the Catholic hierarchy. Protestant liberties in Bohemia were undermined in the 1610s, sparking renewed opposition to the Habsburg dynasty. After the resistance of Protestant estates in Bohemia, Moravia and Austria had been overcome by 1620, Ferdinand II equated Protestantism with disloyalty and saw confessional uniformity as essential for the stability of the monarchy. Indeed, Catholic piety was elevated to become the core ideology behind Habsburg dynastic authority, and the objectives of state policy became interlinked with those of the Catholic Church.[53] In Bohemia the religious liberties granted to Protestants by the 1609 'Letter of Majesty' were abrogated, and all non-Catholic religions were declared illegal under the 1627 'renewed' consitution. Meanwhile Protestant churches in Royal Hungary retained their hard-won constitutional freedoms during the seventeenth century. Unlike the dramatic reversal in Bohemia during the 1620s, the Habsburgs were more constrained in Hungary by the support given to Protestants from the Transylvanian principality, and by the need for noble cooperation in defending Royal Hungary against the Ottomans. The Catholic hierarchy in Hungary concentrated on improving the effectiveness of the clergy and on winning over noble converts. The Jesuits also managed to create

---

[52] Mączak, 'Confessions, Freedoms and the Unity of Poland Lithuania' (1991), pp. 278–9; Müller, 'Late Reformation and Protestant confessionalization in the major towns of Royal Prussia' (1997), pp. 192–210.

[53] Evans, *The Making of the Habsburg monarchy* (1979), pp. 68–73; Hsia, *Social Discipline in the Reformation* (1992), pp. 39–52; Robert *Bireley, Religion and politics in the age of the Counterreformation. Emperor Ferdinand II, Williama Lamormaini S.J. , and the formation of imperial policy* (Chapel Hill [NC]: University of North Carolina Press, 1981); Gernot Heiss, 'Princes, Jesuits and the origins of Counter-Reformation in the Habsburg lands' in Evans, Thomas eds, *Crown Church and Estates* (1991), pp. 92–109; Rona Johnston Gordon, 'Patronage and parish. The nobility and the recatholicization of Lower Austria' in Maag ed., *The Reformation in Eastern and Central Europe* (1997), pp. 211–18.

a network of residences, and by 1650 there were forty Jesuit colleges in Hungary's main towns.[54]

The Habsburgs regarded the freedoms which had been granted to Protestants within their monarchy as temporary measures imposed upon them during difficult political circumstances. As Protestant strength in the Hungarian diet weakened over time with noble conversions to the Catholic Church, only intervention by the armies of the Reformed prince of Transylvania during the mid-1640s offered some respite to growing Protestant grievances. When faced with noble conspiracy in response to the 1664 compromise peace of Vasvár between the Habsburgs and Ottomans, the court promoted more aggressive policies against Protestants in Hungary during the 1670s. Protestant church buildings were confiscated, clergy arrested and Protestant books banned. This policy was curtailed after Leopold's settlement in 1681 with the diet at Sopron. However, Protestant freedoms were by now carefully circumscribed, and only limited numbers of places of Protestant worship were permitted, Protestants were prevented from holding public offices, faced educational restrictions, and were obliged to celebrate Catholic feasts. Although Habsburg monarchs strove to ensure the dominance of Catholicism in Hungary, state stability and Catholic interests were hardly harmonized successfully. Many gentry, especially in eastern Hungary, remained committed to their Calvinist faith, and although some active revolts were mounted, county-party Protestantism mostly became a localist and conservative force in eighteenth-century Hungarian politics.[55]

In Transylvania, even more than in Hungary, the Habsburgs could not overlook local arrangements favouring toleration of a range of churches, which were confirmed by Leopold's diploma of 1690. The Catholic cause in Transylvania was, however, able to take advantage of the weak legal position of the Romanian Orthodox Church. Orthodox churches in east-central Europe were not officially approved religions, and both Catholics and Protestants had pursued mission strategies towards the Orthodox faithful. There were precedents for union between the Eastern and Latin churches, most significantly from the Council of Florence of 1438–39. At Florence both parties had agreed to

---

54 Evans, *The Making of the Habsburg Monarchy* (1979), pp. 121–40; István Bitskey, 'The *Collegium Germanicum-Hungaricum* in Rome and the beginning of Counter-Reformation in Hungary' in Evans, Thomas eds, *Crown, Church and Estates* (1991), pp. 110–22

55 Evans, *The Making of the Habsburg Monarchy* (1979), pp. 272–3; László Benczedi, 'Hungarian national consciousness as reflected in the anti-Habsburg and anti-Ottoman struggles of the late seventeenth century', *Harvard Ukrainian Studies* 10 (1986), pp. 429–30.

union on the basis of the Greeks retaining their rites, but accepting Papal primacy, the existence of purgatory, the use of unleavened bread in the Eucharist, and Catholic understanding of the Holy Spirit. Catholic interest in union resurfaced at the end of the sixteenth century in the context of plans for a crusade against the Ottomans, but thereafter plans for a general union were replaced with attempts within Catholic states to forge particular unions with local Orthodox churches.[56]

Negotiations between the two sides resulted in unions agreed in the Polish-Lithuanian commonwealth in 1595–96, in Hungary in 1611, 1646 and the 1690s, and in Transylvania in the late 1690s.[57] In return for accepting Papal authority and agreeing to the points of Catholic doctrine which had been raised at Florence, Ruthenian and Romanian clergy obtained legal privileges equivalent to those of Roman Catholic clergy. While the previously Orthodox clergy imagined that they were participating in an ecclesiastical union based on the Florentine model, for Catholics these agreements marked the return and integration of the easterners within the Catholic world. Whilst these unions cannot be explained simply as efforts by Catholics to strengthen their cause, the political importance of the Greek Catholic (or Uniate) Church in Transylvania at the turn of the eighteenth century was widely recognized. In Poland and Hungary the state authorities also soon realized the political importance of union to Catholic interests and became firm supporters of Greek Catholic churches in the region.

The focus of this volume is not primarily on assessing the political forces behind the success of different reform efforts in east-central Europe. Nevertheless, the relationship between state power and churches was crucial to the progress of reform, and both Reformed domination of the Transylvanian principality in the seventeenth century and the promotion of Catholic interests across the Habsburg monarchy are discussed here. In particular, Joachim Bahlcke considers the implications for the Catholic Church of the Habsburgs' acquisition of Transylvania at the end of the seventeenth century, the balance in policy between pursuing political and religious goals, and the place of the

---

[56] Oscar Halecki, *From Florence to Brest* (Rome: Sacrum Poloniae Millenium, 1958); Wilhelm Ploechl, 'The Church Laws for Orientals of the Austrian Monarchy in the age of the Enlightenment', *Quarterly Bulletin of the Polish Institute of Arts and Sciences in America* (1944), p. 7.

[57] Borys A. Gudziak, *Crisis and Reform. The Kyivan Metropolitanate, the Patriarchate of Constatinople and the Genesis of the Union of Brest* (Cambridge [MA]: Harvard University Press, 1998); Michael Lacko, 'Die Union in Kroatien (1611)' in Wilhelm de Wries ed., *Rom und die Patriarchate des Ostens* (Freiburg in Bresgau: Alber, 1963), pp. 108–13; Michael Lacko, *Unio Uzhorodensis Ruthenorum Carpaticorum cum Ecclesia Catholica* (Rome: Institutum Orientalium Studiorum, 1955).

Romanian Greek Catholic Church in the principality's new political and confessional order.

As Churches sought constitutional recognition and rights to worship freely, they also conveyed the essence of their various systems of belief and attempted to establish support for religious ideas. Alongside preaching and discussion, Protestant reformers were the first to harness print technology to broker the social reception of religious doctrine. Even so, a vernacular version of Bible was only completed in Polish at Cracow in 1561, and it took until 1590 for Reformed minister Gáspár Károlyi to publish the first complete translation of the Bible in Hungarian at Vizsoly, while Bohemian Brethren only produced a vernacular Bible at Kraliče in Moravia in 1593. Printed literature was produced from the latter decades of the sixteenth century by all the different confessions of the region, asserting the orthodoxy of different creeds, rejecting accusations of heresy, attacking the errors of rival churches, instructing clergy, and developing historical narratives about the origins of each church.[58] A wide range of devotional and pedagogical printed books and tracts was also produced across the region, including catechisms, creeds, confessions of faith, Psalters, hymnals, prayer books and children's instruction manuals.

Many of the contributions to this volume focus on the role played in east-central Europe by catechisms, which reformers hoped to use to establish and consolidate loyalty to their ideas. Some catechisms were home-grown products of reformers from this region, others were translated or adapted from western texts, particularly by Luther, Canisius and the Heidelberg doctors. Various essays here assess how readily available catechisms and other forms of printed literature were in this region, and the intended audience for these printed texts. To what extent did the clergy continue to mediate between ordinary people and the printed words found in catechisms and other religious books? Some catechisms were produced in Latin, but the production of catechisms using local vernacular languages was of crucial significance, an issue taken up by Krista Zach. A connection has often been made between the various linguistic communities of east-central Europe and different churches, but how far was the production of catechisms and other printed literature in the vernacular important in shaping such allegiances? The importance of the vernacular words used to describe theological issues, and how successfully those words resonated within local communities, is also examined by Graeme Murdock and Csilla Gábor for Hungary and Transylvania.

---

[58] Norbert Kersken, 'Reformation and the writing of national history in East-Central and Northern Europe' in Maag ed., *The Reformation in Eastern and Central Europe* (1997), pp. 50–71.

Catechisms served a variety of functions in east-central European societies. Catechisms provided basic instruction for ordinary people about the core elements of their faith, presenting theology in a structured and ordered format. Thomas Fudge examines the content of catechisms compiled in Bohemia to communicate the core themes of Hussite groups, and reflects on how catechisms function as a window on to the theological and religious priorities of Hussites. Catechisms instructed believers in the orthodoxy of their faith, were meant to strengthen the commitment of existing believers, and to lead to correct religious practice and pious behaviour. Catechisms were also produced in an effort to define clearly the boundaries of accepted belief. Although catechisms mostly concentrated on explaining doctrine without reference to opposing views, they sometimes served to highlight points of error in the doctrine of rivals.

Carmen Florea discusses how catechisms were used in the anti-Trinitarian Church of sixteenth-century Transylvania, first in polemic battles with confessional rivals, and then to shape the religious knowledge of the wider community of anti-Trinitarians in the principality. Anti-Trinitarian catechisms highlighted different views on the doctrine of the Trinity, but elsewhere understanding of the sacraments, and especially the Eucharist, was strongly emphasized by all sides. What impact did such explanations of differences between religions in catechisms make in the multi-confessional environment of east-central Europe? Pompiliu Teodor and Ovidiu Ghitta also examine the role of catechisms in the development of the Greek Catholic Church in Hungary and Transylvania. They highlight how catechisms reflected the difficult position of the Greek Catholic Church between the Latin Catholic and Orthodox worlds. Maria Crăciun considers how far catechisms also came to be used as instruments of conversion in her assessment of the catechisms produced by Transylvanian Protestants and addressed to the Romanian Orthodox community. Confessional identity in this region was often at least partly negatively defined, as establishing what a community should not believe was frequently seen to be as important as determining those beliefs which all were supposed to accept. Judith Kalik's work considers how other religious groups, and in this case Poland's Jewish community, could affect the development of the confessional identity of a church.

Catechisms also played a role in attempting to distance communities from traditional religious practices, and studies here raise the question as to whether catechizing can be equated with the imposition of religious values on ordinary people. Printed literature might be seen not to increase the free flow of information but become a new and more effective means of elite domination of society. To what extent was the process of catechizing coercive, and how far was it linked with attempts to improve standards of moral and social discipline? The role of reliable and well-trained clergy was crucial in this regard, and some catechisms even seem to have been primarily aimed at the clergy with a view to ensuring their orthodoxy. On the other hand, catechisms were intended to allow ordinary people not only to commit texts to memory but also to internalize the main tenets of their faith. How well catechisms worked as vehicles to transmit ideas is considered in a number of different social contexts, including the use of catechisms in congregational classes, in schools, in households and by individuals. To what extent were catechisms successful in overcoming the barrier of widespread illiteracy to the spread of ideas? Graeme Murdock questions how far catechisms ever lived up to the expectations of their authors, and whether repeating written words aloud and committing them to memory could shape or alter systems of belief in this region. Not only catechisms made such demands on readers, and other forms of devotional literature, as discussed here by Csilla Gábor, also required reflective religious activity in individual prayer and private meditation.

The circulation of printed books in east-central Europe from the mid-sixteenth century suggests that, for some, decisions about religious allegiance were made by autonomous individuals, informed by private reading to embrace or resist a particular wave of religious reform. However, many more encountered the religious book from a distance, second or third hand, or in groups. Nevertheless, the impact of the contents of printed books certainly seemed to all the religious elites of the region to promise much. Catechisms and other printed religious literature appeared to be vital in providing parishes with well-educated clergy, and possibly also able to inculcate words in the minds and hearts of ordinary believers, words with the power to shape belief, to persuade doubters, to inform religious practice and to order moral behaviour. Whilst the focus here is on the role of printed literature in shaping religious belief and confessional identity, churches also continued to use a variety of other means to convey religious ideas and to establish the particular identity of their church, including styles of preaching, the appearance of church-buildings, the use of music and the clothing of priests.

Across east-central Europe the spread of ideas about reform and attempts to encourage confessional loyalty were pursued against the background of contested political power. To be identified with a particular religion in east-central European society reflected a set of social relationships, and marked a balance of loyalty drawn between sovereign, feudal lord, town, neighbourhood and family. Confessional identity could also indicate a sense of community with those who spoke the same language, or had the same occupation or social status, or were from the same ethnic community. Religious affiliation was also a matter of legal privilege, and could reflect individual judgements upon personal economic and political advantage. Support for different churches was therefore undoubtedly shaped by the political and social environment of east-central Europe from the sixteenth century. However, the amalgam of relationships and individual considerations which ordered religious identity included the attraction of particular ideas about religious reform, encountered by most in the publicity of the church or the school room, but by some privately and alone. The essays in this volume suggest that the coherence of religious ideas and the effectiveness of the means adopted to transmit them, often by printed books, and especially by catechisms, was crucial to the outcome of the Reformation and to the development of confessional identity in communities across east-central Europe.

CHAPTER TWO

Luther and the 'Hussite' catechism of 1522

Thomas Fudge

Pure Hussite religion was never Protestant.[1] Before the famous 'here I stand' of Martin Luther at Worms, lasting reform had swept the lands of the Czech crown. Before John Calvin took up his pen to compose *The Institutes of the Christian Religion* a reformation had transpired in the kingdom of Bohemia. A tumultuous century before Luther challenged the right of the Church to distribute and sell indulgences for the forgiveness of sins, Hussite reformers had broached the fundamental issue of the Church's authority. While the vast majority of the Hussite-Utraquist Church continued to adhere to many of the teachings and practices of the Catholic Church, the more radical face of religious reformation was exemplified by the Táborites and later by the Unity of Brethren (*Jednota Bratrská*). Late medieval heresy had successfully transformed itself into movements of religious *reformatio* and *renovatio*. Thus, before the dawn of the European Reformations, Bohemian Christendom had achieved a unique status. Many Czechs had gone over to a faith and to a religious practice which the Catholic Church, in both papal and conciliar decrees, had condemned as heretical. They had joined themselves to an alternative church which was at first simply schismatic but then, through protracted disobedience, deliberately heretical. During the Hussite century, this reformation of heresy attracted peasants, farmers, gentry, townsfolk, nobility, churchmen, even kings and archbishops, to say nothing of university masters, magnates and their subordinates. The heresy of Jan Hus had transmuted, and by the time Jan Želivský, Jakoubek of Stříbro, Mikuláš of Pelhřimov, Jan Žižka as well as the Táborite and Orebite 'warriors of God' had concluded their work, Bohemia had been transformed and the institutionalization of heresy completed. With the advent of Protestantism there was a three-way theological and religious division in

---

[1] I have suggested elsewhere that the term 'Hussite-Protestant' is effectively an oxymoron. 'Review of Rudolf Říčan, *The History of the Unity of Brethren*', *Communio Viatorum* 36 (1994), p. 65.

the Czech lands. When the Protestant Reformation arrived in Bohemia, it encountered a religious structure already reformed.[2]

Reformation aside, the bane of religious dissent is dissent. Schism breeds schism and heresy, when it has been conceived, brings forth even further heresy. Intolerance looms, and dissent is rarely permitted among dissenters. The shattering of Christendom in the course of the sixteenth century is a grim witness to the possibilities of religious zeal and the tragedy of theological imperialism. In the fie:y furnace between orthodoxy and heresy, survival for dissenters was rarely assured. Synergisms often existed uneasily and the age of confessionalism produced accords which did not always live up to their promises. Political and confessional compromise in the course of the fifteenth century left the future of the Hussite tradition in doubt. The pioneers of the days of Hus and Žižka became settlers, and desiring to preserve their heritage, erected buildings in which to dwell. The construction of those dwellings, however, had first to contend with the burgeoning forces of Protestant movements.

By the sixteenth century Hussitism had evolved into two distinct entities: Utraquism and the Unity of Brethren. It is misguided to assign doctrinal reformulation exclusively to the former. It is equally fatal to regard the Unity of Brethren as interested mainly in ethics and practical affairs and unconcerned with theology. It is true, none the less, that the Unity did not promote a theological monolithic unanimity, and they produced up to forty confessional statements.[3] Heirs of the Táborites, the Unity retained many of their radical tenets. Among that inheritance was the preservation of learning. Even reports from hostile witnesses underscore the value radical Hussites placed on religious education.[4]

---

2 Winfried Eberhard, 'Reformation and Counterreformation in East Central Europe' in Thomas Brady, Heiko Oberman and James Tracey eds, *Handbook of European History, 1400–1600: Late Middle Ages, Renaissance and Reformation, vol. 2. Visions, Programmes and Outcomes* (Leiden: Brill, 1995), (Grand Rapids [MI]: William B. Eerdmans, 1996), p. 554.

3 The first Czech catechism dates from the early sixteenth century. The catechism *Dětinské otázky prvnie (Questions for Children)* is no longer extant in its original Czech version. Anton Gindely, *Geschichte der Böhmischen Brüder* (Osnabrück: Biblio-Verlag, 1968), p. 122. Numerous other catechisms then appeared until 1661 when Jan Amos Comenius published *Die uralte christliche catholische Religion, in kurze Frag und Antwort verfasset. Vor alle Christen-Menschen, alt und jung, seeliglich zu gebrauchen* (Amsterdam, 1661); Miloš Štrupl, 'Confessional Theology of the Unitas Fratrum', *Church History* 33 (1964), pp. 291–2.

4 Aeneas Sylvius Piccolomini noted after visiting Tábor in 1451 that even women in that town knew the Bible better than many Italian bishops; *Libros Antonii Panormitae poetae, de dictis et factis Alphonsi regis memorabilibus, commentarius; Aeneae Sylvii Piccolominei Opera* (Basel, 1571), p. 480.

Important strides were made by radical Hussites in the area of popular education and the Brethren became pioneers in the field of primary education.[5] Later in Bohemian history the book might have been regarded as a sign of heresy but this was not the case in the early sixteenth century.[6] Reformation progress notwithstanding, the Hussite tradition did not maintain an expression of dogmatic immutability when it came to catechetical and confessional identity.[7] Still, the vagaries of religious change in the early decades of the sixteenth century caused the inheritors of the Hussite tradition to cast about for a new identity. There were many elements involved in the process of reinventing Hussite confessional identity, among which the use of catechisms and the influence of Luther were particularly significant.

The Lutheran Reformation and later, Calvinist impulses penetrated Bohemian Christianity in the course of the sixteenth century. The immediate dominant presence of the Reformation in Bohemia was that of Luther, and his influence on the sixteenth-century Hussite tradition has been often noted.[8] After 1530 the Augsburg Confession gained a place of ascendancy in the Czech lands, although Czech confessions were still produced and the Lutheran creed adapted to better suit the Hussite tradition.[9] Later in the century Calvinist theology engulfed the Hussite tradition and the first Reformation became indistinguishable

---

[5] Peter Brock, *The Political and Social Doctrines of the Unity of Czech Brethren in the Fifteenth and Early Sixteenth Centuries* (The Hague and Paris: Mouton, 1957), pp. 99–101.

[6] Marie-Elisabeth Ducreux, 'Reading unto Death: Books and Readers in Eighteenth-Century Bohemia' in Roger Chartier ed., *The Culture of Print: Power and Uses of Print in Early Modern Europe* (Oxford: Polity Press, 1989), pp. 199–201.

[7] Amedeo Molnár, 'The Brethren's Theology' in Rudolf Říčan ed., *The History of the Unity of Brethren: A Protestant Hussite Church in Bohemia and Moravia* (Bethlehem and Winston-Salem: The Moravian Church in America, 1992), p. 390.

[8] S. Harrison Thomson, 'Luther and Bohemia', *Archiv für Reformationsgeschichte* 44 (1953), pp. 160–81; Frederick Heymann, 'The Impact of Martin Luther upon Bohemia', *Central European History* 1 (1968), pp. 107–30; Jaroslav Pelikan, 'Luther's Negotiations with the Hussites', *Concordia Theological Monthly* 20 (1949), pp. 496–517; Josef Čihula, 'Martin Luther a Čechové podobojí', *Český časopis historický* 3 (1897), pp. 274–88, 329–49; Josef Čihula, 'Poměr Jednoty Bratří českých k Martinovi Lutherovi', *Věstnik české akademie nauk a umění* 4 (1897), pp. 1–70; František M. Bartoš, 'Jednota bratrská a reformátoři', in František M. Bartoš, Josef L. Hromádka eds, *Jednota bratrská. Sborník*, (Prague: Kalich, 1956), pp. 108–45; František M. Bartoš, 'Lutherovo vystoupení a Jednota Bratrská', *Reformační Sborník* 3 (1929), pp. 3–17; Scott H. Hendrix, '"We are all Hussites"? Hus and Luther Revisited', *Archiv für Reformationsgeschichte* 65 (1974), pp. 134–60.

[9] Otakar Odložilík, 'Education, Religion, and Politics in Bohemia, 1526–1621', *Cahiers d'Histoire Mondiale* 13 (1971), p. 176.

from the second Reformation. However, acknowledgement of Luther's role in the new emerging identity of Hussite Christianity is striking. Pavel Příbram, professor at Charles University in Prague, for example commented that;

> We Czechs walked in darkness ... until God in his mercy showed us his Son and his Truth, in order that we would be his chosen people ... In his grace he sent us Master Hus and others whose names have been written down in heaven, who would direct us in the way to a correct understanding and enlighten our minds ... And what he first granted to the Czechs, he now grants to other nations as well. He grants it to a people who for hundreds of years wandered in darkness, and did not see the light of Christ, and staggered about aimlessly ... For when God graciously showed the way of salvation to us initially and revealed to us true faith in Christ, they opposed us and arrogantly referred to us as heretics ... But now God has sent Martin Luther to them, in order that the closed hearts of that people might awaken and understand the foolishness of their ways ... And God has given that man Martin such power to proclaim truth as only St Paul has done before.[10]

What Master Hus once had been, now Luther had become.[11] Many in the Hussite tradition saw in Luther the opportunity once again to enter the mainstream of Christianity without at the same time reverting to the Catholicism of Rome. For a century the Hussites had unsuccessfully attempted to shake off their heretical reputation as a land of '*damnosa heresis*', rife with a '*pestiferum virus*' which four kings had been unable to eradicate.[12] Negotiations had been entered into with representatives from Rome, the Orthodox Church and even the Waldensians, but all had been abortive attempts at ecclesiastical reconciliation.[13] The

---

[10] Intro. to Czech translation of Luther's sermons, 'Decem praecepta Wittenbergensi praedicata populo', *D. Martin Luther Werke. Kritische Gesamtausgabe* (113 vols), (Weimar, 1883–1996), vol. 1, pp. 398–521 (hereafter *WA*); Pavel Příbram, *Kázání velebného a nábožného otce Martina Luthera na desatero přikázání Božích, které lidu obecnému zjevně v městě Witemberce kázal jest* (Prague, 1520), pp. 2–3.

[11] A characterization used by Václav Rožďalovský, provost of the *Collegium Carolinum* in Prague; quoted in *WA*, Br. 1, p. 420.

[12] Assessment of Hartmann Schedel in his *Chronica Nurembergense* (Nuremberg, 1493). John Capistrano warned that the Hussite heresy was the most sinister the Christian Church had ever encountered in a 1456 letter to Pope Callistus III; Lucas Wadding ed., *Annales Minorum seu Trium Ordinum a S. Francisco institutorum* (Rome, 1735) vol. 12, pp. 318–19. Aeneas Sylvius Piccolomini judged Bohemia to be a barbarian land on account of its heresy; *Historia bohemica*, ch. 1 in *Aeneae Sylvii Piccolominei Opera* (Basel, 1571), p. 82.

[13] E. F. Jacob, 'The Bohemians at the Council of Basel, 1433' in Robert Seton-Watson ed., *Prague Essays*, (Oxford: University Press, 1949), pp. 81–123; Gerald Christianson, 'Wyclif's Ghost: The Politics of reunion at the Council of Basel', *Annuarium historiae conciliorum* 17 (1985), pp. 193–208; František M. Bartoš, 'A Delegate of the Hussite

Compactata agreed upon by the Council of Basel proved to be an indefinite arrangement, and were in any event unilaterally repealed in 1462 by Pope Pius II. The fall of Constantinople in 1453 ended the chances for Hussite recognition in the east. Despite concessions gained from the official Church in the fifteenth century, union was no longer possible. Thus, in the 1520s, with 'Catholicism ... on the run in every part of the Bohemian lands', it was to the massive upheavals which shook Europe's multiple religious worlds that the Hussite tradition turned its attention in search of identity, recognition and legitimacy.[14] The turn to Luther was at once obvious and yet surprising. The close proximity of Wittenberg to Prague facilitated the former, but the historic animosity between Czechs and Germans, exacerbated by the recent Hussite wars, made the prospective alliance unlikely.

The Hussite tradition in its manifestation as the Unity of Brethren cannot rightly be considered Protestant, at least not before the 1530s, and even then not without some significant modification of its fifteenth-century heritage. What the Brethren were chiefly concerned with, in their ongoing communication with Luther, was exploring the possibility of a common religious identity or relationship. The sixteenth century produced two confessions from the Hussite tradition in 1535 and again in 1575.[15] These documents reflect the degree of Protestant influence in Bohemia by the end of the century. Prior to these declarations of faith, there were other steps along the road of building up the church. One of those important steps in the Hussite Church was the production of pedagogical literature aimed at shaping religious life, encouraging the faithful and setting forth the religious identity of the old tradition in a new and expanding religious world. This educational process had deep roots in Bohemia. Beguine communities in Prague, numbering close to twenty by 1415, had been actively engaged in teaching children from the late thirteenth century.[16] However, the Czech Reformation constituted a revolutionary

---

Church to Constantinople in 1451–1452', *Byzantinoslavica* 24 (1963), pp. 287–92; 25 (1964), pp. 69–74; Susan K. Treesh, 'Europe's Peasant Heretics: The Waldensians 1375–1550' (Rutgers University Ph.D, 1988), pp. 150–75.

[14] Kenneth J. Dillon, *King and Estates in the Bohemian Lands 1526–1564* (Brussels: Editions de la Librairie Encyclopédique, 1976), p. 71.

[15] Hermann A. Niemeyer ed., *Collectio Confessorum in Ecclesiis reformatis publicatarum* (Leipzig, 1840); Jaroslav Pelikan, 'Luther's Endorsement of the *Confessio Bohemia*', *Concordia Theological Monthly* 20 (1949), pp. 829–43; Amedeo Molnár, 'The Czech Confession of 1575', *Communio Viatorum* 16 (1973), pp. 241–7; Ferdinand Hrejsa, *Česká konfese, její vznik, podstata a dějiny* (Prague, 1912).

[16] Anna Kolářová-Císařová, *Žena v hnutí husitském* (Prague: Knihy Sokolice, 1915), pp. 120–22.

breakthrough with respect to the medieval view of children.[17] They were admitted into full participation in the Eucharist by all Hussite parties, and there are extant eucharistic hymns for children, with evidence that catechetical singing also performed a significant role in church worship by the second and third decades of the fifteenth century.[18]

Catechetical instruction specifically, and the process of *catechesis* generally, has been present in one form or another throughout Christian history. Catechisms emerged as a literary genre in the fifteenth century and became widely known and used in the sixteenth century. There are several reasons for this, including the rise of vernacular writing, growing literacy rates, the invention of movable-type printing, and perhaps the pervasive anxiety which characterized the later medieval centuries.[19] It is inaccurate to connect the rise of catechisms with the Protestant Reformation. One of the first to advocate the value of catechetical instruction was Jean Gerson, who advanced the notion that ecclesiastical reform might best be inaugurated through the religious instruction of children.[20] Among several significant fifteenth-century catechisms must be numbered Dietrich Kolde's *The Mirror of Christian Faith*, the first printed lay German catechism and perhaps the most popular.[21] Kolde's catechism went through forty-seven printed editions in the late fifteenth and early sixteenth centuries. Kolde attempted to set out the basic tenets of the Christian faith by explaining the Apostles' Creed, the Ten Commandments, ecclesiastical laws, the seven deadly sins, sins against

---

[17] Noemi Rejchrtová, 'Dětska otázka v husitství', *Československý časopis historický* 28 (1980), pp. 53–77.

[18] Thomas A. Fudge, *The Magnificent Ride: The First Reformation in Hussite Bohemia* (Aldershot: Ashgate, 1998), pp. 186–216.

[19] Denis R. Janz, 'Catechisms' in Hans J. Hillerbrand ed., *The Oxford Encyclopedia of the Reformation*, (Oxford: University Press, 1996), vol. 1, pp. 275–80.

[20] Jean Gerson (1363–1429), *Tractatus de parvulis trahendis ad Christum*; *L'ABC des simples gens, de trés grands utilitié et proufit*; M. L. Ellies du Pin ed., *Johannis Gersonii Opera Omnia (5 vols)*, (Antwerp, 1706); James L. Connolly, *John Gerson: Reformer and Mystic* (Louvain: Libraire Universitaire, 1928); Mark S. Burrows, *Jean Gerson and De Consolatione Theologiae (1418): The Consolation of a Biblical Reforming Theology for a Disordered Age* (Tübingen: Mohr [Siebeck], 1991).

[21] Albert Groeteken, 'Der älteste gedruckte deutsche Katechismus und die niederdeutschen Volksbücher des seligen Dietrich Kolde von Münster', *Franziskanische Studien* 37 (1955), pp. 53–74, 189–217, 388–410; Steven Ozment, *The Reformation in the Cities* (New Haven [CT]: Yale University Press, 1975), pp. 28–32; Christoph Moufang ed., *Katholische Katechismen des 16. Jahrhunderts in Deutscher Sprache* (Hildesheim, 1880); Clemens Drees, *Der Christenspiegel des Dietrich Kolde von Münster* (Werl, 1954); Denis Janz ed., *Three Reformation Catechisms: Catholic, Anabaptist, Lutheran* (Lewiston: The Edwin Mellen Press, 1982), pp. 29–130.

the Holy Spirit, as well as an enumeration of several hundred other sins. There was also instruction on confession and various prayers, including the Lord's Prayer. The emphasis upon sin in Kolde's catechism reflected one aspect of the ethos of the age, and the idea of guilt became a major motif in the catechetical instruction of the later middle ages. Thus, there can be no support for the thesis that religious education was lacking in the century prior to Luther. During the age of Reformation, considerable emphasis was placed upon the appropriation and use of catechisms as a means of communicating reformed religion. However, late medieval catechisms and spiritual pedagogy retained an exclusive concentration on religious or doctrinal matters and almost completely ignored any social application or articulation of religious faith. The proliferation and use of catechisms in the sixteenth century produced a genre of Reformation catechisms, which, unlike their medieval counterparts, also took up the social implications of religion and faith.

Just after the turn of the sixteenth century the Unity of Brethren produced their first catechism. *First Questions for Children (Otázky dětinské prvnie)* was written around 1501 by the bishop, or senior, of the Brethren, Lukáš Pražský (Luke of Prague).[22] Shortly thereafter Lukáš composed a reference book for religious education of *Larger Questions (Otázky větší)*.[23] This catechism was in fact a revision of a much older document which had been in circulation among the Brethren in the fifteenth century. The questions and answers in the catechism largely correspond to Hussite texts dating to the period prior to 1414. Efforts have been made to show that this 'Hussite' catechism was in fact a Waldensian text, but this was demolished by František Palacký. As for relations between Waldensians and Hussites, Palacký showed that the dominant influence went from Hussite to Waldenisan rather than the other way.[24] He also showed that there was no proof that Lukáš had ever been taught by the Waldensians. While there were Waldensian catechisms, there is no basis for assigning priority to them over the 'Hussite' text. Finally, Palacký was able to show textual similarities to

---

[22] Amedeo Molnár, *Bratr Lukáš bohoslovec Jednoty* (Prague: Husova fakulta, 1948), pp. 120–33.

[23] Molnár, *Bratr Lukáš bohoslovec Jednoty* (1948), pp. 107–47; Amedeo Molnár, 'Luther und die Böhmischen Brüder', *Communio Viatorum* 24 (1981), pp. 47–58; Rudolf Vindiš, 'Bratra Lukáše Pražského názory o Eucharistii', *Věstník královské české společnosti nauk* (1921–3), pp. 8–74; Jan B. Lášek, 'Luke of Prague' in *The Oxford Encyclopedia of the Reformation* (1996), vol. 2, pp. 458–9.

[24] Gerhard von Zezschwitz, *Die Katechismen der Waldenser und Böhmischen Brüder* (Erlangen, 1863); Treesh, 'The Waldensians, 1375–1550' (1988), pp. 15–75; Giorgio Tourn, *The Waldensians: The First 800 Years* (Turin: Claudiana, 1980), pp. 59–63.

earlier Hussite texts alluded to above.[25] While the catechism itself is eclectic and has little pedagogical value, especially as it relates to the instruction of small children, it is revealing of the vicissitudes of struggle and change which the later 'Hussite' tradition found itself in. A German translation of the catechism came to Luther's attention in 1522 when Lukáš sent several documents to Luther. Evidently the catechism was reprinted several times between that time and 1524, and in all there were no fewer than fourteen editions of this 'Hussite' catechism in German between 1522 and 1530.[26]

Catechisms, in their varied forms, function as a window on to the theological and religious emphases of religious communities. The ways in which this 1522 'Hussite' catechism set forth its own particular teachings provides us with a glimpse of the later Hussite tradition. What did the catechism teach? The main components of sixteenth-century catechisms are present in this text: the Ten Commandments, the Apostles' Creed and the Lord's Prayer. In response to the question, 'what are the commands of God?', the catechism asserts that obeying the law depends on love for God which is also demonstrated in love for one's neighbours. The Apostles' Creed is presented as a summary of universal Christian faith. The Lord's Prayer is given in response to a query about the proper method of praying. Unlike other catechisms, notably Luther's *Shorter Catechism*, there is no expansion or explanation of what the various components of these texts mean. The 'Hussite' catechism then goes on to enumerate several soteriological concepts. First, that the roots of salvation are in creation. Second, that salvation is dependent on faith, hope and love, although the primary ground of salvation is faith. Third, that obedience to the Word of God produces salvation. Related to salvation and Christian life is the idea of faith. Faith is the primary ground of salvation, it is impossible to please God without it, and faith means trusting in God apart from any other subsidiary consideration or basis. Living faith is contrasted with dead faith, and is explained as that assurance which holds to the triune God. Faith in Christ means to accept God's promises, to know God and to be united with God. Indeed, the most important commandment of Christ is that Christians believe in him. Truth is grasped through faith and this same faith honours God. The saints as well as Mary were received by God on account of their living and humble faith. Serving God is rooted in faith, and Christian hope is likewise of faith.

---

[25] František Palacký, 'O stycích a poměru sekty Waldenské k někdejším sektám v Čechách' *Časopis českého musea* 42 (1868), pp. 291–320; Jaroslav Palacký ed., *Jaroslav Charvát* (4 vols), (Prague, 1941), vol. 3, pp. 115–44.

[26] Jarold K. Zeman, *The Anabaptists and the Czech Brethren in Moravia 1526–1628* (The Hague and Paris: Mouton, 1969), pp. 327–9.

The life Christians should lead is described in terms of love, ethical behaviour and good deeds. Love is one of the pillars upon which salvation depends. Love for one's neighbour is explained in the golden rule of doing for others what one would wish others to do for you. Ethical responses are enumerated in avoiding anger, lust and swearing, while doing good to one's enemies, and the Beatitudes of the Sermon on the Mount are likewise included. God is honoured through the giving of alms and other charity. 'Good morals' ought to be practised, as the true service of God is apprehended through good deeds and Christian hope is confirmed through works. The Eucharist is dealt with in only two questions, but the explanations are among the longest in the catechism. Question sixty-one asked how Christ should be honoured in the sacrament? In response, the catechism forbade any adoration of the sacrament. Christ was to be adored in his heavenly form, but not in his sacramental form. The second question asked about the proper reception of the body and blood of Christ. The answer to this question is ambiguous. First, it is stated that the bread and wine are the body and blood of Christ. Notwithstanding this, the bread is flesh sacramentally and the wine is blood in the same sense. Both are understood as providing spiritual nourishment, but there is no indication that the 'Hussite' framers of this catechism regarded the elements in a literal sense.

In the 'Hussite' catechism of 1522 there are several divergences from, or repudiations of, Catholic teachings. There is a considerable effort to distance the Hussite tradition from the cult of the saints and of Mary. The response to a question about belief in the saints is a terse negative. While it is proper to render honour and respect to the saints, the catechism issued several pointed prohibitions. It is improper to worship the saints, make petitions to them, or pray to them. One must not place trust in their ministrations. Saints' days are not to be observed, offerings may not be given to them, acts of charity should not be undertaken in their names. Fasting, swearing an oath or making vows with reference to the saints is likewise rejected. Pilgrimages to their shrines or the building of churches in their memory is also discouraged. Beyond these prohibitions, there is a mandate against kneeling before, or creating images of, the saints. A full ten questions in the catechism were devoted to the matter of the saints. The dogma of transubstantiation promulgated by the Fourth Lateran Council in 1215 and advocated by the official Church is dismissed. The answer to question seventy-one also rejected the notion of extreme unction, obedience to papal authority, the cult of the saints (again), popular forms of piety associated with the rosary, purgatory, the Mass, monastic and other religious orders, and deeds performed on behalf of the dead.

Since this catechism came to the attention of Luther in 1520 and then again in 1522, it is important to explore what elements of the catechism might have been antithetical to Luther's own doctrines. Much of the document would not have been problematic for Luther, but there are elements which were of potential concern. First, the Czech catechism does not enumerate a doctrine of justification *sola fide*. Indeed, the 'Hussite' soteriology in the 1522 catechism generally coupled faith with hope, love or good deeds.[27] One might have expected Luther to react negatively to any doctrine of salvation linked in any way to human deeds or effort. Second, whilst the strident dismissal of the lives of the saints was something Luther did agree with, he generally tempered those denunciations with an underscoring of the pedagogical value of the saints' lives.[28] More seriously, Luther was perturbed with the explanation of the Eucharist, a point which will be taken up in some detail below. Beyond these points, it is noteworthy that nowhere in the catechism is there any mention of the atonement or the cross. There are four allusions to it: first, by citing the Apostles' Creed; second, in a brief statement of the idea of redemption; third, by reference to being 'made clean through his [Christ's] blood', although again there is no development of this idea, and finally, there are four references to the blood of Christ which was shed for many for the redemption of sins. Each of these references appears in the context of discussing the Eucharist, but there was no separate discussion or development of a theology of the cross. By comparison, in Luther's *Shorter Catechism* there is a detailed explanation of redemption in his discussion of the Apostles' Creed.

By the time this 'Hussite' catechism was composed, the Hussite Revolution had come to an end and the Bohemian Church was engaged in the process of institutionalization and constructing a post-revolutionary identity. There are few explicitly 'Hussite' elements in the catechism, but the most obvious 'Hussite' motif does remain. Since the 1370s the Eucharist in general, and later, the chalice in particular, was the focal point of Hussite religion. Alongside the commands of God, and instruction concerning the saints and other potential errors of faith, the

---

27 Hus preached a doctrine of salvation consistent with the medieval idea of 'faith formed by love'; *Magistri Iohannis Hus, Tractatus de ecclesia*, S. Harrison Thomson ed. (Boulder [CO]: University of Colorado, 1956), pp. 53–4; Anežka Schmidtová ed., *Magistri Iohannis Hus Opera Omnia, vol. 7. Sermones de tempore qui Collecta dicuntur* (Prague: Academia, 1959), p. 189.

28 Robert Kolb, *For all the Saints: Changing Perceptions of Martyrdom and Sainthood in the Lutheran Reformation* (Macon: Mercer University Press, 1987), pp. 11–18; James Michael Weiss, 'Luther and his Colleagues on the Lives of the Saints', *Harvard Library Bulletin* 33 (1985), pp. 174–95.

Eucharist occupies a central position in the catechism of 1522. The distinctive aspects of *communio sub utraque specie* were made clear in the catechism. Other aspects of the catechism running counter to the doctrine of the official Church, enumerated above, cannot be regarded as essentially 'Hussite'. Some are indicative of late medieval heresy, while others are also to be found in Protestant polemics, while still others are common to both. The better question is: what is missing from a 'Hussite' document which one might otherwise expect to find? Radical Hussite literature constantly referred to the evils of the official Church, condemned the use of images, advocated iconoclasm, unequivocally insisted upon the practice of utraquism, placed considerable emphasis on preaching, and called for the thorough divesting of ecclesiastical wealth and a return to lives of apostolic poverty in the fashion of the primitive Church. Punishment of all serious sins was held as a virtue, and there was a persistent preoccupation with eschatology and the advent of Antichrist. Most of these ideas are absent from the catechism, and those which do appear are treated briefly. In short, the catechism has no true self-defining motifs worthy of 'Hussite' attribution.

The revised composition of the catechism in the 1520s falls within the period of the profusion of Reformation ideas. Are there elements of these ideas present in the language and formulation of the 'Hussite' catechism? Among the major elements of Reformation theology should be numbered the ideas of *sola fide, sola gratia, sola scriptura, solus Christus*, the priesthood of all believers, Christian liberty, a revised emphasis on the sacrament, and a theology of the cross. There is no definite indication of *sola fide* or *sola gratia* in the text. The doctrine of *sola scriptura* is not formally articulated, but nine of the catechism's questions refer in one way or another to the 'Holy Scriptures' or the 'Word of God.' God is known through his Word, believing in God implies unity with the Word and a practice of that Word, and salvation is promised to those obeying the Word. The witness of scripture is regarded as essential, as Christians are to receive Christ through the Word, hope is rooted in the Word of God, obedience to the Word of God is essential, while those who err ignore the Word. Finally, Christian unity is achieved through those things promoted by scripture. Beyond these allusions to scripture, it is significant that while there are two references to ecclesiastical tradition and a single reference to non-canonical scripture, there are no fewer than thirty-six direct quotations or references to Biblical texts (twenty-six to the New Testament and ten to the Old Testament). Such reliance on scriptural authority, however, does not equate to a full doctrine of *sola scriptura*. There is no immediate doctrine of *solus Christus*, the priesthood of all believers, Christian liberty or a theology of the cross. As already noted there is considerable revision in the area of sacramental theology. The only sacrament mentioned in the catechism is the Eucharist, and whilst there are elements of ideas taken up by Protestants in discussion of the sacrament, they are not immediate products of sixteenth-century thought.

The Czech catechism of 1522 can be understood in its basic three-fold division: salvation, faith and religion. In the first instance, salvation is linked to faith subjectively as the basis of redemption and objectively in the tenets of the Apostles' Creed. The section on faith distinguishes between inactive and living faith. Faith which is useful and living is linked, for the Brethren, to the fulfilment of divine commands (in this case the Decalogue) and to a relationship with the triune God. This articulation is probably based upon the scholastic definition of faith which employed a tripartite division: *credere de Deo*, *credere Deo* and *credere in Deum*. Distinguishing between the different elements of faith in this way was also used by Jan Hus.[29] True religion is delineated in the same fashion as faith, with fundamental distinctions drawn between genuine and false worship, and the guiding principles of Brethren theology are here clearly linked to soteriology and eschatology.[30] The incomplete nature of the 'Hussite' catechism may seem incongruous as it was intended to be used for the religious instruction of children, but the 'Hussite' catechism of 1522 is in fact only the first part of a larger work. This explains the absence of any instruction on baptism and confirmation, or any systematic treatment of the Lord's Supper, or of the function of the Church.[31] The first part of the catechism under consideration here was composed not to instruct new catechumens but rather for those children who had been born into the Hussite tradition. Once this instruction had been mastered, children in the Brethren were then allowed to proceed on to the process of confirmation contained in the second part of the catechism. Once confirmed, the third part of the catechetical education was then undertaken.[32] In other words, the Unity promoted a tripartite membership of their communities, and without understanding this it is difficult to see any coherence or useful educational structure in this catechism. The catechism does not, however, break from medieval catechisms in its focus on religious truth, and applications of religious truth to daily life are ignored.

---

[29] Jan Hus, *Výklad víry* in Karel J. Erben ed., *Mistra Jana Husi Sebrané spisy české* (3 vols), (Prague: Tempský, 1865–8), vol. 3 (1868), p. 7.

[30] Zeman, *The Anabaptists and the Czech Brethren* (1969), p. 334.

[31] The complete Czech catechism appeared in November 1523 under the title *Spis tento otázek trojiech*; Zeman, *The Anabaptists and the Czech Brethren* (1969), pp. 333–5.

[32] Amedeo Molnár ed., *Českobratrská výchova před Komenským* (Prague: Státní pedagogické nakladatelství, 1956), pp. 66–9.

This 'Hussite' catechism appeared during a decade when a range of catechisms were in use among different religious communities across the Continent. Kolde's aforementioned *Mirror* continued to be printed and used. The radical sector of the Protestant movement joined the urge to engage in religious instruction, and in 1527 Balthasar Hubmaier published an Anabaptist catechism.[33] A series of visitations to Saxon parishes in 1527 provided the impetus for the creation of Luther's catechisms. The appalling ignorance of even basic Christian teachings discovered in the parishes prompted the production in April 1529 of Luther's *Catechism*. This was followed in May 1529 with the publication of the so-called *Shorter Catechism*.[34] If Kolde seemed to emphasize sin and guilt, and Hubmaier focused on the distinctive tenets of the Radical Reformation, Luther paid close attention to the Ten Commandments, the Apostles' Creed and the Lord's Prayer. Both Hubmaier and Luther utilized a question-and-answer format similar to the 'Hussite' catechism. In 1520 Luther had insisted that there were three things a person should know which were essential to salvation. First, the law which pointed out human need; second, the creed which provided evidence of available assistance to meet that need, and third, the Lord's Prayer which demonstrated how to find and appropriate this assistance.[35] Luther's *Shorter Catechism* was originally printed on broadsheets which could be hung on the walls of houses. The Nuremberg city council was among several to adopt the *Shorter Catechism* as a basic textbook in schools, in the expectation that children instructed in its precepts would grow up in true faith.[36] Luther was elated with what he perceived as the early success of the new catechetical process: 'I declare, I have created a reform that will cause the ears of the Popes to ring and their hearts to burst.'[37] The *Shorter Catechism* must certainly be numbered among the most influential and

---

[33] Balthasar Hubmaier, *Ein Christennliche Leetafel, die ein yedlicher mensch, ee und er im wasser getaufft wirdt, vor wissenn solle* (1527); Gunnar Westin, Torsten Bergsten eds, *Quellen zur Geschichte der Täufer, vol. 9. Balthasar Hubmaier: Schriften* (Gütersloh: Gerd Mohn, 1962); Janz ed., *Three Reformation Catechisms: Catholic, Anabaptist, Lutheran* (1982), pp. 131–78.

[34] *Deutsch Catechismus* in WA 30/1, pp. 125–238; *Der kleine Catechismus für die gemeine Pfarherr und Prediger* in WA 30/1, pp. 243–425; Theodore G. Tappert ed., *The Book of Concord: The Confessions of the Evangelical Lutheran Church* (Philadelphia [PA]: Fortress Press, 1959), pp. 337–461; WA 30/1, pp. 1–122; John W. Doberstein ed., *Luther's Works, vol. 51* (Philadelphia: Fortress Press, 1959), (hereafter *LW*), pp. 137–93.

[35] WA 7, pp. 195–6.

[36] Gerald Strauss, *Luther's House of Learning: Indoctrination of the Young in the German Reformation* (Baltimore [PA]: Johns Hopkins University Press, 1978), p. 155.

[37] Luther's 1528 preface for Stephen Klingebeil's work 'Von Priester Ehe'; WA 26, p. 530.

far-reaching of all Luther's writings and indeed of the Lutheran Reformation.

The 'Hussite' catechism of 1522 came to Luther's attention during the reaction to his 1520 book, *The Babylonian Captivity of the Church*, and provided the occasion for his composition of a subsequent book on the Eucharist.[38] Sparked by Luther's knowledge of the 'Hussite' catechism, in some ways this later text constituted a response to Lukáš and the Brethren.[39] The most significant problem Luther had with the Czechs was with respect to their theology on the Eucharist. Luther feared the rise of heresy and the destruction it could wreak on inchoate movements for reform. The dissenter wished to permit no dissent, posing a significant problem for medieval heresies being assimilated into the streams of Reformation in the sixteenth century. Luther feared the potential for blind enthusiasm from the 'Hussite' catechism. The context of the state of Saxony in the 1520s is essential for understanding what might otherwise be regarded either as irrational insecurity on one hand, or dictatorial pettiness on the other. By 1523 Luther had already been called upon to deal with the 'Wittenberg disturbances' of late 1521, the Zwickau prophets, iconoclastic campaigns in early 1522, the restless fervour of Andreas Karlstadt, Gabriel Zwilling and Thomas Müntzer, to say nothing of the escalating agitation among the German knights, the German peasants and other disparate strands which later would form aspects of the Radical Reformation in Germany and elsewhere.

By 1529 Protestant battles about the Eucharist had come to full expression, and the reformers were bitterly divided over the sacrament of the altar. Zwingli suggested that his scriptural proofs would break stubborn necks, but Luther stood on a Marburg hillside and pounded his fist against a table upon which he had written the words, 'this is my body', and refused either to budge or suffer his neck to be broken. Luther was fully prepared to reform what he regarded as the errors of the Mass perpetuated by the official Church from medieval times. However, he was not prepared to abandon the Lord's Supper to some sacramentarian three-headed devil.[40] The matter of the real presence was of ultimate concern to Luther, and he was not convinced that the Czechs held to that premise. Indeed, the Táborite position clearly had not done

---

[38] *WA* 6, pp. 497–573; *LW* 36, pp. 11–126.

[39] *Von aubeten des Sakraments des heiligen Leichnams Christi* in *WA* 11, pp. 431–56; *LW* 36, pp. 275–305.

[40] This was Luther's description of his Eucharistic opponents. The three heads were comprised of Karlstadt, Johannes Oecolampadius, Huldrych Zwingli and other unidentified 'fanatics' from a 1526 letter to a congregation at Reutlingen; *WA* 19, pp. 118–25.

so, with claims to orthodoxy compromised by their congenial reception of Wyclif's remanentism. When it came right down to it, Luther declared that he would rather drink real blood with papists than mere wine with fanatics.[41] Rumours about the position of the Czechs on this issue stretched back to Hus and beyond. More immediately, the Lutheran pastor in the Moravian town of Jihlava, Paul Speratus, had spread tales to Luther of the Brethren's alleged belief that adoration of the sacrament was not proper. Luther was therefore deeply worried about the interpretation among Hussites of the words of institution of the sacrament and about their understanding of the real presence.[42]

Luther's reading of the 1522 'Hussite' catechism caused him to conclude that the Czechs believed that Christ should not be adored in the sacrament, and that Christ was not really present in the bread and wine.[43] The emphasis in Luther's own doctrine on these issues came down to the words of institution. Everything depended on those words, for in them was the sum and substance of the entire gospel. For Luther, the words themselves were even more important than the sacrament. Without the words and the reality related in them, the sacrament became yet another human work or effort.[44] In this respect Luther gave tacit approval to the dictum of Augustine, 'believe and you have eaten already'.[45] Placing heavy emphasis on the doctrine of the real presence, Luther categorically assailed the idea that in the sacrament there is merely bread and wine.[46] Admitting that there was a distinction to be maintained between Christ in heaven at the right hand of God, and Christ in the sacrament or in the hearts of believers, Luther stoutly defended the concept that Christ is present in the sacrament.[47] Since true worship is nothing but faith, Luther advised that no one ought to be condemned of heresy or theological irregularity on the basis of not adoring the sacrament. By the same token, those who do adore the sacrament must equally not be subjected to censure and condemnation on the same principle that scripture nowhere says it is improper. Summarily, Luther concluded that there was less danger in not adoring

---

[41] 'Sooner than have mere wine with the fanatics, I would agree with the pope that there is only blood'; 'Confession concerning Christ's Supper' (1528) in *WA* 26, p. 462; *LW* 37, p. 317.

[42] Luther's 1522 letters to Speratus; *WA* Br 2, pp. 531, 560–61.

[43] *WA* 11, p. 431; *LW* 36, p. 275.

[44] *WA* 11, p. 432; *LW* 36, pp. 277, 288–9; 'There is a great difference between faith and good works, just as vast as the difference in value between the tree and the fruit.'

[45] 'Tractate XXV on the Gospel of St. John 12' in Jacques Paul Migne ed., *Patrologia Latina* (217 vols), (Paris, 1843–73), vol. 35, col. 1602.

[46] *WA* 11, p. 434; *LW* 36, p. 279.

[47] *WA* 11, p. 447; *LW* 36, p. 294.

the sacrament, but asserted that the entire question ought not to be a matter of contention. Each person should make up his or her own mind.[48] Therefore, Luther took exception to the Czechs because they appeared actively to forbid sacramental adoration. However, for Luther the apparent rejection of the doctrine of the real presence in the 'Hussite' catechism was an altogether more serious matter.

The last few pages of Luther's reply to the 'Hussite' catechism provide a commentary on the religious practices of the Unity of Brethren. Luther praised the successful implementation of utraquism among the Czechs and complained that the Germans had thus far failed to make satisfactory progress in that direction. Notwithstanding this accolade, Luther took issue with the Bohemian practice of baptizing children on the basis of future, rather than present, faith. Moreover, he commented disparagingly on the idea that good works are essential to a living faith, a suggestion implied in the Czech catechism and, as noted previously, categorically stated by Hus. Furthermore, Luther decried the lack of clerical marriage among Czech priests as 'damaging to the gospel'.[49] Luther strongly suggested that Czech clerics become more competent in their knowledge of biblical languages, as well as Latin, in order more fully to understand the truths of scripture.[50] Luther concluded his book by stating that although many regarded the Czechs as the 'worst kind of heretics', he was convinced that they were 'much nearer to the gospel than any others' known to him, adding that the moral lives of the Czechs were infinitely better than those of the Germans.[51]

The 'Hussite' catechism of 1522 provides a valuable piece of the complex puzzle to judge the effectiveness of catechizing in early modern Europe. Many of the leaders of the Lutheran Reformation, despite Luther's enthusiasm about early catechetical successes, came to suspect that their efforts had failed. Sixteenth-century Protestant impulses had, in the end, effected little change either in popular religion or in the manner in which ordinary people lived their lives. Compulsory catechizing bred resentment, boredom, apathy and in some cases outright hostility. There is little evidence from the 1522 catechism to suggest the need to modify this assessment.[52] A mixture of Hussite and Reformation thinking had coalesced to form a codified attempt to inculcate specific religious convictions. That amounted, as did all similar attempts, to an imposition of confessional values on popular religion.

---

48 WA 11, pp. 448–9; LW 36, pp. 295, 297.
49 WA 11, pp. 452–3, 454–5; LW 36, pp. 300, 302, 303.
50 WA 11, pp. 455–6; LW 36, p. 304.
51 WA 11, p. 456; LW 36, pp. 304–305.
52 Strauss, Luther's House of Learning (1978), pp. 2, 299, 305, 307.

While clearly a vehicle for the dissemination of information, there was always an element of coercion which also accompanied the process of *catechesis*. In the end, even though catechisms in some places were actually ascribed special sacral power and were used as sacred objects, there are few indications to support the claim that catechisms either helped to preserve the Hussite faith or indeed stimulated further religious Reformation.[53]

The 1522 catechism was made widely available as the numerous editions of the 1520s testify. Although most, if not all, Brethren pastors were educated and capable of reading and providing religious instruction, much religious education was expected to go on in homes where there is insufficient evidence to suggest that more than a few families were able to do this effectively. There is little to be learned from counting the number of books available, since, as Robert Scribner has shown, the real question is how many could read?[54] Some German texts addressed the gulf between learned ideas and popular culture, and wood-block pamphlets were produced which sometimes featured a condensed catechism in visual form from which non-readers could find instruction.[55] These pictures avoided complex and complicated depictions and, while interpretation was still necessary, sought to communicate a clear and concise message. However, the Brethren seem to have failed to utilize this pedagogical strategy and did not use images in printed texts during the sixteenth century to the extent the Lutheran Reformation did, or even as much as previous generations of Czechs had done.[56]

What does this 'Hussite' catechism of 1522 tell us about the development of Czech religion and the formation of Hussite religious identity? Hussite faith had never been established through a clearly defined set of beliefs. The impulse to publish the 1522 catechism cannot,

---

[53] Robert W. Scribner, 'The Impact of the Reformation on Daily Life' in *Mensch und Objekt im Mittelalter und in der Frühen Neuzeit Leben–Alltag–Kultur* (Vienna: Österreichischen akademie der Wissenschaften, 1990), p. 328; Hans-Christoph Rublack, 'New Patterns of Christian Life' in Thomas Brady et al. eds, *Handbook of European History 1400–1600*, pp. 585–605; John Bossy, *Christianity in the West 1400–1700* (Oxford: University Press, 1985), p. 119.

[54] Robert W. Scribner, 'How many could read?: Comments on Bernd Moeller's "*Stadt und Buch*"' in Wolfgang J. Mommsen ed., *Stadtbürgertum und Adel in der Reformation studien zur Sozialgeschichte der Reformation in England und Deutschland* (Stuttgart: Klett-Cotta, 1979), pp. 44–5.

[55] Robert W. Scribner, *For the Sake of Simple Folk: Popular Propaganda for the German Reformation* (Oxford: Clarendon Press, 1994).

[56] One representative example which summarized the entire catechism in nine pictures is *Ein kurze ordenliche summa der rechten waren lehre unseres heyligen christlichen glaubens* ... (Regensburg, 1554).

however, be regarded as merely a reaction to the German Reformation. Instead, it represents an ambivalent attempt to forge a new identity in a rapidly changing world. The exclusive concentration on religion in the 'Hussite' catechism and the complete neglect of its social implications or applications leave this text not in the realm of Reformation catechisms but squarely within the medieval genre. This effort to provide religious education for small children was partly based on the past, and partly on what its framers thought might be the appropriate route through the theological thickets growing everywhere in the multiple religious worlds of Europe. Uncertainty, ambiguity and hesitancy characterize the 'Hussite' catechism of 1522. Hussite religion had become short-circuited by the accommodation of the Church's teaching to the needs of dominant social groups which mitigated the original, and popular, appeal of the movement. The catechism of 1522 is certainly a far cry from the radical Hussite religion personified in its purest form at Tábor. Having rejected official Christendom, this 'Hussite' document represents an attempt to construct a *via media* between radical medieval heresy and burgeoning Protestantism. It constitutes one of the steps of the Hussite movement from heresy to legitimation.

CHAPTER THREE

Protestant vernacular catechisms and religious reform in sixteenth-century east-central Europe

Krista Zach

While public religious instruction in medieval Europe was largely reliant on imagery, some of which remains on the walls of the Continent's Romanesque and Byzantine churches, Protestant reformers were able to take advantage of technological change and more widespread literacy in the sixteenth century to use catechisms to convey ideas about salvation to ordinary lay believers. However, both the Byzantine and Latin Churches had to some degree already established the practice of catechizing from between the eighth and eleventh centuries. Although Protestant reformers did not therefore invent catechisms, they renewed the importance of catechizing as the prime means of educating ordinary people about their faith, and also developed new structures and functions for their catechisms.[1]

The titles which sixteenth-century reformers gave to their catechisms explained their central purposes. Martin Luther called his 1529 *Shorter Catechism*, 'The Layman's Bible', and suggested that it ought to be used to instruct the young about their faith either at schools or in homes. Other early Protestant catechisms included Luther's *Longer Catechism* of 1529, *A Small Bible* completed by Johannes Brenz in 1535, and *A Catechism for Children* compiled by Philipp Melanchthon in 1540. Protestant catechisms normally included explanations of five key elements of doctrine: the Ten Commandments, the Apostles' Creed, the Lord's Prayer, and the sacraments of baptism and Holy Communion.[2]

---

[1] The name 'catechism' was used in this sense for the first time in 1528 by Andreas Althamer and Johannes Brenz; see Gerhard Müller, Gerhard Krause *et al.* eds, *Theologische Realenzyklopädie* (to date 31 vols), (Berlin: Walter de Gruyter, 1977–) (hereafter *TRE*), vol. 17 (1988), p. 711.

[2] *Martin Luther, Werke. Kritische Gesamtausgabe (Weimarer Ausgabe [WA])* (60 vols), (Weimar: Böhlau, 1883–1983), vol. 30/ 1, Georg Buchwald, Otto Albrecht eds (1910), p. 27; Christoph Weismann, *Eine kleine Biblia. Die Katechismen von Luther und Brenz* (Stuttgart: Calwer, 1985), pp. 14, 22–8; Christoph Weismann, *Die Katechismen des Johannes Brenz. Vol. 1: Entstehungs-, Text- und Wirkungsgeschichte* (Berlin: Walter de Gruyter, 1990), pp. 10–15, 22, 32, 617–19, 711; *TRE*, vol. 17 (1988), pp. 713–17.

The central ideas of Evangelical religion were conveyed through German catechisms from the 1520s, and Huldrych Zwingli encouraged the use of catechisms to educate people about their faith in the Zurich church.[3] Different catechisms included varying additional elements of doctrine, expressed sometimes quite simply but elsewhere in considerable detail. Reformed Churches also adopted catechisms to aid instruction about key ideas, from John Calvin's *Genevan Catechism* of 1541 to the very successful Heidelberg *Catechism* of 1563, which was adopted by Reformed Churches across the Continent.[4] Last in line came anti-Trinitarian catechisms published from the late 1560s in Transylvania.[5]

Johannes Honterus, leading reformer of the Saxon Germans in Transylvania, commented that the message of religious reform soon spread 'onto the very fringes of the occidental Church'.[6] Most east-central European reformers followed the view taken by western reformers on the role which catechisms could play in instructing their communities and in developing Protestant churches. Committing answers from catechisms to memory was seen to have the potential to spread ideas about salvation across the largely illiterate societies of the region. Literature which set out the ideas of Evangelical reformers was available in Hungary from the mid-1520s, whilst the local production of catechisms began from the 1540s. Johannes Honterus attempted to consolidate the progress of reform in the Saxon towns of Transylvania by publishing *A Short Catechism for Priests and Fathers* at Braşov (Brassó/Kronstadt) in 1548.[7] Although by no means all the catechisms which were published during the sixteenth century in east-central Europe have surviving copies, some catechisms were attached to new confessions of faith produced by reforming synods or included in regulations for school curricula.[8] Catechisms were widely used by

---

3 Huldrych Zwingli, *Kurze christliche Unterweisung* (Zurich, 1523); Johann Bugenhagen, *Büchlein für die Laien und die Kinder* (Wittenberg, 1525).

4 Weismann, *Die Katechismen von Luther und Brenz* (1985), pp. 22–4; *TRE*, vol. 17 (1988), pp. 729–31.

5 Zoltán Balázs, 'Gab es eine unitarische Konfessionalisierung im Siebenbürgen des 16. Jahrhunderts?' in Volker Leppin, Ulrich A. Wien eds, *Konfessionenbildung und konfessionelle Kultur in Siebenbürgen (16. Jahrhundert)* (Stuttgart: Steiner, 2001).

6 Johannes Honterus, *Die Reformation der Kronstädter Kirche und des ganzen Burzenlandes* (Kronstadt, 1543), also known as 'Reformationsbüchlein'; Ludwig Binder, *Johannes Honterus. Schriften, Briefe, Zeugnisse* (Bucharest: Kriterion 1996), p. 170.

7 Johannes Honterus, *Der Kleine Catechismus für die Pfarrherr vn(d) Hausväter* (Kronstadt, 1548) in Ludwig Binder, *Johannes Honterus. Schriften, Briefe, Zeugnisse* (1996), pp. 113, 238.

8 Mihály Bucsay, *Der Protestantismus in Ungarn 1521–1978* (Vienna: Böhlau, 1977), pp. 96–9; Mathias Bernath, Felix v. Schroeder eds, *Biographisches Lexikon zur Geschichte Südosteuropas* (4 vols), (Munich: Oldenbourg, 1974–81), vol. 3 (1979), p. 153 (hereafter

Protestants across east-central Europe because translating existing catechisms into the vernacular languages of the region proved by far a 'simpler task' than dealing with longer and more complex literature. Certainly the Slovene reformer Primus Trubar conceded this in 1549 as he worked to promote Lutheran ideas among Slavs in south-western Hungary (modern Slovenia and coastal Croatia).[9]

As one of the main printed sources of ideas about Protestant reform, and the most common printed text of the period, the role of catechisms in religious and social change across early modern Europe deserves further research and analysis. In discussing the impact of catechisms in east-central Europe, it is particularly important to highlight several key issues. First, sixteenth-century catechisms were mostly published in the vernacular languages of east-central Europe. They played an important role in establishing linguistic norms across the region, and also set standards for the spoken vernacular used in church services. Second, although the production of catechisms in, and for, east-central European communities during the sixteenth century has been considered in a number of studies, these tend to concentrate rather narrowly on enumerating localized developments, particularly in studies of Hungarian and Transylvanian literature. Even this work is of an inconsistent standard. Research on variations between different texts, and the degree to which ideas from these catechisms penetrated communities across the region, has so far been almost entirely neglected.[10] Third, catechisms were mostly produced in the region during the four middle decades of the sixteenth century. The period between the 1540s and 1580s was marked by intensive cultural communication between centres of western education and the eastern lands of Europe's periphery. It is important to examine this process of cultural exchange, consider the reasons behind the rapid and intensive reception of Protestant catechisms in east-central Europe, and the significance of the uneven spread of catechisms across this region. Some

---

BioLex); *TRE*, vol. 17 (1988), pp. 715–17; Ernst Benz, *Wittenberg und Byzanz. Zur Begegnung und Auseinandersetzung der Reformation und der östlich-orthodoxen Kirche* (Marburg/Lahn: Verlagsbuchhandlung, 1971), pp. 64–6; Oskar Sakrausky, *Primus Trubar. Deutsche Vorreden zum slowenischen und kroatischen Reformationswerk* (Vienna: Evangelischer Presseverband, 1989), pp. 12–15. For bibliographic references on literature from Hungary and Transylvania see Gedeon Borsa ed., *Régi magyarországi nyomtatványok 1473–1600* (3 vols), (Budapest: Akadémiai kiadó, 1971), vol. 1; Gedeon Borsa ed., *Alte siebenbürgische Drucke (16. Jahrhundert)* (Cologne: Böhlau, 1996).

9 Primus Trubar, *Abecedarium, und der klein Catechismus in der windischen Sprach* (Tübingen, 1551), foreword; Balduin Saria, *Was hat uns Primus Trubar heute zu sagen?* (Munich: Südostdeutsches Kulturwerk, 1963), p. 15.

10 Sakrausky, *Primus Trubar* (1989), p. 73.

of these issues will be assessed in this chapter, looking here at the publication of catechisms in the different languages of the region, the purposes behind their production, and examining the relationship between linguistic community and confessional identity in east-central Europe.

The Hungarian kingdom never recovered from the catastrophic defeat inflicted by the Ottomans at the battle of Mohács in 1526. From the siege of Vienna in 1529 to the capture of Buda in 1541, fear of the Ottoman empire turned into a reality of territorial losses and ongoing border conflicts. Hungary was dismembered into three parts. The western region, later known as Royal Hungary, came under Habsburg rule. This territory stretched from the German-speaking towns and rural regions mainly inhabited by Hungarians and Slovaks in Upper Hungary down to the Slav and Italian regions of the Adriatic coast. Slovenia and Istria became borderlands between the Habsburgs and the Ottomans, who now controlled most of central and southern Hungary. To the east, Transylvania, including the Hungarian *Partium*, became an autonomous principality under rather loose Ottoman suzerainty, with native princes also holding influence over some of the counties of Upper Hungary. In Transylvania, the progress of Protestant preaching was consolidated in the 1560s and 1570s, when communities oriented towards Lutheranism, Calvinism and anti-Trinitarianism won legal protection, the right to worship freely and to publish printed literature in the principality.[11] The Ottoman invasion of Hungary not only brought political upheaval and social dislocation, but also a crisis of confidence in the Catholic Church. Protestant reformers were able to win support for their attempt to renew religion both in towns and from nobles, with little obstruction from weakened Catholic Church structures. Part of their rapid success was also due to the continuing 'Turkish peril', hinted at in much reform preaching.[12] Protestant communities also set up their own printing-presses, especially in the Transylvanian principality, where there were at least six major centres

---

11 Bucsay, *Der Protestantismus in Ungarn* (1977), pp. 104–64; Ján Adam, 'Bemerkungen zur Kalvinischen Reformation in der Slovakei' in Karl Schwarz, Peter Svorc eds, *Die Reformation und ihre Wirkungsgeschichte in der Slowakei* (Vienna: Evangelischer Presseverband, 1996), p. 91; Krista Zach, 'Stände, Grundherrschaft und Konfessionalisierung in Siebenbürgen. Überlegungen zur Sozialdisziplinierung (1550–1650)' in Joachim Bahlcke, Arno Strohmeyer eds, *Konfessionalisierung in Ostmitteleuropa. Wirkungen des religiösen Wandels im 16. und 17 Jahrhundert in Staat, Gesellschaft und Kultur* (Stuttgart: Steiner, 1999), pp. 367–91.

12 Honterus, *Die Reformation der Kronstädter Kirche und des ganzen Burzenlandes* (1543), p. 170; Sakrausky, *Primus Trubar. Deutsche Vorreden zum slowenischen und kroatischen Reformationswerk* (1989), p. 15.

of printing, and where a number of smaller printing-presses were also being established.[13]

From the 1540s to the 1580s between twenty-five and thirty different versions of Protestant catechisms were produced in the languages of this region, most of them in print, marking a period of intensive dissemination of religious knowledge in east-central Europe.[14] These catechisms provided the very first printed texts in Romanian, Slovene, Croat and Slovak, and were among the first texts produced in Hungarian, as they were elsewhere in Europe in the Finnish, Romany, Basque and Baltic languages. German-speakers in east-central Europe also developed their own versions of catechisms, adapting texts published in Germany.[15] Most of these catechisms were produced by humanists or reform-minded theologians, and most printed with the support of urban magistrates. Among these scholars were Primus Trubar (1508?–86) and Jurij Dalmatin (1546?–89), who translated the Bible into Slovene in 1584. Among Transylvanian Saxons involved were Johannes Honterus (1498?–49) and Kaspar Helth, who later called himself by the Hungarian version of his name, Gáspár Heltai (1520?–74), the Hungarian Péter Méliusz Juhász (1536–72), Leonhard Stöckel (1510–60) from the Spiš (Szepes/Zips) region of Upper Hungary, and the much younger Slovak parson Severín Skultéty (1550?–99).[16]

These translators and authors had mostly studied in German and Swiss universities such as Wittenberg, Basel, Geneva and Heidelberg, and returned home determined to introduce reform in their own regions. As these reformers produced printed religious literature, not only catechisms but also creeds, confessions of faith, textbooks and regulations for schools, they remained in constant contact with their former teachers such as Johann Bugenhagen, Johannes Oecolampadius,

---

13 Borsa ed., *Régi magyarországi nyomtatványok 1473–1600* vol. 1 (1971); Borsa ed., *Alte siebenbürgische Drucke (16. Jahrhundert)* (1996). In the 1570s prince István Báthory ordered the printing of religious pamphlets in the principality to be discontinued, but this was of little effect. Gedeon Borsa, 'Die Verbreitung der Druckereien im ehemaligen Ungarn' in Leppin, Wien eds, *Konfessionenbildung und konfessionelle Kultur in Siebenbürgen (16. Jahrhundert)* (2001).

14 Weismann, *Die Katechismen des Johannes Brenz* (1990), pp. 18, 623–30, 633–6; Borsa ed., *Alte siebenbürgische Drucke* (1996); Sakrausky, *Primus Trubar. Deutsche Vorreden zum slowenischen und kroatischen Reformationswerk* (1989).

15 Binder, *Johannes Honterus* (1996); Bucsay, *Der Protestantismus in Ungarn* vol. 1 (1977). For catechisms and other religious books printed in Brașov from 1548 and in Cluj from 1550 see Borsa, *Alte siebenbürgische Drucke* (1996), nos. 39, 45, 46, 60, 61, 130, 140, and pp. 49, 86; Weismann, *Die Katechismen von Luther und Brenz* (1985), p. 34.

16 For biographical details see *BioLex* (4 vols), (1974-81).

Philipp Melanchthon and Heinrich Bullinger among others.[17] It is difficult to assess the degree to which east-central European reformers asked for and adopted the advice of western teachers on programmes for reform and ways to improve local schools, but most catechisms seem to have been written or translated on the personal initiative of local reformers.[18] The translation and publication of catechisms involved more than simply copying out original versions, although the five central elements of doctrine were normally left unchanged. Reformers also often made additions to the original text, such as Primus Trubar's translation of sections from the Pentateuch and inclusion of some rhymes at the beginning of his first catechism in 1550. Johannes Honterus also added Old Testament king Manasseh's apocryphal prayer as well as advice on catechizing at home to his 1548 catechism.[19]

German reform literature, and later catechisms, especially those by Luther and Brenz, seem to have been known in Upper Hungary and Transylvania as early as the 1530s. Johannes Honterus produced the first catechism adapted for German-speakers in Transylvania in 1548. Then Gáspár Heltai published another version of Luther's *Shorter Catechism* at Cluj (Kolozsvár/Klausenburg) in 1550. Evangelical reform was also accepted in the German towns of Upper Hungary, and in 1548 Leonhard Stöckel produced a trilingual confession of faith (*Confessio Pentapolitana*) for the communities of the region. Then in 1556 Stöckel published a *Catechism* of Lutheran ideas at Bardejov (Bártfa/Bartfeld) for use in the town's school.[20]

Protestant preaching among Hungarians is suggested to have begun in the late 1520s, thanks to the efforts of Márton Kálmáncsehi Sánta (d. 1557) and Mátyás Devai Biró (d. 1545). However, Hungarian translations of western catechisms were somewhat slow to appear. In

---

[17] There were positive reactions from Bugenhagen, Luther and Melanchthon in 1544 to the Reformation booklets of the Transylvanian Saxons; Binder, *Johannes Honterus* (1996), pp. 248–50; Schwarz, Svorc eds, *Die Reformation in der Slowakei* (1996), pp. 85–6.

[18] Trubar and other reformers in Dalmatia and Slovenia strongly advocated this; Saria, *Primus Trubar* (1963), p. 19; Weismann, *Die Katechismen des Johannes Brenz* (1990), p. 627; Andreas Müller, *Reformation zwischen Ost und West. Valentin Wagners Griechischer Katechismus (Kronstadt 1550)* (Cologne: Böhlau, 2000), pp. xvi, xxx–xxxii.

[19] Sakrausky, *Primus Trubar* (1989), p. 73; Johannes Honterus, *Der Kleine Katechismus* (1548); Binder, *Johannes Honterus* (1996), p. 113.

[20] Borsa, *Alte siebenbürgische Drucke* (1996), nos. 39, 53; Honterus, *Der Kleine Katechismus* in Binder, *Johannes Honterus* (1996), pp. 113, 283; Gáspár Heltai, *Catechismus minor* (Kolozsvár, 1550); Martin Luther, *Summa christlicher Lehre, anderst der kurze Catechismus ... durch Caspar Helth* (Kolozsvár, 1551); Leonhard Stöckel, *Catechesis ... pro juventute Bartphensis composita* (Bartfeld, 1556); Borsa, *Alte siebenbürgische Drucke* (1996), nos. 39, 46, 53.

1550 Gáspár Heltai was the first to translate Luther's *Shorter Catechism* into Hungarian, and in 1553 the longer version of Luther's work soon followed, both printed at Cluj.[21] The last Hungarian Lutheran catechism published in Transylvania was produced by András Batizi at Cluj in 1555.[22] In 1559 Gál Huszár published a catechism influenced by the ideas of Heinrich Bullinger at Magyaróvár in western Hungary. Reformed catechisms were then published in Hungarian in greater numbers, notably by superintendent Péter Méliusz Juhász at Debrecen from 1562. These mostly followed Calvin's 1545 edition of the *Genevan Catechism*, and then later the 1563 Heidelberg *Catechism*. At Cluj, a number of Latin catechisms were also printed for schools from the mid-1560s, including Gergely Molnár's 1564 Calvinist *Catechism for the School at Kolozsvár*.[23] Hungarian catechisms of the 1560s also reflected doctrinal disputes taking place between theologians in Transylvania at that time. In 1566 the first Hungarian edition of the Heidelberg *Catechism* was produced. However, this was no simple translation of a Reformed text by a local Calvinist, but included ideas questioning the doctrine of the Trinity.[24] At Cluj and Debrecen other catechisms had also been published which explicitly dealt with disputed doctrine between Calvinists and Lutherans, including works of 1558 and 1559 by Ferenc Dávid, a 1559 service order-book by Gáspár Heltai, and a 1559 Apostles' Creed produced by Péter Méliusz Juhász.[25]

---

21 Borsa, *Alte siebenbürgische Drucke* (1996), nos. 46, 60, 61, 86.

22 Borsa, *Alte siebenbürgische Drucke* (1996), no. 86.

23 Péter Méliusz Juhász, *Catekismus. Az egesz keresztieni tudomannac fondamentoma es sommaia a szent irasbol esve szedettetet es meg emendaltatot* (Debrecen, 1562); Gergely Molnár, *Catechesis scholae Claudiopolitanae ad pietatis studiosam iuventutem in doctrina Christiana fideliter exercenda(m)* (Kolozsvár, 1564); Borsa, *Alte siebenbürgische Drucke* (1996), no. 130.

24 *Catechismus Ecclesiarum Dei in Natione Hungarica per Transilvaniam; quae relicto Deo Papistico quaterno, Verbum Dei de Sancto Sancta Triade Uno vero Deo, Patre, Filio ejus Domino Nostro Jesu Christo, ac amplorum Spiritu amplexae sunt, simplicitateque pia ac puritate illut credunt ac profitentur* (Kolozsvár, 1566); Borsa, *Alte siebenbürgische Drucke* (1996), no. 140, and pp. 148–9. This catechism was followed by decrees on the Trinity from clergy synods at Târgu Mureş (Marosvásárhely/Neumarkt) and Alba Iulia (Gyulafehérvár/Weissenburg).

25 Ferenc Dávid, *Consensus doctrinae de sacramentis Christi pastorum et ministrorum ecclesiarum in inferiori Pannonia et nationis utriusque in tota Transilvania. Conscriptus et publicatus in sancta sinodo Claudiopolitana Transylvainae* (Kolozsvár, 1557); Ferenc Dávid, *Acta synodi pastorum ecclesiae nationis Hungaricae in Transilvania ... in oppido Thorda caelebratae* (Kolozsvár, 1558); Ferenc Dávid, *Apologia adversus maledicentiam et calumnias Francisci Stancari, iussu et voluntate omnium docentium coelestem doctrinam incorrupte in ecclesiis Transylvanicis conscripta* (Kolozsvár, 1559); Ferenc Dávid, *Defensio orthodoxae sententiae de caena[!] Domini ministrorum ecclesiae Claudiopolitanae et reliquorum recte docentium in ecclesiis Transylvanicis* (Kolozsvár, 1559); Gáspár Heltai,

Protestant catechisms were not only published by and for German- and Hungarian-speakers in east-central Europe. In 1550 Primus Trubar published his translation of a *Catechism* using the spoken Slovene he encountered in the duchy of Carniola. In 1551 he published an *ABC and Short Catechism* aiming to encourage support for Lutheranism among Slovene-speakers. These catechisms were published at Tübingen, but because of local censorship laws in Carniola, both texts were claimed to have been published in Transylvania.[26] After 1553 a number of Slovene versions followed of Johannes Brenz's Württemberg *Catechism*, as well as translations of Luther's *Shorter Catechism*. Catechisms for the region were also published at Urach in the 1560s, and translated into Slovene, Croat and Italian using Latin, Glagolite and Cyrillic lettering.

These catechisms were the product of the particular interest of some German princes, nobles and towns in the progress of reform in regions of east-central Europe bordering on the Ottoman Empire. Christoph of Württemberg and Hans Ungnad of Sonnegg in Inner Austria supported the production of books for the region from printing-presses at Tübingen, Urach and Reutlingen. Indeed the printing press at Urach near Tübingen was established in the early 1560s precisely in order to print Protestant books using Latin, Cyrillic and Glagolite scripts.[27] To give some idea of the scale of this enterprise, a 1561 catechism had two thousand copies printed using the Glagolite and Cyrillic scripts, and four hundred additional copies using the Latin alphabet. Glagolitic writing was the most commonly used script in Croatia at this time, but was giving way to the increased use of Latin letters infiltrating the region from the coast.[28] In 1566 Sebastian Krelj's Croat *Bible for the Young* was

---

Agenda (Kolozsvár, 1559); Gáspár Heltai, *Libellus epistolaris a pio et doctissimo viro Heynricho Bullingero, Tygurine ecclesiae in Helvetia pastore ... ecclesiis in Hungaria earundemque pastoribus et ministris transmissus* (Kolozsvár, 1559); Borsa, *Alte siebenbürgische Drucke* (1996), nos. 102, 105, 106, 109–12; Borsa, *Régi magyarországi nyomtatványok 1473–1600*, vol. 1 (1971); Bucsay, *Der Protestantismus in Ungarn* (1977), pp. 114–18. After Dávid's 1579 trial on charges of rejecting the adoration of Christ, his main opponent, István Basilius, produced a catechism in 1583 of which no copies survive. Mihály Balázs, *Gab es eine antitrinitarische Konfessionalisierung im Siebenbürgen des 16. Jahrhunderts?* (2001) suggests that, 'In den letzten Jahrzehnten des 16. Jahrhunderts ist eine ganze Fülle von antitrinitarischen Katechismen mit unterschiedlicher theologischer Nuancierung zu bemerken ...' Unfortunately only two such works are known from later copies.

   26 Primus Trubar, *Abecedarium, und der klein Catechismus* (1551); Primus Trubar, *Catechismus* (Tübingen, 1550), Mirko Rupel ed. (Ljubljana: NUK, 1970), p. 245; Borsa, *Alte siebenbürgische Drucke* (1996), p. 385.

   27 Benz, *Wittenberg und Byzanz* (1971); Weismann, *Die Katechismen des Johannes Brenz* (1990), pp. 34, 627; Sakrausky, *Primus Trubar* (1989), pp. 12–15.

   28 Christoph Weismann, *Die Katechismen von Luther und Brenz* (Hagenau: Valentin Kobian, 1985), p. 70; Johannes Brenz, *Fragstücke* (1535).

added to the stock of books destined for Istria and Dalmatia.[29] Catechisms were not only published in the Slav languages of south-western Hungary, and in 1581 Luther's *Shorter Catechism* was translated into Slovak, probably by Severín Skultéty. This catechism was published at Bardejov, and was the first printed text using the Slovak language.[30]

The production of this remarkable range of catechisms in the mid-sixteenth century is indicative of the close links and frequent exchanges between east-central Europe and western Europe during the Reformation. Local reformers were not only concerned to use western texts as aids to spread knowledge about religious reform to the urban centres and countryside of their own linguistic and regional communities, but also sought to address neighbouring communities of different languages and confessions. This was indeed encouraged by leading western reformers who took a strong interest in the region such as Melanchthon and Bullinger.[31] These efforts particularly applied to followers of Orthodox Churches. In 1544 the first known vernacular catechism to be printed in east-central Europe was produced in Romanian using the Cyrillic alphabet. This text of *Christian Questions* was probably translated from Luther's *Shorter Catechism* by Filip Moldoveanul, a Wallachian who worked for the council at Sibiu (Nagyszeben/Hermannstadt). Unfortunately no copies of this work have survived, and indeed there may have been other catechisms printed in the region during this period which have since been lost. A second edition of this Romanian catechism was printed in 1559 or 1561 at Braşov, produced by a Greek Orthodox priest known as Diacon Coresi.[32] Catechisms are also known to have been published in Greek during this period. They included Valentin Wagner's *Catechism*, based on Melanchthon's 1540 *Catechism*, which was printed at Braşov in 1550 and aimed at Greek traders who lived around Braşov in the south of Transylvania.[33]

---

[29] Weismann, *Die Katechismen des Johannes Brenz* (1990), p. 628; Sebastian Krelj, *Catechesis quinque linguarum* or *Otrozhia Biblija* (Urach, 1566) in Slovene, Croat, German, Latin and Italian.

[30] An eighteenth-century source dated an unpublished hand-written translation from before 1546; Andej Hájduk, 'Severín Skultéty' in Schwarz, Svorc eds, *Die Reformation in der Slowakei* (1996), pp. 80–89.

[31] Benz, *Wittenberg und Byzanz* (1971), pp. 100–103; Krista Zach, *Orthodoxe Kirche und rumänisches Volksbewusstsein im 15. bis 18. Jahrhundert* (Wiesbaden: Harrassowitz, 1977), pp. 158–67, and see note 25.

[32] Filip Moldoveanul, *Intrebare Creştinească* (Sibiu, 1544). The first edition is completely lost, and from the second only a fragment has survived; Borsa, *Alte siebenbürgische Drucke* (1996), nos. 28, 117.

[33] Valentin Wagner, *Katichisis* (Kronstadt, 1550); Borsa, *Alte siebenbürgische Drucke* (1996), no. 43; Müller, *Valentin Wagners Griechischer Katechismus* (2000), p. xii.

During the mid-sixteenth century Protestant reformers in east-central Europe were supported by local authorities and nobles, both within the region and elsewhere, to publish a variety of catechisms using vernacular languages. Some sense of the intentions of the translators, publishers and patrons of these catechisms can be gauged from the forewords and epilogues of the books concerned, and from other contemporary sources. Reformers intended catechisms to be used in a variety of environments to instruct the young in the fundamentals of their faith, to spread knowledge about true religion, and effect the salvation of individuals and communities. Preachers also hoped to be able to use catechisms to explain complex points of doctrine, particularly contested areas such as understanding of the Eucharist.[34] The Transylvanian reformer, Johannes Honterus, expressed the reasons behind his translation of catechisms in the following terms:

> Many people have experienced through their own ruin, how great errors in Christian belief have been obscured until now by the Antichrist ... various writings by highly educated men easily testify ... that no one can continue to excuse his ignorance, [only] if he blocks his ears and keeps his eyes closed ... [The] foolish audacity of false prophets had grown to such an extent, that this [ruin] would soon have happened to those with true faith, if God had not spread the writing of his holy word across the world.[35]

Other translators also stressed the importance of public instruction about religion, and the need for people to hear or read the word of God in their own language. Coresi, responsible for the 1559 Romanian catechism published at Braşov, and who also translated a Gospel, wrote that 'students should understand the Lord's Word: but how can they understand it, if they have to learn about it in a foreign language which nobody understands.' Coresi also commented in the early 1560s that 'in the Church it is better to speak five comprehensible words than ten thousand incomprehensible words in a foreign tongue.'[36] There was a close connection between the production of vernacular catechisms and

---

34 Weismann, *Die Katechismen von Luther und Brenz* (1985), p. 32; *TRE*, vol. 17, p. 712, and see note 25.

35 'Viele Menschen haben es durch eigene Verderbnis erfahren, mit wie grossem Irrtum der christliche Glaube bisher durch den Antichrist verdunkelt ... es ist auch durch mannigfaltige Schriften hochgelehrter Männer genugsam bezeugt ... dass sich fortan niemand mit seiner Unwissenheit entschuldigen kann, es sei denn, dass er seine Ohren verstopft und seine Augen zugeschlossen hält ...'; Johannes Honterus, *Reformationsbüchlein* (Kronstadt, 1543), foreword; Binder, *Johannes Honterus* (1996), pp. 113, 169–70.

36 Zach, *Orthodoxe Kirche und rumänisches Volksbewusstsein* (1977), p. 166; Diacon Coresi, *Intrebare creştinească* (Braşov, 1561).

attempts to improve standards of learning more generally. Primus Trubar explained that he included a number of songs and rhymes in his catechism so that 'God may also give his mercy and spirit ... that young Slovenes may learn to read.'[37] Catechisms were therefore intended as authoritative sources of knowledge about true religious doctrine. As Trubar had commented in 1550:

> A religious person's first concern and habit is to love God's Word, to listen to it and to read it gladly, to regard this Word alone as true and to believe it. No matter what people speak, teach or do – be they the Holy Fathers of the old or of the new faith, the false Christian Church, councils, popes, bishops, priests, monks, or anyone else – the religious man shall look and consider if their teaching and actions agree with God's Word as written in the Holy books, in the Bible. If they do not agree, he shall not believe them and shall not follow their teaching. On this account, this person will be religious and wise, understanding, rich and happy – regardless of the opinion of other people who hold him for a fool.[38]

Reformers also thought that catechisms could spread hope of being rescued by God from the miseries of political upheaval and social dislocation brought by Ottoman invasion. Most of the forewords and epilogues of printed catechisms and the confessions of faith adopted by reforming synods in the 1550s and 1560s connected the need to understand the word of God with their immediate political environment. The continued threat of further Ottoman advances heightened the sense of the region as a threatened bastion of Christianity during the mid-sixteenth century, but it was widely thought that a true reform of religion would lead to political and military recovery.[39] As Johannes Honterus wrote in 1543; 'we believed on these and other grounds, that in the present times, so full of danger, that we should not wait any longer' to introduce reforms to religious practices.[40] This may

---

[37] 'Auff das hub ich an den Catechismum zu verdolmetschen, und ins Gesang vnd Reimen zu bringen. Darzu gab Gott auch sein Gnad und Geist ... darauß die Jungen Windischen lesen lernen mügen ...'; Primus Trubar, *Teütsche Vorred* to *Na pervi deil tiga Noviga Testamenta* (1557); Saria, *Primus Trubar* (Tübingen: Morhart, 1963), p. 15.

[38] Trubar, *Catechismus* (1550); Boris Paternu, *Protestantism and the Emergence of Slovene Literature*. *Slovene Studies 6/1–2* (Munich: Trofenik, 1984), pp. 81–2.

[39] Harald Roth, 'Autostereotype als Identifikationsmuster. Zum Selbstbild der Siebenbürger Sachsen' in Konrad Gündisch, Wolfgang Höpken and Michael Markel eds, *Das Bild des Anderen in Siebenbürgen. Stereotype in einer multiethnischen Region* (Cologne: Böhlau, 1998), pp. 179–90.

[40] 'Gleichwohl glaubten wir aus diesen und anderen Gründen, in den gegenwärtigen so gefahrvollen Zeiten nicht mehr warten zu sollen [mit Einführung der Neuerungen ...]'; Johannes Honterus, *Apologie* (Kronstadt, 1543) in Binder, *Johannes Honterus* (1996), p. 170.

also explain in part why leading western reformers took such a deep interest in the progress of reform in east-central Europe. Certainly Primus Trubar wrote in his 1557 translation of part of the New Testament about the call to produce texts using Slavonic languages, which had received support among some of the German Protestant elite:

> Both nations, in the Slovene and Croatian provinces, grieved me to the heart; they should raise sympathy in anyone not only because of the fact that they must live on the border with the Ottomans ... but I also feel sympathy for them because they know very little or almost nothing ... about the most necessary and comforting fundamentals of our real Christian faith which should be known by every sensible man for the benefit of his soul and for his highest consolation.[41]

Catechisms in sixteenth-century east-central Europe therefore had didactic purposes, polemic purposes and political purposes. They were also produced as part of a concerted attempt to bring reform to the Orthodox communities of the region. It is unclear how far western reformers may have encouraged this mission to the Orthodox Church. Whilst there may have been outside encouragement, it seems that printed works directed to Romanians and other Orthodox communities mostly resulted from local initiatives.[42] The first two Romanian catechisms of 1544 and 1559 were works commissioned by the Saxon magistrates of Sibiu and Braşov, apparently inspired by a feeling of responsibility towards the Romanian Orthodox peasantry living in their territory. These urban German elites met the cost of translating, printing and distributing the catechisms to local Romanian communities. Unfortunately no evidence survives about the scale of this enterprise, or on the reception which the catechisms received from Orthodox priests or Romanian communities.[43]

The Romanian catechisms and Bible translations published by Saxon Germans in Transylvania during the second half of the sixteenth century have long been recognized as a significant achievement in the development of Romanian literature.[44] However, Romanian scholars of the nineteenth and twentieth centuries balanced this recognition with

---

[41] 'Und dieser obgemelten zweien Völckern erbarmlich und grosse gfar, angst vun nott ... haben mich verursacht ... .'; Saria, *Primus Trubar* (1963), p. 14, from Trubar's German foreword.

[42] Benz, *Wittenberg und Byzanz* (1971); Zach, *Orthodoxe Kirche und rumänisches Volksbewusstsein* (1977), pp. 130–31, 161–3.

[43] Zach, *Orthodoxe Kirche und rumänisches Volksbewusstsein* (1977), pp. 163, 166.

[44] Alexandru Rosetti, *Istoria limbii române de la origini până în secolul al xvii-lea* (Bucharest: Editura Academiei, 1968).

deep suspicion about the real intentions of Protestant reformers.[45] Romanians in Transylvania did not have the constitutional status of a recognized estate or 'nation' alongside German towns and villages, the mostly Hungarian nobility and the community of free Szeklers. For some Romanian historians, attempts to convert Orthodox believers marked a further social evil perpetrated by 'foreign forces' and 'false creeds' against Transylvania's Romanians. Rather than suggest an agenda of seeking to undermine Romanian identity, more recently some Romanian historians have, however, looked again at the reasons why Orthodox and Protestant piety and religious practices in the end proved incompatible and why the Saxon Protestant mission to the Romanians failed.[46]

Protestant reformers in east-central Europe were faced with the advance of Ottoman military might and political power, which made the need for religious reform seem urgent. Within the fragmented Hungarian kingdom, communities speaking Hungarian, German, Romanian and Slav languages were all perceived to require clear information about 'true' faith in their own languages. There was no reason to suppose that some linguistic or ethnic communities within the Latin Church were more predisposed than others to accept reform. The reception of Reformation ideas in this region was certainly influenced by factors including shared language, ethnic ties and communication linkages. In the sixteenth century, German-speaking towns in Transylvania and Upper Hungary became very strongly associated with Lutheranism, a cohesiveness which later allowed for religion and ethnicity to become tightly linked within Transylvanian Saxon or Zipser Saxon identities.[47] Meanwhile, Hungarian towns and nobles in Transylvania and Upper Hungary mostly became Calvinist, although there was strong support for anti-Trinitarianism in some areas. While,

---

[45] Zach, *Orthodoxe Kirche und rumänisches Volksbewusstsein* (1977), pp. 130, 162–7; compare with Mircea Păcurariu, *Istoria bisericii ortodoxe române* (Bucharest: Editura Institutului biblic şi de misiune al Bisericii Ortodoxe Române, 1994), vol. 1, pp. 495, 545.

[46] Maria Crăciun, 'Orthodox Piety and the Rejection of Protestant Ideas in xvith Century Moldavia' in Maria Crăciun, Ovidiu Ghitta eds, *Ethnicity and Religion in Central and Eastern Europe* (Cluj: University Press, 1995), pp. 70–91.

[47] The rather misleading concept of a Saxon 'Volkskirche' originates from the work of Georg Daniel and Friedrich Teutsch, *Geschichte der Siebenbürger Sachsen für das sächsische Volk* (4 vols), (Hermannstadt: Krafft, 1920–26) and (Cologne: Böhlau, 1984); compare with Krista Zach, 'Religiöse Toleranz und Stereotypenbildung in einer multikulturellen Region. Volkskirchen in Siebenbürgen?' in Konrad Gündisch et al. eds, *Das Bild des Anderen in Siebenbürgen* (1998), pp. 109–53.

by the early seventeenth century, Hungarians dominated the Reformed and eventually also the anti-Trinitarian Church, some Hungarian-speakers in the Transylvanian principality as well as Slovaks in Upper Hungary also belonged to the Lutheran and Catholic Churches. For example, Catholicism never completely lost its grip among the Hungarian-speaking northern Szekler communities of eastern Transylvania. Thus, links between religion, language and ethnicity in this region need to be treated with great care in order not to offer support to simplistic nationalist paradigms.[48]

Among the factors which shaped the social reception of religious reform in east-central Europe, how should the role of vernacular texts, and particularly of catechisms, be assessed? Evidence about how catechisms were received within local communities is almost non-existent, and analysis rests heavily on the ideas of those who produced this material.[49] The number of copies of catechisms circulating in the region, and the variable density of coverage in different areas also requires further investigation. However, it is clear that as reformers attempted to spread Protestant religious ideas across east-central Europe, they were certain that vernacular catechisms had a vital role to play. By printing texts in the vernacular to instruct people about religion, reformers aimed to reach all the linguistic communities of their region, not limiting their appeal to urban communities or social elites. Reform was required for each ethnic and confessional community, even, according to some, including the Turks. Primus Trubar and his colleagues turned their attention to Slovene- and Croat-speakers, and whilst Transylvanian Saxon magistrates ordered schoolbooks to be printed for their own community they also addressed neighbouring Romanians. While the ethnic and linguistic contexts of confessional difference in east-central Europe later became prominent, in the mid-sixteenth century such barriers to reform were simply not recognized.

---

[48] Bucsay, *Der Protestantismus in Ungarn* (1977), pp. 69–86; Krista Zach, 'Bild-Gegenbild-Spiegelbild. Ethnotypische Chiffren aus einer Region multikultureller Übergänge am Beispiel Siebenbürgens' in Wernfried Hofmeister, Bernd Steinbauer eds, *Durch aubenteuer muess man wagen vil. Festschrift für Anton Schwob* (Innsbruck: Institut für Germanistik, 1997), pp. 567–88; Graeme Murdock, 'International Calvinism, Ethnic Allegiance, and the Reformed Church of Transylvania in the Early Seventeenth Century' in Crăciun, Ghitta eds, *Ethnicity and Religion in Central and Eastern Europe* (1995), pp. 92–100.

[49] For consistent consideration of these issues see Ádám Dankanits, *Lesestoffe des 16. Jahrhunderts in Siebenbürgen* (Bucharest, Kriterion, 1982); Murdock, 'International Calvinism, Ethnic Allegiance, and the Reformed Church of Transylvania in the Early Seventeenth Century' (1995), pp. 92–100. Sakrausky, *Primus Trubar* (1989), p. 184.

This was also a period when western Protestant centres took a particular interest in the region, training young ministers, corresponding with local leaders, and providing financial support for the publication of religious books. However, reform was initiated and shaped by locals, influenced by contact with the west, but at the same time remaining autonomous in deciding how best to advance the cause of reform in east-central Europe.

The production of catechisms in the mid-sixteenth century made a significant impression upon the development of the languages of the region, but in many areas catechisms failed to make a long-term impact on systems of religious belief. Catechisms were widely used in schools and parishes across the region in the mid-sixteenth century, including very remote areas of the former Hungarian kingdom in modern Slovenia and Slovakia. However, this success came during a period of weak central political authority, immanent fear of Ottoman power, and disrupted ecclesiastical structures in many areas. From the last decade of the sixteenth century, support for Protestant ideas fell away in the face of Catholic Counter-Reform sponsored by the Habsburgs. Catholic recovery was most marked in Inner Austria, Royal and Upper Hungary, including lands where people spoke Slovene, Croat and Slovak. When the Habsburgs were able to push the Ottomans out of the northern Balkans at the end of the seventeenth century, they also gained control over eastern Hungary and Transylvania. Among the effects of the reversion of many Hungarian magnates, gentry and urban elites to Catholicism was the prohibition of Protestant publishing and the destruction of Protestant books, as had happened before in Slovenia. Only in the Transylanian principality did constitutional protection continue to be afforded to Protestant confessions, and here the production and use of catechisms was sustained. A Calvinist catechism was even published for Slovak-speakers at the Reformed town of Debrecen in the Hungarian *Partium* as late as the end of the eighteenth century, but such attempts to revive Protestant fortunes were but a pale reflection of the sixteenth-century production of catechisms in support of religious reform across all the communities of east-central Europe.[50]

---

[50] Weismann, *Die Katechismen des Johannes Brenz* (1990), p. 627; Adam, 'Bemerkungen zur Kalvinischen Reformation in der Slovakei' (1996), pp. 90–97.

CHAPTER FOUR

Shaping Transylvanian anti-Trinitarian identity in an urban context

Carmen Florea

After the collapse of the medieval Hungarian kingdom, the Ottomans and Habsburgs battled to establish their supremacy over Transylvania. The Transylvanian estates were left uncomfortably lodged between these two powers and, under the leadership of elected native nobles, attempted to bring stability to the region. In 1568 the Transylvanian diet, meeting at Turda (Torda/Thorenburg), reacted to the further challenge posed to domestic order by the spread of Reformation ideas by attempting to unite the estates around a 'tolerant' constitutional settlement, and granted freedoms to all Christian faiths in the principality. The history of Cluj (Kolozsvár/Klausenburg), one of Transylvania's largest towns, provides particularly important evidence about the nature and impact of this Turda settlement within the principality. Cluj was also the centre of support for anti-Trinitarianism in Transylvania, a cause which received some backing from the court of prince János Zsigmond Zápolyai. After János Zsigmond's death in 1571, prince István Báthory worked to recover the position of the Catholic Church in Transylvania and invited Jesuit missionaries to move to Cluj in the 1580s. This more hostile political environment left the new anti-Trinitarian Church reliant upon some noble supporters, but especially dependent upon its urban base of support in Cluj.[1]

This chapter focuses on the role which the town of Cluj played in Transylvanian religious life, and in the development of anti-Trinitarianism

---

[1] Róbert Dán, Antal Pirnát eds, *Antitrinitarianism in the second half of the sixteenth century* (Budapest: Akadémiai kiadó, 1982); Mihály Balázs, *Az erdélyi antitrinitarizmus az 1560-as évek végén. Humanizmus és Reformáció 14* (Budapest: Balassi kiadó, 1988); Mihály Balázs, *Teológia és irodalom. Az Erdélyen kívüli antitrinitarizmus kezdetei. Humanizmus és Reformáció 25* (Budapest: Balassi kiadó, 1998); Earl Wilbur, *A History of Unitarianism in Transylvania, England and America* (Cambridge [MA]: Harvard University Press, 1952); George Williams, *The Radical Reformation* (Philadelphia [PA]: Westminster Press, 1962), pp. 708–32.

within the principality during the second half of the sixteenth century. While anti-Trinitarian ideas spread right across Transylvania, in particular to some Hungarian-speaking towns and to eastern counties, the institutions of an anti-Trinitarian Church emerged from Cluj. Radical theological speculation was also pursued in other Transylvanian urban centres, such as at Sibiu (Nagyszeben/Hermannstadt) and Braşov (Brassó/Kronstadt), but failed to establish institutional support there.[2] The radical religious ideas which were supported in Cluj will be examined here, as will the means by which an anti-Trinitarian (or later Unitarian) Church established a superintendent resident in Cluj, whose influence reached far beyond the town's walls. The second part of this article will consider the production of anti-Trinitarian catechisms in Cluj, and assess the impact which these catechisms made on anti-Trinitarianism across Transylvania. The focus here will not only be on the theological content of these texts, which marked significant developments in anti-Trinitarian doctrine, but also suggest that they represented a concerted attempt by anti-Trinitarian clergy in Cluj to establish wider social understanding of anti-Trinitarianism in their town and across the principality. I will investigate the production and reception of catechisms from the 1566 publication of *Catechismus Ecclesiarum Dei*, and will examine the anti-Trinitarian Church up to the death in 1601 of János Kósa, author of the last anti-Trinitarian catechism to be discussed here.

Despite the dramatic political changes to afflict Transylvania during the sixteenth century, Cluj maintained its status as a royal free town throughout the period. A charter of privileges was first issued for Cluj in 1405, which was confirmed by later Hungarian kings. In 1554 the town's privileges were upheld by the Transylvanian prince, who took over the powers of the royal governor of medieval Transylvania. The status of Cluj as a royal free town was confirmed again in 1560 by János Zsigmond, and by István Báthory in 1577. This status meant that the citizens of Cluj had the right to choose a judge and twelve jurors for a local court, and the right to present the town's *plebanus*. Members of the town's court and council were required to be citizens of Cluj in order to hold their offices, and were empowered to take decisions concerning all local administrative, judicial and financial matters.[3] The town's

---

2 Christine Peters, 'Mural Paintings, Ethnicity and Religious Identity in Transylvania: The Context for the Reformation' in Maria Crăciun, Ovidiu Ghitta eds, *Ethnicity and Religion in Central and Eastern Europe* (Cluj: University Press, 1995), pp. 49–50.

3 Elek Jakab, *Oklevéltár Kolozsvár története első kötetéhez* (Buda: Magyar kir. Egyetemi Könyvnyomda, 1870), no. lxxxvi, pp. 123–6; Elek Jakab, *Oklevéltár Kolozsvár története második és harmadik kötetéhez* (Budapest: Magyar kir. Egyetemi Könyvnyomda, 1888), nos. xxx, liii, pp. 55–7, 101–103; Elek Jakab, *Kolozsvár története. Első kötet* (Buda: Magyar kir. Egetemi Könyvnyomda, 1870), pp. 435–62.

importance as a commercial centre developed greatly during the sixteenth century. This was based on its prime location on the main route west out of Transylvania from the German-speaking towns of the principality to urban centres in eastern Hungary such as Oradea (Nagyvárad/Grosswardein), or towards Košice (Kassa/Kaschau) to the north.[4] Commercial activity in Cluj also benefited from the support of princes, and in 1558 the town was granted the right to hold four 'national fairs', and the statutes of a number of local guilds gained princely approval during this period.[5]

From the late middle ages Cluj, unlike most other major towns in Transylvania, had a linguistically mixed population, divided between German- and Hungarian-speaking residents. These two communities shared control of the town's offices. In 1458 it was established that the town's judge would be a Hungarian-speaker one year and a German in the following year.[6] The twelve jurors were elected on the same basis, six were Hungarians and six were Germans. It was also decided that half of the one-hundred-strong council was to be drawn from the ranks of the town's guilds, a decision confirmed in 1486.[7] During the second half of the sixteenth century this balance of power was maintained between the local German and Hungarian communities, and arrangements between the two linguistic groups were approved by prince János Zsigmond in 1568.[8] However, the proportion of Hungarian-speaking citizens in the town seems to have progressively increased during this period, and the Hungarian community was particularly well represented among the growing ranks of artisans who gradually became more involved in the town's administrative structures.[9]

Turning to examine the framework for religious life in Cluj, this was maintained with a strong degree of continuity across the period despite the impact of doctrinal reform. Cluj traditionally had only a single parish church, with the *plebanus* for St Michael's church in the town's central square chosen by the town council. However, one sign of the growing strength of the Hungarian-speaking community in Cluj was their use of the church of Sts Peter and Paul from the mid-fifteenth

---

[4] Béla Köpeczi ed., *Erdély története* (3 vols), (Budapest: Akadémiai kiadó, 1988), vol. 1, László Makkai, András Mócsy eds, pp. 471–2.

[5] Jakab, *Oklevéltár* (1870), nos. v, xi, xxi, xxii, xxvi, xxxii, xxxvii, xlvi, lxvii, pp. 9–10, 20–24, 34–5, 35–8, 44–8, 58–60, 69–75, 94–5, 98–102, 139–42; Samuel Goldenberg, *Clujul în secolul al XVI-lea. Producţia şi schimbul de mărfuri* (Bucharest: Editura Academiei Populare Române, 1957).

[6] Jakab, *Oklevéltár* (1870), no. cxv, pp. 192–3.

[7] Jakab, *Oklevéltár* (1870), no. clxxii, p. 275.

[8] Jakab, *Kolozsvár története. Második kötet* (1888), no. xli, pp. 80–88.

[9] Jakab, *Kolozsvár története. Második kötet* (1888), p. 292.

century. There were also Mendicant establishments within Cluj, with a Dominican convent and nunnery, a Franciscan friary and a Poor Clare convent.[10] On the whole, the balance in the public life of Cluj between Hungarians and Germans was preserved in the sixteenth century. From the mid-sixteenth century the salary of the *plebanus* in Cluj was provided by the town council, and the salary of any other preachers employed in the town was then established by the *plebanus*. It started to be the practice that when the town's judge was Hungarian, St Michael's church was used by Hungarians, while Germans used the chapel of St John which was affiliated to St Michael's. In the following year under a German-speaking judge, the German community worshipped in St Michael's church, whilst the Hungarian community attended services in the chapel of St John.[11]

The involvement of the magistrates of Cluj in selecting and providing financial support for the town's *plebanus* and in taking responsibility for the employment of parish preachers took on a new significance when Reformation ideas began to make an impact in Cluj from the 1540s. Indeed, the involvement of magistrates in the religious life of towns across Hungary and Transylvania was highly significant in gaining acceptance for reform.[12] This was particularly the case in Transylvania after the collapse of Catholic institutions in the principality. From 1556 the diet agreed that all church property within the bishoprics of Transylvania should be brought under the control of the prince, and the prince took up residence in the former episcopal palace at Alba Iulia (Gyulafehérvár/Weissenburg). The Transylvanian bishop had traditionally taken part in the investiture of a newly-elected *plebanus* in Cluj, but in the absence of a bishop, local magistrates now dominated the ceremony. Investitures were held in front of St Michael's church in the central square. At his investiture, the new *plebanus* met representatives of the town council and other citizens, and conducted a short service. Then, two jurors presented the *plebanus* with symbols representing the income of the parish. The *plebanus* was charged to take good care of the state of religious life in the town, and promised to act only in the interests of the town and its council.[13]

The traditional privilege granted to the council in Cluj to choose a

---

10   Marie Madeleine de Cevins, 'L'Église dans les villes hongroises aux XIV–XV siècles' (Paris-Sorbonne University Ph. D, 1995), pp. 412–13.

11   László Makkai, *Koloszvár. Egy magyar város ezer esztendeje* (Koloszvár: Város Kiadása, 1942).

12   de Cevins, 'L'Église dans les villes hongroises aux XIV–XV siècles' (1995), pp. 1190–92.

13   Jakab, *Kolozsvár története. Második kötet* (1888), pp. 412–13.

plebanus thus became more significant, and magistrates came to control the direction of the town's church and therefore the reception of Reformation ideas. While the German-speaking towns of Upper Hungary and Transylvania had adopted Lutheran ideas in the 1540s, the free practice of Lutheranism in the Transylvanian principality was only sanctioned by the diet in 1557. However, in 1545 the council in Cluj had already decided to give control of St Michael's to the Lutheran Church, and in 1556 the Dominicans and Franciscans were ordered to leave the town. The altars and images in the chapels of these orders were destroyed, and in 1565 the council decided that the Dominican nunnery and the church of Sts Peter and Paul should be demolished altogether, leaving St Michael's as the focal point for religious life in Cluj. In 1558 the council decided to transfer control of the town's church to 'sacramentarians'.[14] Debates had been held in Transylvania that year between Lutheran clergy and those ministers who supported Calvinist views on communion theology. However, there are also indications of the uncertain state of religion in the town at this time. The council decided to permit the Hungarian and German communities to maintain separate preachers subordinate to the *plebanus*. In 1558 Hungarian-speaking preachers were allowed to serve in the former Dominican church and in St John's chapel. Meanwhile, from 1560 another German-speaking preacher was appointed by the council.[15] Faced with apparent differences between the religious preferences of the two linguistic communities, in 1565 the magistrates ordered preachers employed in the town not to argue about religious issues unless the council specifically gave them permission to do so.[16]

The turbulent state of religious life in Cluj was then unsettled again by the arrival of anti-Trinitarian ideas during the 1560s. Interest in anti-Trinitarianism developed in the principality after the arrival of Giorgio Biandrata in 1563. Biandrata was one of a number of exiled Italian reformers, who worked in Poland before coming to Transylvania. Biandrata served at the Transylvanian court as personal physician to the regent Isabella Zápolyai, daughter of the Polish king, and then to her son János Zsigmond.[17] Biandrata certainly contributed to the spread of

---

[14] Jakab, *Kolozsvár története. Második kötet* (1888), pp. 74, 186–7, 337; Géza Entz, András Kovács, *A koloszvári Farkas utcai címerei* (Budapest: Balassi kiadó, 1995), pp. 10–12; Edit Grandpierre, *A koloszvári Szent Mihály templom* (Cluj: Minerva, 1936), pp. 28–32. Compare with *Quellen zur Geschichte der Stadt Brassó* (4 vols), (Brassó: Gust, 1903), vol. 4, pp. 81, 535, for iconoclasm in Sibiu and Braşov in 1544.

[15] Jakab, *Kolozsvár története. Második kötet* (1888), pp. 111, 135.

[16] Jakab, *Kolozsvár története. Második kötet* (1888), p. 178.

[17] Domenico Caccamo, *Eretici Italiani in Moravia, Polonia, Transilvania (1558–1611)* (Chicago: Newberry Library, 1970); Cesare Alzati, *Terra romena tra Oriente*

interest in anti-Trinitarian ideas at the court, and public debates were held with rival Calvinist preachers in 1564 at Aiud (Nagyenyed/ Grossenyed), and in 1566 at Alba Iulia, Turda and Odorheiu Secuiesc (Székelyudvarhely/Odorhellen). Further debates about the scriptural basis for the doctrine of the Trinity were then held in 1568, 1569 and 1571, all in the presence of prince János Zsigmond.[18]

One participant in these debates was the Cluj *plebanus*, Ferenc Dávid. Dávid had been educated at schools in Cluj and Alba Iulia, and in the 1540s was listed among students at the University of Wittenberg. After 1552 he became a Lutheran and was elected as *plebanus* of Cluj in 1556. In 1558 Dávid shifted his loyalty to the Reformed cause, and then in the 1560s, under the influence of Biandrata, began to move towards anti-Trinitarianism, all the time remaining as *plebanus* in Cluj.[19] Dávid became increasingly familiar with anti-Trinitarian theology during the debates of the 1560s, and started to formulate his own ideas about the biblical basis for ideas about the Trinity and about traditional Christology. In 1565 he formed a group of young anti-Trinitarians at Cluj with the aim of providing an accurate translation of the Bible in Hungarian. Once the Transylvanian diet had decided in 1568 to accept all the Christian faiths of the principality, Dávid led the further Reformation of the church in Cluj in 1570, and St Michael's church became the main centre of anti-Trinitarian preaching in Transylvania.[20]

In 1571 the constitutional freedoms of the anti-Trinitarian Church were confirmed, and the church was able to hold its first clergy synod at which Ferenc Dávid presided as superintendent. Theoretically, Dávid held jurisdiction over anti-Trinitarian churches across the former Catholic bishopric of Alba Iulia.[21] Anti-Trinitarianism received support from some prominent Hungarian noble families, including figures such as Gáspár Békes, Gáspár Kornis, Kristóf Hagymási, János Gerendi and

---

e Occidente. Chiese ed etnie nel tardo '500 (Milano: Jaca, 1981), pp. 49–51; Antal Pirnát, 'Il martire e l'uomo politico' in Dán, Pirnát eds, *Antitrinitarianism in the second half of the sixteenth century* (1982), pp. 157–82.

18 Sándor Székely, *Unitária vallás történetei Erdélyben* (Kolozvár, 1840), pp. 53–5; György Fekete, 'Az unitárius szabadságának alkotmányos biztositékai' in György Boros ed., *Az unitárius vallás Dávid Ferenc korában és azután* (Kolozsvár, 1910), pp. 28–30.

19 Balázs, *Az erdélyi antitrinitarizmus* (1988); Elek Jakab, *Dávid Ferenc emléke. Éitéltése és halála* (Budapest, 1879); János Erdő, 'The Biblicism of Ferenc Dávid' in Dán, Pirnát eds, *Antitrinitarianism in the second half of the sixteenth century* (1982), pp. 45–62.

20 The preachers in Cluj at this time were Demeter Hunyadi, István Basilius, Pál Kozárvári, István Szatmári and Johann Eppel; Székely, *Unitária vallás történetei Erdélyben* (1840), p. 46.

21 Székely, *Unitária vallás történetei Erdélyben* (1840), p. 68; Pirnát, 'Il martire e l'uomo politico' (1982), p. 154.

Mihály Csáki. Some of the works published in Transylvania by Biandrata and Dávid were indeed dedicated to Békes, Csáki and Hagymási.[22] Anti-Trinitarianism was also particularly well received among some Szekler villages in the eastern counties of Transylvania. It is difficult to be certain about the extent of the authority exerted by the anti-Trinitarian superintendent in the early years of the church's existence, and how far Dávid's authority in reality extended beyond Cluj. In 1571 the death of János Zsigmond caused further disruption to the development of the institutions of an anti-Trinitarian Church in Transylvania, as restrictions were soon imposed on the fledgling church by the new Catholic prince, István Báthory. The Transylvanian diet restricted the right of the anti-Trinitarian Church to hold synods, which in future could only take place in the towns of Cluj and Turda.[23] In 1576 the diet met at Mediaş (Medgyes/Mediasch) and confirmed Ferenc Dávid in his post as superintendent. However, this diet also expressly forbade any religious innovation among Transylvania's churches, which confirmed previous decisions taken by diets in 1571, 1572 and 1573.[24] The loss of court support and limits placed on anti-Trinitarian institutions and doctrinal development in the 1570s, left the church increasingly reliant on its urban base in Cluj, and in particular on its *plebanus*, preachers and the town council.

During the 1570s Transylvanian anti-Trinitarianism came to be based primarily at Cluj, in an environment which had recently seen rapid changes in religious sympathies, and which maintained autonomous control over local religious affairs. It is perhaps hardly surprising given these circumstances that the anti-Trinitarian Church soon faced a major internal debate over the exact nature of the doctrines which the church should adhere to. The crucial point of debate between anti-Trinitarians in Cluj came over the issue of Christ's double nature and whether he should be adored in worship. Some radicals working in Cluj, such as Jacobus Paleologus and Johannes Sommer, contributed to the ongoing development of Ferenc Dávid's thinking about the nature of Christ. Dávid came to believe that Christ should neither be invoked in prayer nor adored in worship. Dávid preached on these ideas in the church at Cluj, which eventually brought him into direct conflict with the state authorities. Dávid's non-adorantist anti-Trinitarianism seemed to imply clear doctrinal innovation, and he was accused of breaking the restrictions imposed in 1576 against such innovation by anyone within

---

[22] János Kénosi Tűzsér, *De typographiis et typographis unitariorum in Transylvania*, Ferenc Földesi ed. (Szeged: KFT, 1991), pp. 120–25.

[23] Fekete, 'Az unitárius szabadságának alkotmányos biztositékai' (1910), p. 30.

[24] Jakab, *Kolozsvár története. Második kötet* (1888), pp. 186.

the four 'received' religions of Transylvania. At a diet held in Alba Iulia in 1579, Dávid again expressed his ideas about non-adorantism of Christ, while Giorgio Biandrata and Demeter Hunyadi, along with other leading anti-Trinitarian clergy, supported the adoration of Christ in worship. Dávid was found guilty of breaking the diet's restriction against religious innovation and was imprisoned at Deva (Déva/ Diemrich) castle, where he died later in 1579.[25]

Meanwhile, with princely backing, Giorgio Biandrata called a synod of anti-Trinitarian clergy to Cluj in July 1579, at which Demeter Hunyadi was chosen as the church's new superintendent. There were also clear signs from this synod of growing hierarchical controls being imposed on the church. All clergy present were compelled to sign a declaration in support of the adoration of Christ in anti-Trinitarian worship, and the synod agreed that all further doctrinal debate on the issue of the adoration of Christ was expressly forbidden.[26] The new superintendent was also given powers to control the movement of clergy between parishes, and to prevent any rogue clergy escaping from disciplinary sanctions imposed by the clergy hierarchy.[27] Demeter Hunyadi remained as superintendent and *plebanus* for Cluj until his death in 1592. The next superintendent chosen to lead the anti-Trinitarian Church in Transylvania was György Enyedi, who could claim to have as many as 425 congregations under his jurisdiction across the principality.[28] Whilst Enyedi was superintendent, he was not elected as *plebanus* in Cluj because of the agreement between Hungarian and German residents which required that a German should take the office after Demeter Hunyadi. Instead John Erasmus, already an anti-Trinitarian preacher in Cluj, became the town's *plebanus*.[29] György Enyedi attempted to provide firm institutional leadership for the anti-Trinitarian Church. In 1592 a synod held at Turda decided that all anti-Trinitarian clergy must attend each synod, threatening to deprive from their offices those who failed to comply.[30] Also a group of three ministers, including the Cluj preacher, János Kósa, was established to

---

25 Pirnát, 'Il martire e l'uomo politico' (1982), pp. 157–82.

26 Székely, *Unitária vallás történetei Erdélyben* (1840), p. 85.

27 György Tóth, *Az Unitárius egyház rendszabályai, 1626–1859* (Cluj: Minerva, 1922), pp. ix–x.

28 Székely, *Unitária vallás történetei Erdélyben* (1840), p. 69; see also Mihály Balázs, Gizella Keserű eds, *György Enyedi and Central European Unitarianism in the sixteenth and seventeenth centuries* (Budapest: Balassi, 2000).

29 The preachers in Cluj at this time were János (Várfalvi) Kósa, Péter Enyedi, István Basilius, Miklós Bogáthi and Ferenc Balasi; Jakab, *Kolozsvár története. Második kötet* (1888), pp. 263, 332–5.

30 Tóth, *Az Unitárius egyház rendszabályai* (1922), p. xii.

investigate suspected problems in the church at Deva. Enyedi also attempted to provide the church with clear statements about anti-Trinitarian doctrine, and completed extensive texts explaining and clarifying the church's central beliefs.[31]

János Kósa became the next anti-Trinitarian superintendent in 1597 and, although a Hungarian, he was also able to serve as Cluj *plebanus* until 1601. There are further indications of the growing authority of the superintendent over the anti-Trinitarian Church during Kósa's period in office, such as the synod's requirement that ministers should only discuss directly with the superintendent any questions which they had about contested points of theology. Anti-Trinitarian superintendents thus played an ever more significant role in the organization of the church and in the formulation of statements about anti-Trinitarian doctrine. With the exception of György Enyedi, the church's superintendents were also all elected to serve as the *plebanus* of Cluj and, with the exception of John Erasmus, all preached to the Hungarian-speaking community in the town. Anti-Trinitarianism entirely dominated the religious life of Cluj in the latter decades of the sixteenth century, controlling the only functioning church in the town.[32] The German-speaking community in Cluj was also served by anti-Trinitarian preachers, one of whom was made *plebanus*, but Hungarians took the lead in the religious life of Cluj and in anti-Trinitarianism across Transylvania.

Education also played a crucial role in the development of anti-Trinitarianism in Cluj. The school in Cluj was granted a quarter of the town's tithe by princely decrees in 1556, 1562, 1571 and 1576, all of which were backed by the town council.[33] The school was led by a rector, who was supported by four staff. As in other aspects of public life in Cluj, these offices were appointed in rotation between the two linguistic communities, so that when the rector was a Hungarian the main teacher was a German. From 1568 the school in Cluj was staffed by anti-Trinitarians, under the leadership of Ferenc Dávid, who was rector until 1577. Dávid worked alongside teachers such as Johannes Sommer, Jacobus Paleologus and Christian Francken, and surviving volumes from the school library preserve some of the most important works by these radical thinkers.[34] The school proved to be an important

---

31 György Enyedi, *Explicationes, locrum veteris et novi Testamenti, ex quibus Trinitati dogma stabiliri solet* (Kolozsvár, 1598).

32 Székely, *Unitária vallás történetei Erdélyben* (1840), p. 64–129; Jakab, *Kolozsvár története. Második kötet* (1888), pp. 337–42, 413; Tóth, *Az Unitárius egyház rendszabályai* (1922), pp. ix–xv.

33 Jakab, *Kolozsvár története. Második kötet* (1888), pp. 104–107.

34 Works by Johannes Sommer, 'Refutatio Scripti Petri Carolij ... ', 'Declamatio contra Baptismum Adultorum', 'De fide in Christum', 'De Peccato', and 'De remissione

channel for the dissemination of anti-Trinitarian ideas, and was the only working school in Cluj until the 1580s. Some leading anti-Trinitarian clergy, including Demeter Hunyadi, were educated in Cluj, and all of the anti-Trinitarian superintendents from this period also at one stage held teaching positions in the school. Their teaching activity made a major contribution to the formulation and expression of anti-Trinitarian doctrine in Transylvania, and the important role of schools in the church was emphasized in 1592 when all rectors of anti-Trinitarian schools across Transylvania were required to attend synods. The Cluj school was another arena in which the town's magistrates and clergy worked in close cooperation to develop anti-Trinitarian institutions, aiming to provide the church with well-trained clergy.[35]

The development of anti-Trinitarianism in Transylvania also benefited from having access to the printing workshop of Cluj, with only one other press in Alba Iulia producing anti-Trinitarian books in Transylvania during the sixteenth century. The printing-press in Cluj was established in 1550 by Georg Hoffgreff. From 1551 until 1553 Hoffgreff ran the press together with Gáspár Heltai, and thereafter the press was run solely by Heltai. Initially the press published Lutheran and Calvinist texts, but in 1569 Heltai identified himself as an anti-Trinitarian, and thereafter most of the works he published were by anti-Trinitarian authors. However, after István Báthory's decree requiring princely sanction for the publication of religious books in 1571, Heltai was compelled to print only secular books. After Heltai died in 1574, the Cluj press was managed by his wife, and after her death by their son Gáspár until 1594. From the end of the sixteenth century the output of the press declined, and it was finally destroyed in the major fire which damaged much of Cluj in 1655. Despite restrictions on its activity, Heltai's press contributed greatly to the propagation of anti-Trinitarian ideas in Transylvania.[36] Most of the works published in Cluj between 1569 and 1571 were reflections on the theological debates held between Calvinists and anti-Trinitarians in those years.[37] After censorship was

---

Peccatorum'; Jacobus Paleologus, 'De providentia', 'De Matrimonio', 'De peccato originis', 'An omnes ab uno Adamo descenderint', 'De Sacramentis', 'De Eucharistia', 'De Anima', 'De Discrimine Veteri et Novi Testamenti' and 'De ressurectione mortuorum'; Christian Francken, 'De bestialissime idolatria' and 'Disputation inter Faustum Socinum et Christianum Francken de honore Christi'; see Elemér Lakó ed., *The Manuscripts of the Anti-Trinitarian College of Cluj/Koloszvár in the Library of the Academy in Cluj-Napoca. Catalogue* (Szeged, 1997).

[35] Kelemen Gáll, *A kolozsvári unitárius kollégium története (1568–1900)* (2 vols), (Cluj, 1935); Tóth, *Az Unitárius egyház rendszabályai* (1922), p. xii.

[36] Kénosi, *Typographis unitariorum in Transylvania* (1991), p. xviii.

[37] Ferenc Dávid published works in Hungarian in Cluj in 1570 and 1571; *Az Egy ő*

imposed in 1571, the only anti-Trinitarian work which was allowed to be published in the 1570s was a 1579 work which aimed to prevent the infection of non-adorantism spreading among anti-Trinitarians.[38] Once rules on publishing religious books in Transylvania were relaxed, later anti-Trinitarian works to be published in Cluj included books by Biandrata, Dávid, Faustus Sozzini, György Enyedi and János Kósa. The press published Latin works which were mainly theological debates and polemical treatises contributing to the needs of the clergy, and also books in Hungarian intended to explain anti-Trinitarian beliefs to a wider audience.

The anti-Trinitarian clergy elite in Cluj, with the support of the town's magistrates, gradually developed institutional controls over the church through the office of the superintendent during this period, debated and established the church's doctrine, and spread anti-Trinitarian ideas to a wider public. Compiling catechisms proved to be one crucial means which promoted debate over the contours of accepted anti-Trinitarian doctrine, and assisted clergy to explain doctrine to lay believers. Three texts in particular highlight this process over the latter decades of the sixteenth century: *Catechismus Ecclesiarum Dei in Natione Hungarica per Transilvaniam*, 'Catechesis Christiana' written by Jacobus Paleologus in 1574, and the *Catechesis* compiled by János Kósa at the end of the sixteenth century. Kósa was also responsible for the production of a catechism printed in Hungarian which was directed for children to use.[39] These catechisms were distinctive from the texts produced in the region by Lutherans, Calvinists and Catholics. Their structure and content highlighted key points of theological difference between the anti-Trinitarian Church and its confessional rivals, and focused on controversial areas of debate within the anti-Trinitarian community.[40] Anti-Trinitarian catechisms presented core ideas in a

---

magától való Felséges Istenről, és az igaz Fiáról az Názáreti Jésusról az igaz Messiáról, az Sz. Irásból vett Vallástétel, Az Egy Atya Istennek és az ő Áldott Sz. Fiának az Jezus Kristusnak Istenségekről igaz Vallástétel, az Prófétáknak és Apostoloknak irásaink igaz folyása szerént, and *Az Egy Atya Istenről és az ő Fiáról, az Jesus Kristusról, és az Szent Lélekről való rövid Vallás, az Prófétáknak és Apostoloknak irások szerént.*

38 Kénosi, *Typographis unitariorum in Transylvania* (1991), pp. 68, 121–41.

39 János (Várfalvi) Kósa, 'Az Üdvességnek Fundamentumárol rövid Kérdezkedés az Szent Irás szerént az küsdedeknek Tudományában, és az Urnak szólgálattyában és félelmében való fel nevelésére', and 'Az Üdvességnek Fundamentumárol ki adott Tanúságnak Szent Irásból való meg mutogatása az öregekért, kik az Kérdéseket és Feleleteket meg tanúlták, az fellyül meg irt Kérdezkedésnek rendi szerént'.

40 András Mózes, *Az Erdélyi román reformáció káteirodalma* (Cluj: Orient Nyomda, 1942), pp. 20–22; László Makkai, 'Un catéchisme hongrois contre les Antitrinitariens' in Dán, Pirnát eds, *Antitrinitarianism in the second half of the sixteenth century* (1982), pp. 92–3.

relatively simple form, and while some were intended to inform debate among the clergy elite, others aimed to educate believers by actively engaging them in learning about anti-Trinitarian beliefs rather than, as during sermons, remaining passive recipients of information about their faith.

In 1566 the Cluj press produced *Catechismus Ecclesiarum Dei*, which emerged from theological debates held at Alba Iulia between Hungarian-speaking clergy about the doctrine of the Trinity in 1565 and in the spring of 1566.[41] While Calvinist orthodoxy was defended by the minister from Debrecen, Péter Méliusz Juhász, anti-Trinitarianism was espoused by Ferenc Dávid and Giorgio Biandrata. The format and content of the 1566 *Catechismus* was in fact largely Calvinist, and was based on the 1563 Heidelberg *Catechism*. However, in addition some elements of the disputes held in Alba Iulia were reprinted, and clear statements of anti-Trinitarian belief were quoted on the nature of God and the person of Christ. The text affirmed the fundamental unity of God as the basis of true faith in the clearest possible terms: 'For there cannot be many and diverse gods, since God the Father is one, as from all eternity, united in perfect fullness with the Son and the Holy Spirit.'[42] From this starting point, the catechism explained the double nature of Christ, with human and divine attributes, and denoted only a limited role for the Holy Spirit, principally expressed through the sacrament of baptism.[43] The scriptural basis of the theology espoused in the catechism, and especially on the Trinity, was constantly stressed. This keynote of exact and clear biblical support for all elements of anti-Trinitarian theology was also sustained in all the later catechisms of this period.[44] The *Catechismus Ecclesiarum Dei* emerged from theological debate and served as a polemic text. However, it was also a crucial first step in crystallizing the beliefs of Transylvanian anti-Trinitarians, and was later also used in instruction at the school in Cluj.

Transylvanian anti-Trinitarianism emerged from the crucible of debate with local Calvinists. Pointing out areas of difference between the two emerging confessions was therefore a crucial function for anti-

---

[41] *Catechismus Ecclesiarum Dei in Natione Hungarica per Transilvaniam; quae relicto Deo Papistico quaterno, Verbum Dei de Sancto Sancta Triade Uno vero Deo, Patre, Filio ejus Domino Nostro Jesu Christo, ac amplorum Spiritu amplexae sunt, simplicitateque pia ac puritate illut credunt ac profitentur* (Kolozsvár, 1566).

[42] *Catechismus Ecclesiarum Dei* (1566); 'Plures enim ac diversae Deitates esse non possunt, sed una est Deitas Patris, quam ab anni aeternitate, Filio et Spiritus Sancto perfecta plenitudine communicat'.

[43] *Catechismus Ecclesiarum Dei* (1566); 'Christus et verus Deus, et verus homo: Itaque secundum naturam humanam jam non est in terra'.

[44] *Catechismus Ecclesiarum Dei* (1566), pp. 50–63, 93–9, 101–106.

Trinitarian printed texts. The articulation of coherent anti-Trinitarian ideas in Transylvania was achieved above all by the 1566 *Catechismus*, published before the first synod of the anti-Trinitarian Church was even held. If the 1566 *Catechismus* affirmed belief in the unity of God for Transylvanian anti-Trinitarians, the years between 1566 and 1570 were marked by an evolution in anti-Trinitarian thought under the leadership of Ferenc Dávid. Dávid produced a work in 1567 to refute the writings of Péter Méliusz Juhász, and in 1568 a further anti-Trinitarian work appeared called *De falsa et vera unius Dei patris, filii et spiritus sancti cognitione*. In this second text, the idea of the Trinity was depicted as a creation of Antichrist, a thesis supported with dramatic visual representations of the false three-headed deity supposedly invoked by Trinitarians (see Figure 4.1).

These works concentrated on the two key concerns of Dávid's theology; the nature of Christ, and the need for exact scriptural foundation for all belief. Dávid described himself a humble servant of the crucified Jesus, placing great emphasis on the human nature of Christ and how his sacrifice provided an example for every Christian to follow. Dávid also considered the crucial issue of the divine nature of Christ, but argued that God the Father had delegated part of his absolute divine nature to the Son, and that by virtue of this delegation, Christ could still be rightly adored in worship.[45] The Reformed superintendent, Péter Méliusz Juhász, responded in 1568 and 1569 with works which labelled the Cluj theological party as 'heretics' and 'atheists', and identified anti-Trinitarians as traitors to the Christian and Hungarian cause against the Ottomans.[46]

After 1570 the anti-Trinitarian Church became split over the issue of the adoration and invocation of Christ. One contribution to this debate was the 'Catechesis Christiana' written by Jacobus Paleologus. Paleologus came to Transylvania in 1571 at Ferenc Dávid's invitation.

45 Ferenc Dávid, *Refutatio scripti Petrii Melii, quo nomine synodi Debrecinae docet Jehoualitatem et trinitarium Deum patriarchis, prophetis et apostolis incognitum* (Gyulafehérvár, 1567) translated into Hungarian as *Rövid magyarazát miképpen az Anti-Christus az Istenről való Tudományt meg homályosittotta: És az Kristus az ő Hiveinek általa tantitván minket, miképpen épittette meg az ő Mennyei Sz. Attyáról, és ő magáról, és az Sz. Lélekről, bizonyos értelmet adván előnkben* (Gyulafehérvár, 1567); *De falsa et vera unius Dei patris, filii et spiritus sancti cognitione libr duo. Authoribus ministris ecclesiarum consentientium in Sarmatia et Transylvania* (Gyulafehérvár, 1568); Balázs, *Az erdélyi antitrinitarizmus az 1560-as évek végén* (1988), pp. 35–50.

46 Péter Méliusz Juhász, *Propositiones de Jah et Jehovah, seu de unitate et trinitate in Deo vero* (Nagyvárad, 1568); Péter Méliusz Juhász, *Disputatio in causa sacrosanctae Trinitatis* (Debrecen, 1569/70); Makkai, 'Un catéchisme hongrois contre les Antitrinitariens' (1982), pp. 92–3.

Idolum hoc Trifrons paſsim in delubris viſitur,
Deum Trinum & vnum Antichriſti deſignans,
vnde illud Papiſticum carmen.

Menſe Trifrons iſto Ianũ pater vrbe Bifrontem
Expulit, vt ſolus regnet in orbe Trifrons.

4.1 The anti-Trinitarian depiction of the Triune God from Ferenc Dávid, *De Falsa et Vera Unius Dei Patris, Filii et Spiritus Sancti Cognitione* (Alba Iulia, 1568), Latin copy from the nineteenth century. Reproduced with kind permission of the Romanian Academy Library, Cluj.

Paleologus was interested in studying the history of biblical Israel, and considered Jesus as merely one of the prophets. Paleologus took up a teaching position at the anti-Trinitarian school in Cluj, where he worked until 1575. After leaving Transylvania, he was later condemned as a heretic and was executed at Rome in 1583.[47] Paleologus wrote the 'Catechesis Christiana' while at Cluj, probably in 1574 or 1575, but the text remained unpublished possibly because of the restrictions imposed by prince István Báthory on religious publishing during the 1570s. However, the manuscript surivived as part of the 'Codex Thoroczkay' of Máté Toroczkai, anti-Trinitarian superintendent between 1601 and 1616. This 'Codex' also contains other radical anti-Trinitarian works of the period by Johannes Sommer and Christian Francken.[48] Paleologus' catechism was constructed as a dialogue, divided into twelve days of debates held between a priest and his guests, who included Peter, Paul, Samuel, Luther and Calvin. These debates highlighted similarities between the faith of Jews and Christians, and attached great significance to the Old Testament. The description of the nature of God in Paleologus' 'Catechesis Christiana' was similar to previous expressions of the unity of God in Transylvanian anti-Trinitarian writings. However, discussion of Christ's nature placed a new emphasis on his role as a human messenger from God to Israel, who did not come to initiate a new faith but to reform the existing one. Paleologus argued that Christ only became divine after his death, through his adoption by God the Father, and suggested that Christ should not therefore be adored in worship.[49]

Both these catechisms, *Catechismus Ecclesiarum Dei* and 'Catechesis Christiana', were written in Latin and produced as part of debates between clergy to determine the theology of the emerging anti-Trinitarian Church. These catechisms were channels for Cluj preachers and teachers to elaborate their theology, in a period when the powers of superintendents to exert discipline over anti-Trinitarian clergy were still in the process of being established. Although superintendent of the Transylvanian Church and *plebanus*

---

[47] Róbert Dán, '*Judaizare*; the career of a term' in Dán, Pirnát eds, *Antitrinitarianism in the second half of the sixteenth century* (1982); Caccamo, *Eretici Italiani in Moravia, Polonia, Transilvania* (1970).

[48] Jacobus Paleologus, 'Catechesis Christiana' (1574/5); also in this 'Codex' his 'Disputatio Scholastica', 'De ressurectione mortuorum', 'De eucharistia', 'Summa omnium et prius de justitia', 'De Christo cognomine', 'De tribus gentibus' and 'Theodoro Bezae pro Castillione et Bellio'.

[49] Paleologus, 'Catechesis Christiana' (1574/5), pp. 3–6, 55. See also Robert Dán, 'Eőssi András és az erdélyi szombatosság genezise', *Irodalomtörténeti Közlemények* 78 (1974), pp. 572–7.

of Cluj until 1579, Ferenc Dávid could not impose his developing non-adorantist ideas on fellow clergy, but could influence the direction of the church through his own writings and through tracts by other radicals such as Paleologus. Therefore Paleologus' 'Catechesis Christiana', although only a Latin manuscript circulating amongst the elite of Cluj, was influential within Transylvanian anti-Trinitarianism. Another preacher in Cluj, István Basilius, made a similar attempt to establish the core ideas of the anti-Trinitarian Church with a 1583 Latin manuscript catechism, which was also used as a basis for instruction at the local school.[50]

After the crisis of 1579, the adoration of Christ and celebration of the Eucharist were confirmed as part of worship in the anti-Trinitarian Church. This consensus was reflected in the *Catechism* compiled by János Kósa. Unfortunately, no copies of the first editions of this catechism have survived, but Kósa's *Catechism* was republished several times during the seventeenth century. The publication of these catechisms in Hungarian seems to mark the end of internal debate about accepted doctrine within the church, and indicate a new concentration on presenting anti-Trinitarian doctrine to children in schools and to ordinary lay members of the church. Kósa's *Catechism* opens with the question of how a Christian can be saved, and then moves on to discuss the role of prayer, the sacraments and the law in anti-Trinitarian faith. The *Catechism* also offers instruction on appropriate behaviour during church services, and details the requirement on Christians to obey their lawfully appointed rulers. The declared purpose of this *Catechism* was to present Christian teachings exactly as they were described in the Bible, and every element of doctrine was accompanied by copious scriptural quotations. Some references were also made to the Apostles' Creed, especially to its treatment of the humanity and divinity of Christ. The structure of Kósa's *Catechism* particularly focuses on the unity of God, and how his almighty power makes the consideration of anything else as divine completely impossible. The attitude to Christ must be one of subjection, because he is a necessary intercessor between man and God the Father, from whom alone heavenly reward can come. This confirmed the ideas which had been circulating from the late 1560s on the delegation of elements of the Father's divinity to the Son. The *Catechism* also clearly asserted that the Holy Spirit was part of the essential unity of God. Overall, Kósa's *Catechism* offered a clear and

---

[50] István Basilius, 'Exercitium Pietatis Puerilis per Catechism in Schola Claudiopolitana'; see also Basilius, *Az Credonak vagy Apostoly Vallásnak Magyarázattya* (Alba Iulia, 1568); Kénosi, *Typographis unitariorum in Transylvania* (1991), p. 91.

concise explanation of the fundamentals of anti-Trinitarian doctrine.[51] This text did not serve any polemic purposes, nor was part of a theological debate between anti-Trinitarian clergy in Cluj, but was rather aimed primarily to assist the education and devotion of the laity of the anti-Trinitarian Church.

Catechisms played a significant role in the development of anti-Trinitarianism in Transylvania during the late sixteenth century. Study of these catechisms reveals the profound difficulties which the church experienced to establish the limits of their radical challenge to the mainstream of Protestant reform. With the loss of princely support from the death of János Zsigmond in 1571, direction of the church was assumed by the clergy of Cluj, dependent for their offices, salaries and school on the town's magistrates. Anti-Trinitarian religion emerged in Cluj after polemic debate with local Calvinists, and much internal discussion of radical ideas followed in the town. As anti-Trinitarian texts from the 1570s show, some clergy moved to abandon the worship of Christ and towards a Judaistic religion. The reception of these ideas within Cluj's urban community is mostly obscured from our sight, but Ferenc Dávid was able to retain the loyalty of the Cluj magistrates until he was condemned for doctrinal innovation by the Transylvanian diet in 1579. Further research is needed to understand the development of other aspects of anti-Trinitarian religious life during this period, for example attitudes towards the sacraments and to moral discipline. From the 1580s the doctrinal limits of anti-Trinitarianism were firmly drawn, and a structured system of beliefs was advanced by organized church institutions. Published literature in the vernacular increasingly focused on bolstering the knowledge of a mostly Hungarian-speaking community about the fundamentals of their religion. The anti-Trinitarian Church's superintendent remained resident in Cluj, and almost always also served as the *plebanus* in Cluj during this period. The emergence of Transylvanian anti-Trinitarianism during the late sixteenth century was therefore a product of the urban privileges of Cluj, which provided a base for debating radical religious ideas and became the centre of the Transylvanian anti-Trinitarian Church.

---

[51] János (Várfalvi) Kósa, *Catechesis az idvessegnek fundamentomarol, rövid kerdesekre szent iras szerent vala feleletek* (Kolozsvár, 1623) is the first edition with surviving copies. Kénosi, *Typographis unitariorum in Transylvania* (1991), p. 89; Székely, *Unitária vallás történetei Erdélyben* (1840), pp. 103–106 claims that this catechism was still used during the nineteenth century in anti-Trinitarian schools in Transylvania.

CHAPTER FIVE

Calvinist catechizing and Hungarian Reformed identity

Graeme Murdock

By the end of the sixteenth century more than three-quarters of over 5,000 parish churches across Hungary and Transylvania were being used for Protestant worship, and a majority of these Protestant parishes were held by clergy from the Reformed Church. Since communities in urban centres had overwhelmingly abandoned the Catholic Church, perhaps as much as eighty per cent of the population of Hungary and Transylvania attended Protestant services towards the end of the sixteenth century.[1] The success of the Reformation in sixteenth-century Hungary was partly a result of political change, above all the catastrophic collapse of the medieval Hungarian kingdom and dramatic expansion of Ottoman power. These troubled circumstances provided the context for the rise in support for various Protestant churches, as the Hungarian noble elite adopted Reformed or Lutheran religion both from sincerely held personal convictions about the failure of the spiritual powers of the Catholic Church, and also in order to bolster their political ambitions for greater autonomy from monarchical power. The remnant of the Hungarian kingdom which was not occupied by the Ottomans was divided between Habsburg Royal Hungary and the Transylvanian principality, ruled by princes elected from the ranks of the native nobility. By the late 1560s the weakness of princely power in Transylvania resulted in legal status being offered to four 'received' religions (Catholic, Lutheran, Reformed and anti-Trinitarian) of the three estates or nations (Hungarian nobles, German towns and Szeklers) represented in the diet. Meanwhile nobles in Royal Hungary also tried

---

1 Kálmán Benda suggested that fifty per cent of Hungarian society was Reformed in 1600, with twenty-five per cent Lutheran, and the remainder Unitarian, Catholic or Orthodox; 'La réforme en Hongrie', *Bulletin de la Société de l'histoire du Protestantisme Français* 122 (1976), pp. 30–53. Katalin Péter agreed that seventy-five to eighty per cent of Hungarians were Protestant between 1570 and 1620 in *Papok és nemesek. Magyar művelődéstörténeti tanulmányok a reformációval kezdődő másfél évszázadból* (Budapest: Ráday Gyűjtemény, 1995), p. 10; Jenő Zoványi, *Kisebb dolgozatok a magyar protestantizmus történetének köréből* (Sárospatak, 1910), pp. 97–100.

to establish a balance between their corporate privileges and Habsburg sovereignty over religious affairs, as over other spheres of public life.[2]

Within this context of divided political authority, feudal, regional, local and family loyalties, as well as geography, communication networks and pre-Reformation patterns of religiosity and ecclesiastical organization largely decided emerging patterns of religious adherence across Hungary and Transylvania. Although a sense of ethnic or linguistic solidarity was not decisive in establishing continued loyalty to the Catholic Church or in inspiring conversions to one of the Protestant churches, ethnic cohesiveness and linguistic community cannot be discounted in reinforcing attachment to a particular religion. Certainly Calvinism quickly became almost exclusively the preserve of Hungarian-speaking communities, but Hungarian-speakers also became Lutherans, anti-Trinitarians, or remained within the Catholic Church.[3]

Hungarian noble loyalty to Protestant churches was severely tested from the late sixteenth century by Counter-Reformation pressure exerted by the Catholic hierarchy and Habsburg dynasty in Royal Hungary, and by the disruption of renewed war against the Ottomans. Protestant strength in Royal Hungary was closely linked with the political power of the diet, and the depth of commitment among noble converts proved crucial to the later fortunes of Protestant churches. This pattern of mostly Protestant estates clashing with the ruling Catholic dynasty was repeated across the Habsburg monarchy, but the nobility of Royal Hungary held a particularly strong bargaining position. In return for religious freedoms, Protestant magnates and gentry could offer not only royal solvency and stable local administration but also military cooperation to defend Hungary against Ottoman attack. The Turkish threat certainly constrained the Habsburgs' freedom to act against Protestants across Hungary, but their enduring determination to promote the interests of the Catholic Church also weakened any plans to challenge Ottoman power. The period of the Fifteen Years' War demonstrated the limits of the Habsburgs' ability either to reverse

---

[2] Robert Evans, *The Making of the Habsburg Monarchy, 1550–1700: an interpretation* (Oxford: Clarendon, 1979); Robert Kann, Zdeněk David, *The Peoples of the Eastern Habsburg Lands, 1526–1918. A history of East Central Europe*, 6 (Seattle: University of Washington Press, 1984); Peter Sugar, *Southeastern Europe under Ottoman rule, 1354–1804. A history of East Central Europe*, 5 (Seattle: University of Washington Press, 1977); Orest Subtelny, *Domination of Eastern Europe. Native nobilities and foreign absolutism* (Kingston [ONT]: McGill University Press, 1986).

[3] Graeme Murdock, 'International Calvinism, Ethnic Allegiance, and the Reformed Church of Transylvania in the Early Seventeenth Century' in Maria Crăciun, Ovidiu Ghitta eds, *Ethnicity and Religion in Central and Eastern Europe* (Cluj: University Press, 1995), pp. 92–100.

Ottoman advances or to enforce Catholicism on the Hungarian nobility. In the wake of István Bocskai's revolt in 1604, the Habsburgs were forced to compromise with the Hungarian estates and freedom of worship was granted to Lutherans and Calvinists by the terms of the 1606 peace of Vienna, ratified by the Hungarian diet in 1608.[4]

The advance of Protestant religion in Hungary was not solely a result of political and social circumstances, but was also a consequence of the perceived attractions within Hungarian society of Calvinist and other Protestant ideas about religious renewal. The Reformed Church developed in Hungary and Transylvania during the second half of the sixteenth century as reform-minded clergy collected together insights from a range of western theologians. Reformed religion was distinctive from local confessional rivals primarily through Calvinist sacramental theology, and Calvinists in Hungary were initially described as 'sacramentarians'. A fledgling Reformed Church was supported by some magnates and gentry, especially in eastern Hungarian counties and in some Hungarian-speaking towns. This church united around the 1567 *Confessio Catholica*, drawn up at Debrecen by Péter Méliusz Juhász and Gergely Szegedi, and also accepted the Second Helvetic Confession. Clergy synods across Hungary and in Transylvania soon recognized similar confessions of faith, established hierarchical church institutions under provincial superintendents, and endorsed alterations to the conduct of religious services and ceremonies.[5]

To identify with the Reformed Church in sixteenth-century Hungary and Transylvania was to make a statement about feudal loyalty to a local lord, especially in the countryside, or about solidarity with family and neighbourhood, and was perhaps in part related to a sense of linguistic community, but also indicated attachment to a particular set of ideas. Although the preferences of the social elite largely determined the emerging pattern of the multi-confessional environment in Hungary and Transylvania, the medieval Hungarian kingdom had also become, to some degree, a marketplace of ideas about religion during the middle

---

4 Kálmán Benda, 'Habsburg absolutism and the resistance of the Hungarian estates of the sixteenth and seventeenth centuries' in Robert Evans, Trevor Thomas eds, *Crown, Church and Estates. Central European politics in the sixteenth and seventeenth centuries* (London: Macmillan, 1991), pp. 123–8.

5 Robert Evans, 'Calvinism in East Central Europe: Hungary and her neighbours' in Menna Prestwich ed., *International Calvinism, 1541–1715* (Oxford: Clarendon, 1985), pp. 167–96; Graeme Murdock, *Calvinism on the Frontier, 1600–1660. International Calvinism and the Reformed Church in Hungary and Transylvania* (Oxford: Clarendon, 2000), pp. 10–45; Mihály Bucsay, *Der Protestantismus in Ungarn, 1521–1978. Ungarns Reformationskirchen in Geschichte und Gegenwart. 1. Im Zeitalter der Reformation, Gegenreformation und katholischen Reform* (Vienna: Böhlau, 1977).

decades of the sixteenth century. In Royal Hungary, Catholic, Lutheran and Calvinist clergy competed for support, and these rivals were joined by anti-Trinitarian ministers and Eastern Orthodox priests in Transylvania.

If the relative attractiveness of different sets of religious beliefs was a significant factor in establishing and retaining the loyalty of the Hungarian social elite, and perhaps also the loyalty of ordinary people who lived in Royal Hungary and the Transylvanian principality, then how were such ideas transmitted in a mostly illiterate society? For the Reformed Church, preaching and the spoken word remained a significant means through which clergy communicated ideas about religious reform to local communities. Gradual improvements in the standards of Hungarian colleges and schools aided the ability of Reformed ministers to broaden understanding about the changes which they believed needed to be made to customary beliefs and religious practices. Vernacular printed books also played an important part in spreading Reformed ideas among the clergy and, to some extent, more broadly within Hungarian and Transylvanian society. The Reformed clergy hierarchy certainly perceived books and the vernacular written word to be vital sources of truth and authority, able to alter and shape the beliefs of a community and to aid individuals' understanding of their religion. Reformed synods consistently stressed the need for every Christian to understand the fundamentals of their faith, and initially expressed the hope that reading the Bible would play a primary role in achieving this. However, canons for the Transylvanian Reformed Church province, drawn up by superintendent Mihály Tasnádi Ruber in 1606, only emphasized the importance of books in building up the knowledge and abilities of the clergy. Every minister was required to obtain a copy of the Bible, if he did not have one already, as well as possess other unspecified theological works.[6]

During the late sixteenth century and early decades of the seventeenth century Reformed students and ministers furnished the church with translations of scripture, creeds, collections of sermons, prayers and catechisms. Whilst the numbers and range of available vernacular books certainly increased, the reception of printed ideas within Hungarian society remained limited to those with access to these books. It is impossible to quantify literacy rates for the region, but there is some sense that during the sixteenth century a greater proportion of the population had begun to acquire some reading skills. There was certainly an increasing number of available cheap books, and a broader

---

[6] 'Az erdélyi anyaszentegyház közzsinatainak végzései kivonatban', István Szilágyi ed., *Magyar Protestáns Egyházi és Iskolai Figyelmező* 3 (1872), pp. 1–9.

range of subject matter in printed works. All this, together with the achievements of Reformed schools, suggests that by the early seventeenth century literacy was no longer an exclusive hallmark of social privilege among the clergy, nobility and urban elites, and that some account must be made for books to have also played a part in the religious life of smaller towns and larger villages across the region.[7]

While many printed books were aimed at ordinary members of Reformed congregations, parish clergy undoubtedly continued to play a prominent role in mediating and spreading Calvinist ideas within Hungarian and Transylvanian society. Books were mostly used by parish clergy to explain religious truth to local communities in public services. However, from the 1630s many translations from western languages into Hungarian began to appear of practical theological works, piety tracts, childrens' books, works on personal morality and on the everyday problems of religious life. This trend was epitomized by the enormously successful translation by Pál Medgyesi of Anglican bishop Lewis Bayly's *The Practice of Piety*, first published at Debrecen in 1636.[8] While it is very difficult to assess the wider impact on Hungarian society of this so-called practical theological literature, some ministers by the early decades of the seventeenth century clearly aimed to shape the private religiosity and personal morality of individual Reformed believers directly through such printed material.

Catechisms were the most commonly used form of printed literature through which Hungarian Reformed clergy attempted to spread ideas about their religion. Catechisms bridged the oral and literate worlds, as printed texts which were intended for oral instruction in questions and answer sessions. The remainder of this study will establish the variety of purposes for which catechisms were used in the Hungarian Reformed Church, how this changed during the period from around 1560 to 1660, and the significance of these texts in shaping Reformed religious identity in early modern Hungary and Transylvania. Reformed catechisms contained summaries of ideas about the nature of God, Christ, and the Holy Spirit, about man's redemption, God's law, prayer and the

---

7 Aladár Ballagi, *A magyar nyomdászat történelmi fejlődése, 1472–1877* (Budapest, 1878); Katalin Péter, 'A műveltség hordozói' in Ágnes Várkonyi ed., *Magyarország története* [gen. ed. Pál Zsigmond Pach 10 vols] vol. 3, pts 1–2 (1526–1686), (Budapest: Akadémiai kiadó, 1987), pp. 544–8; Lajos Naményi, 'A nagyváradi nyomdászat története', *Magyar Könyvszemle* 16 (1901), pp. 280–91; Károly Irinyi, Kálmán Benda, *A négyszáz éves debreceni nyomda (1561–1961)* (Budapest, 1961), pp. 7–59, 313–408; Zsigmond Jakó, *A Bethlen kollégium könyvtárának kezdetei és első korszaka* (Kolozsvár, 1973).

8 Pál Medgyesi, *Praxis Pietatis* (Debrecen, 1636), reprinted in 1638, 1640, 1641 and 1643.

sacraments. Catechisms were taught in schools, congregational classes and later more widely in homes, to bring basic knowledge about Reformed religion in a standardized form especially to the young, to women and to the illiterate. Congregations were instructed through catechisms about the orthodoxy of Calvinist beliefs, aiming to strengthen the commitment of believers, but catechisms also pointed out errors in the beliefs of rival churches, and were on occasion directed to assist the conversion of non-believers.

The use of catechisms in the Hungarian Reformed Church was first sanctioned by the 1567 Debrecen synod, which introduced a requirement for Reformed ministers to use catechisms to teach their congregations short explanations of the Apostles' Creed, the Lord's Prayer and Ten Commandments. Reformed Church articles for Upper Hungary in 1595 also promoted the daily use of catechisms among the young, to teach the 'milk' of the fundamentals of Christian faith so that congregations could then move on to more 'solid foods'. The Upper Hungarian Reformed synod also insisted that the same catechism should be used by all clergy, so that when ministers moved from parish to parish their congregations would not be disturbed by different teaching.[9]

These moves to formalise religious instruction required the production of standard texts, and a number of catechisms and summaries of the main areas of Reformed faith were soon published, often accompanied by examples of prayers. Many of the authors of these catechisms explained their own particular reasons for producing their texts. Gáspár Heltai suggested that his *Catechism* published at Cluj (Kolozsvár/Klausenburg) in 1553 should be used to teach young people and the 'simple-minded' a short summary of Christian knowledge.[10] András Batizi's 1555 *Catechism* aimed to build up children and the ignorant in true faith, stressing that 'worthy' Christians needed to understand the fundamentals of their religion. Batizi added that if the Turks advanced further into Hungary then many people would be denied the possibility to hear regular preaching, but instead could keep up their faith through studying catechisms.[11] Gergely Molnár compiled a *Catechism* in 1564 for use in the school at Cluj, in which he

---

9 *A xvi. században tartott magyar református zsinatok végzései*, Áron Kiss ed. (Budapest, 1882), pp. 586–7, 712.

10 Gáspár Heltai, *Catechismus minor, az az a keresztyeni tudomanac revideden valo sumaya* (Kolozsvár, 1550); Gáspár Heltai, *Catechismus, melybe a menynyei tudomannak sommája ... egybe szerzetettöt és befoglaltattot* (Kolozsvár, 1553).

11 András Batizi, *Keresztyéni tudományról való rövid könyvecske. Catechismus az az, a keresztyeni tudomannac revideden valo tanusaga* [first pub. Cracow, 1543–5, 1550] (Kolozsvár, 1555).

summarized 'necessary information' for true faith.[12] In 1574 Bálint Szikszai Hellopoeus, minister at Eger and then at Debrecen, aimed his *Short Catechism* at children and households who needed to learn 'true knowledge' about religion.[13] Meanwhile, Tamás Félegyházi, the minister at Debrecen, argued in 1583 that catechisms were very badly needed in Hungarian to correct error and keep people on the path of true faith. Félegyházi stated in the introduction to his *Catechism* that all Christians, but especially teachers, should know short, plain definitions of the chief points of their religion, and he particularly directed his work to help build up the understanding of 'simple people'.[14]

When János Siderius, the Abaújvár archdeacon, published his *Catechism* in 1597, he claimed that there had recently been a decline in the practice of catechizing, and some confusion caused because of a variety of catechisms being used in different areas. Siderius' *Catechism* of eighty-four questions and answers did much to rectify this problem, as it appeared in more than twenty editions during the seventeenth century and became a standard text for religious instruction used in schools, churches and homes across Hungary and Transylvania. Siderius' *Catechism* was accompanied by a series of prayers, including prayers for children to say when going to bed and getting up in the morning. The tone of these children's prayers sounds more than a little austere to modern ears: 'I lie down in my bed, as in my coffin, in the name of God, Father, Son, and Holy Ghost, Amen!' 'I rise from my bed, as from dreams of sin, in the name of God, Father, Son, and Holy Ghost, Amen!' However, these prayers emphasize how catechisms were both intended to convey information about Reformed religious beliefs and also to play a role in shaping everyday religious life.[15]

---

12 Gergély Molnár, *Catechesis scholae Claudiopolitanae ad pietatis studiosam iuventutem in doctrina Christiana fideliter exercendam* (Kolozsvár, 1564). Also note Péter Méliusz Juhász, *Catekizmus. Az egész keresztyéni tudománynak fundamentoma és sommája ... Calvinus János írása szerint* (Debrecen, 1562) in *Studia et acta ecclesiastica 3. Tanulmányok és szövegek a magyarországi református egyház xvi. századi történetéből*, ed. Tibor Barth (Budapest, 1973), pp. 222–77.

13 Bálint Szikszai Hellopoeus, *Az egri keresztyén anyaszentegyháznak ... rövid catechismus* (Debrecen, 1574); Bálint Szikszai Hellopoeus, *A mi keresztyéni hitünknek és vallásunknak három fő articulusáról ... való könyvecske* (Debrecen, 1574).

14 Tamás Félegyházi, *Az keresztieni igaz hitnek reszeirol valo tanitas, kerdesekkel es feleletekkel, ellenvetesekkel és azoknak meg feitésivel, az hiveknek eppületekre ... ez melle adattattot rövid catechismus* (Debrecen, 1583), p. 3.

15 János Siderius, *Kisded gyermekeknek való katechizmus, azaz a keresztyéni hitnek fő ágazatairúl rövid kérdések és feleletek által való tanitás* (Debrecen, 1597); 'Én felkelek én ágyamból, mint egy bünnek álmából, Atyának, Fiúnak, és Szent Lélek Istennek nevében, Amen! Én lefekszem én ágyamban, mint én koporsomban, Atyának, Fiúnak, és Szent Lélek Istennek nevében, Amen!'; János Barcza, 'Siderius János kátéja' in *Studia et acta ecclesiastica 3* (1973), pp. 849–76.

There appears to have been some revival in interest in using catechisms and summaries of faith to instruct the Reformed faithful from around the turn of the seventeenth century. Tamás Félegyházi's *Catechism* was republished in 1601, thanks to financial support from nobles resident in Debrecen.[16] There was also noticeably greater use in Hungary from this period of the 1563 Heidelberg *Catechism*. The Heidelberg *Catechism* had been first translated into Hungarian in 1577 by Dávid Huszár and published at Pápa, where Huszár was the local minister. Huszár argued in the preface to his translation that Christians needed to understand the fundamentals of their faith if they were to attain salvation. Huszár described the *Catechism* as 'short questions about Christian faith, which every Christian follower ought to know'.[17] A second translation of the Heidelberg *Catechism* was completed by the Debrecen minister Ferenc Szárászi in 1604, who intended his work to assist the spiritual development of children and 'the simple' in Reformed congregations.[18] Albert Szenczi Molnár also published a shorter version of the Heidelberg *Catechism* in 1607 within his Psalter, and the whole Heidelberg *Catechism* was included within Molnár's Oppenheim *Bible* of 1612.[19]

Without ever entirely displacing home-grown catechisms, translations of the Heidelberg *Catechism* soon gained official sanction for use across the Reformed Church provinces of Hungary and Transylvania. In 1619 the Upper Danubian Reformed Church province ordered the use of the Heidelberg *Catechism* in local schools. The 1621 rules adopted by Sárospatak college in north-eastern Hungary stipulated that the Heidelberg

---

[16] Tamás Félegyházi, *Catechesis, az az rövid kerdesek es feleletek az keresztyeni hitnek agairol, az gyermekeknek es az egy-igyüeknek tanitasokra* (Debrecen, 1601).

[17] Dávid Huszár, *A keresztyén hitről való tudománynak rövid kérdésekben foglaltatott summája* (Pápa, 1577); 'a keresztyen hitröl valo rövid kérdésec, mellieket minden hiv keresztyennec tudni kelly'. A Hungarian translation of the Heidelberg *Catechism* in fact appeared in 1566, but in an altered form to support anti-Trinitarian ideas; *Catechismus Ecclesiarum Dei in Natione Hungarica per Transilvaniam quae relicto Papistico Deo quaterno, Verbum Dei de Sacro Sancta Triade Uno vero Deo, Patre, et Filio ejus Domino Nostro Jesu Christo, ac amplorum Spiritu amplexae sunt, simplicitateque pia ac puritate illut credunt ac profitentur* (Kolozsvár, 1566).

[18] Ferenc Szárászi, *Catechesis, azaz kerdesök es feleletök az kerestyeni tudomannak agairol. Az iambor istenfelö harmadik Friderik herczek birtokaban, Palatinatusban levö tudos bölcs doctorok altal irattatot, deakbol penig magyar nyelvre fordittatot, hogy mind az kisdedöknek az scholakben, mind penig az egyigyüeknek az ecclesiaban lelki éppületökre lenne* (Debrecen, 1604).

[19] Albert Szenczi Molnár, *Kis katekizmus, avagy az keresztyén hütnec részeiröl rövid kérdesekben es feleletekben foglaltatot tudomány ... szedetött az haidelbergai öreg Katekizmusból* (Herborn, 1607); Albert Szenczi Molnár, *Szent Biblia ... az palatinatusi katekizmussal* (Oppenheim, 1612); Lajos Dézsi, *Szenczi Molnár Albert* (Budapest, 1897).

Catechism should be taught there on Wednesdays and Saturday mornings. The Western Danubian Reformed Church province supported use of the Heidelberg *Catechism* at their synod held at Pápa in 1630. The synod also repeated the requirement that congregational catechism classes be held across the province on Sunday afternoons and after weekday morning services. Regular visitations of local parishes by the provincial clergy hierarchy were supposed to check that these classes were actually taking place. The Heidelberg *Catechism* also received Transylvanian princely sanction. In 1638 Pál Keresztúri published *The Christian Infant*, an examination of the religious knowledge displayed by the sons of Prince György I Rákóczi, which was based on the Heidelberg *Catechism*. György and Zsigmond Rákóczi had given answers in turn to different questions from the *Catechism* on 15 August 1637 in the church at Alba Iulia (Gyulafehérvár/Weissenburg) in front of their parents, teachers and Reformed clergy.[20] Johann Heinrich Alsted's 1636 Latin-Hungarian shorter version of the Heidelberg *Catechism* then became widely used in Reformed schools across Transylvania. Five editions of Alsted's *Catechism* were published at Alba Iulia before 1660, with prayers attached for pupils to use. Vernacular schools in Transylvania meanwhile continued to use either wholly Hungarian translations of the Heidelberg *Catechism*, or the catechisms compiled by János Siderius or András Batizi.[21]

In 1646 a national synod of Hungarian Reformed Church provinces met at Satu Mare (Szatmár/Sathmar), and issued revised instructions for Reformed ministers to give sermons based on catechisms during Sunday afternoon services and to hold catechism classes each week. The national synod approved both the Heidelberg *Catechism* and Siderius' *Catechism* for general use in the Church. The 1649 canons of the Transylvanian Reformed Church province also stipulated that catechism classes were compulsory for all, and especially for those about to take communion for the first time. Boys were to learn their catechism in schools, adults to receive instruction during

---

20 Pál Keresztúri, *Csecsemő keresztyén, mellyet az tekintetes és nagyságos urak az Rakoczi György és Sigmond Istennek segitségéből, az egész jelen valoknak nagy örvendezésekkel, dicséretesen és igen boldogul el mondottanak, mikor igaz vallásokban való szép épületekről abban az probában bizonságot tennének, mellyet az Erdély Országnak kegyelmes Fejedelme az Ur Vacsorája elött kivánt hallani* (Gyulafehérvár, 1638).

21 Johann Heinrich Alsted, *Catechismus religionis Christianae – Catechismus, azaz: A keresztyéni vallásnak és hütnek rövid kerdesekben és feleletekben foglaltatott* (Gyulafehérvár, 1636); B. Nagy, 'A heidelbergi káté jelentkezése, története és kiadásai magyarországon a xvi és xvii században' in *Studia et acta ecclesiastica 2. Tánulmányok és okmányok a magyarországi református egyház történetéből. A második helvét hitvallás magyarországon és Méliusz életművei*, ed. Tibor Barth (Budapest, 1967), pp. 15–92; *A xvi. században tartott magyar református zsinatok végzései* (1882), Kiss ed., p. 725.

Sunday afternoon services, and classes held for girls and young women at least once a week. The canons' author, Transylvanian superintendent István Geleji Katona, explained that these classes for girls would mark the beginning of their instruction about religion as 'mother's milk', which would then enable women to advance further in understanding of their faith. The canons also stressed the need for the same catechism to be used across the Transylvanian principality, so that when ministers moved from one parish to another congregations' learning would not be disturbed.[22]

In 1640 the Eastern Tisza Reformed Church province superintendent, István Keresszegi Herman, published a series of sermons which he had given at the town of Debrecen based on the Heidelberg *Catechism*. Keresszegi hoped that his book would be used by local ministers to build up their congregations' knowledge of Reformed beliefs, and that it would also be widely used in domestic family devotions. Keresszegi wrote that every householder was a 'prophet and priest in Christ' in their own home, and should read from catechisms aloud and search for supporting Bible passages in order to strengthen the faith of the whole household.[23] Other writers from the 1640s also stressed the practical role which catechisms could play in developing knowledge about faith in homes, as well as in schools and through congregational classes. Improvements were also suggested by various Reformed writers to the ways in which catechisms were being used. Pál Medgyesi wrote in the introduction to his 1645 translation of an English *A-B-C of Salvation* that children should try to learn two or three catechism questions by heart each day, and then repeat on Sunday what they had learned during the previous week. He also advised readers to look up the relevant Bible passages, given in support of the answers in catechisms, and then read them out loud for the benefit of those unable to read. Medgyesi, and other so-called 'puritan' clergy, were particularly concerned to improve understanding of the contents of catechism answers as part of their wider interest in improving standards of personal piety and morality in Hungarian Reformed congregations.[24]

---

22 *Egyházi kánonok – Geleji Katona István 1649 és a Szatmárnémetiben 1646 évben tartott zsinat végzései*, Áron Kiss ed. (Kecskemét, 1875), 1646 resolutions, nos. 2, 19; 1649 canons, no. 50.

23 István Keresszegi Herman, *A keresztyén hitnek ágazatiról való prédikációknak tárháza* (Nagyvárad, 1640); 'minden házi gazda Propheta és Pap a' Christusban házánál, a' ki avagy tsak olvasni tudna-is, erre szert tévén, a' hitnek akar mi ágazatirol-is tselédi között az Könyvet olvasván, és a Bibliábol a' locusokat reá keresvén tanitást tehetne, és a hitben háza népét éppithetné.'

24 Pál Medgyesi, *Lelki A-Bé-Cé. A Christus oskolájába az alsó rendben bé állatandó tsetsemőkuek közönségessen kiváltképpen; penig a' méltóságos kegyes Fejedelem aszszonynak Lorantfi Susannának, aprobb Tselédgyének hasznokra* (Gyulafehérvár, 1645).

János Apáczai Csere's 1650 *Catechism* criticized the practice of many ministers who, he claimed, stopped holding classes in the winter because of the cold weather. Apáczai emphasized the importance of regularly teaching the young and those who were weak in matters of faith, both men and women alike. He also stressed that all the answers to catechism questions needed to be fully understood, and Apáczai provided a series of follow-up questions and supporting Bible passages in his catechism to check on progress. Apáczai's comments are revealing of concern among Reformed clergy in the mid-seventeenth century as to whether many who learned catechism answers off by heart had any real understanding of the words they could recite. Catechisms published in Hungary during the second half of the seventeenth century were indeed marked by attempts to continue to improve methods of catechizing to combat this problem, and by efforts to develop greater use of catechisms in peoples' homes.[25]

Memorizing short passages was crucial to the success of catechizing, and yet there was nervousness among some Reformed clergy about encouraging their congregations to learn and repeat words without entirely understanding their meaning. Apáczai stressed that catechism answers should not be learned by rote without understanding what was being memorized, anxious about the shallow knowledge of many who attended catechism classes. Other ministers were concerned that requiring congregations to recite phrases encouraged superstition, as the words might be seen by some as having magical significance. For example, sections of the Lord's Prayer were learned through catechisms, and the prayer was then repeated aloud by the congregation each week in church services. Pál Medgyesi suggested that the details of the different requests contained within the Lord's Prayer ought to be completely understood by every member of a congregation before they were allowed to recite the words during public worship. Medgyesi was not alone in expressing concern about the dangers of superstition through church-goers repeating a formula of words, and in 1652 István Komáromi Szvertán also published a critique of the customary recitation of the Lord's Prayer by congregations during services.[26]

Catechisms were mostly used to instruct members of the Hungarian Reformed community about their faith, but were also sometimes used as a test to guard against the infiltration of heterodox ideas. Subscribing to

---

[25] János Apáczai Csere, *A keresztyéni vallasra rövid kérdésekben és feleletekben tanito Catechesis* (Amsterdam, 1650).

[26] Pál Medgyesi, *Doce nos orare et praedicare* (Bártfa, 1650); István Komaromi Szvertán, *Mikoron imádkoztok ezt mondgyatok az az: Az uri imadsagnak ... magyarázattya* (Nagyvárad, 1652).

the Heidelberg *Catechism* had become a test of ministers' orthodoxy in Zemplén district by 1630, and in 1646 a synod at Tokaj demanded that student ministers accept the Heidelberg *Catechism* and Second Helvetic Confession before they were given permission to travel to study at foreign universities. Catechisms were also seen as valuable instruments in the defence of Reformed communities against the attacks of rival confessions. István Pathai, minister at Pápa in western Hungary, hoped that through his 1592 *Catechism*, 'God's chosen ones might see the clarity of our true religion, and not afterwards believe the talk of those who blaspheme, but be able to answer them.'[27] In 1669 János Pósaházi envisaged his catechism being used in schools and homes to build up understanding of Reformed faith, as 'milk' to prepare the weak for more 'stout food' in sermons. As is suggested by its title, *A Support for Truth ... teaching of a catechism, which explains Reformed religion, and protects against competing, cunning adversaries*, Pósaházi wanted to provide a resource for people to defend their faith against Catholic attacks, very appropriate to the circumstances of his home at Sárospatak during the late 1660s.[28]

Catechisms were also produced by the Reformed Church as part of attempts to foster reform within the Orthodox Church in Transylvania. In the 1640s Transylvanian Reformed superintendent István Geleji Katona wanted new Orthodox metropolitans to accept a Protestant catechism which had been published in Romanian, agree to found Romanian schools, provide seating in churches and only give communion to adults. The Reformed clergy hierarchy and Rákóczi princely family supported further Romanian translations of the Heidelberg *Catechism* in 1648 and 1656. István Fogarasi, the Reformed minister at Lugoj (Lugos/Lugosch) in south-western Transylvania, complained in his introduction to the 1648 *Catechism* that while Jewish children of five and six could already read from the scriptures, some Christians in their twenties had still hardly touched a copy of the Bible in their lives. Fogarasi acknowledged that Bibles were hardly 'lying scattered in every bush', and so he had produced a catechism or 'little Bible' in Romanian

---

27 'Pathai István kátéja [Pápa, 1592]', ed. Lajosné Pataky in *Studia et acta ecclesiastica* 3 (1973), pp. 837–48; 'az Istennek választottai pedig látván a mi igaz vallásunknak tisztaságát, ne higyjenek ennekutána a minket káromlók beszédnek, de lenne mit felelniök ellenük.'

28 János Pósaházi, *Igazság istápja ... katekizmusi tanítás, melyben a ker. reformáta vallás ... megmagyaráztatik, és az ellen tusakodó fortélyos patvarkodások ellen ... óltalmaztatik* (Sárospatak, 1669); 'a' kik Catechizálás által gyakoroltatnak, azok a' Templombéli Praedikátiokat éppületessebben halgathattyák, jobban meg-foghattyák, és erössebbé meg-tarthattyák'. Géza Nagy, *Fejezetek a magyar református egyház 17. századi történetéből* (Budapest, 1985), pp. 75–8.

for use in the Protestant schools at Lugoj and Caransebeş (Karánsebes/Karansebesch). The 1656 Romanian *Catechism* also sought to defend the position of existing Romanian Reformed communities, outlining biblical support for the teaching of the Heidelberg *Catechism* against Orthodox criticisms of Calvinist theology.[29]

The ways in which catechisms were used in the Hungarian Reformed Church to establish both orthodox and heretical beliefs are particularly clear from examining the key sections which dealt with the Eucharist. Catechisms asserted Reformed understanding of the sacrament and rejected all rival interpretations. In 1562 the *Catechism* compiled by Péter Méliusz Juhász at Debrecen set out Reformed ideas on this critical issue dividing the confessions, explaining how Christ's body was merely represented in the elements of the sacrament. Méliusz described the bread as 'neither Christ's body in form, nor changing into becoming Christ's body, but bread given in the name of Christ's body.'[30] Bálint Szikszai Hellopoeus set out 'true understanding' about communion in his 1574 *Catechism* against Catholic errors. Szikszai discussed the elements of communion in the following terms; 'there is a different use for the bread and wine in the Lord's Supper than in your home, because here it represents the body of Jesus Christ ... as a certain pledge, seal, and sign' of salvation, but without 'a drop of change or combination' to the substance of the bread, because Christ is in heaven.[31]

Tamás Félegyházi described the Catholic mass and teaching on transubstantiation as 'blasphemy against God' in his 1583 *Catechism*, and stated that people could not live with the 'Papist wafer' in communion. Félegyházi explained that Christ's body was only present in the sacrament by faith. According to Félegyházi, the Lord's Supper provided a 'holy sign', in which the bread and wine represented how Christ's body and blood communicate with us by faith.[32] István Pathai

---

[29] István Fogarasi, *Catechismus, azaz: A keresztyén vallásnak és hütnek rövid kérdésekben és feleletekben foglaltatott ... olah nyelvre forditot* (Gyulafehérvár, 1648); A. Mózes, 'A xvi–xvii századbeli protestáns román káték', *Református Szemle* 29 (1936), pp. 340–45; Pál Hunfalvy, 'Az oláh káté', *Századok* 20 (1886), pp. 475–90; Judit V. Ecsedy, 'Dobre mester erdélyi nyomdaja, 1640-2', *Magyar Könyvszemle* 109 (1993), pp. 146–66.

[30] Péter Méliusz Juhász, *Catekizmus* (1562) published in *Studia et acta ecclesiastica 3* (1973), pp. 222–77; 'nem Krisztus teste állatjában, sem Krisztus testévé való létellel, változással: hanem a Krisztus teste nevének a kenyérre való adással.'

[31] Bálint Szikszai Hellopoeus, *Az egri keresztyén anyaszentegyháznak ... rövid catechismus* (1574); Bálint Szikszai Hellopoeus, *A mi keresztyéni hitünknek és vallásunknak három fő articulusáról ... való könyvecske* (1574); 'mas hazna vagion az Ur vaczoraiaban az keniernek bornak hog nem mint az te hazadnal mert it az Iesus Christusnak testenek kepet viseli, annak tisztiben iar es annak bizonios zalogia, peczeti es iele.'

[32] Tamás Félegyházi, *Az keresztieni igaz hitnek reszeirol valo tanitas* (1583); see question 30, and pp. 417–44; 'Christustol szereztetet szent iegy'.

presented three understandings of communion to his audience at Pápa in his 1592 *Catechism*. The 'Christian' in Pathai's text spoke against transubstantiation and ubiquitarianism, and in favour of the Reformed view that the bread 'does not alter, nor does his [Christ's] body dissolve into the bread'.[33] János Siderius' *Catechism* described the bread and wine as outward and visible signs of Christ's sacrifice, but the bread represented Christ's body 'without any alteration or disappearance, but as a visible testimony' to the truth. On the question as to whether Christ's body was really present in the elements of communion, Siderius wrote that it was present:

> ... according to his holy promises and pledges to our faith; but not in the wafer or bread, or underneath the bread, as if someone could chew it with their teeth ... because [Christ] is in heaven, but, because faith has such long hands and great strength, distant and hoped for things ... are made present [in the sacrament]'.[34]

The answers given in Siderius' *Catechism* on communion were very similar to the formula of words found in the text of the Heidelberg *Catechism*, as translated by Dávid Huszár and others. The elements of communion provided visible 'signs and pledges' to the effects of Christ's redemptive sacrifice. Huszár's translation concluded that since Catholic priests attempted to replicate Christ's sacrifice in the mass, they denied the effects of Christ's original passion and practised idolatry. In Szárászi's 1604 translation of the Heidelberg *Catechism* the sacraments provided outer 'signs and pledges' of the working of redemption, and Szárászi also outlined the main differences between Reformed communion and the Catholic Mass.[35] Similarly, according to István

---

33 'Pathai István kátéja [1592]', ed. Pataky in *Studia et acta ecclesiastica* 3 (1973), pp. 837–48; 'sem el nem változik, sem a test a kenyérbe enyészik'.

34 János Siderius, *Kisded gyermekeknek való katechizmus, azaz a keresztyéni hitnek fő ágazatairúl rövid kérdések és feleletek által való tanitás* (Debrecen, 1597); János Barcza, 'Siderius János kátéja' in *Studia et acta ecclesiastica* 3 (1973), pp. 849–76; 'nem valamivel elváltozas avagy eltünésképpen, hanem látható bizonyságtétellel'; 'az ő szent ígérete és fogadása szerint a mi hitünknek; de nem az ostyában avagy a kenyérben, sem nem a kenyér alatt, hogy azt valaki foggal rághatná, hanem hittel foghatyuk meg, noha az mennyországban vagyon; mert a hitnek oly hosszú keze és nagy ereje vagyon, hogy az távoli és reménség alatt való dolgokat is ... jelenvalókká teszi.'

35 Dávid Huszár, *A keresztyén hitről való tudománynak rövid kérdésekben foglaltatott summája* (1577); János Siderius, *Kisded gyermekeknek való katechizmus* (1597); Ferenc Szárászi, *Catechesis* (1604), answer 78, 'csak jele es zaloga ... Azonkepen az Ur vacsorajanak kenyere sem Christus termeszet valo teste'. Hungarian translations all included the section which was added to question 80 of the Heidelberg *Catechism* which attacked the Catholic Mass; 'The Heidelberg Catechism, 1563' in Arthur Cochrane ed., *Reformed Confessions of the 16th Century* (London: SCM Press, 1966), pp. 305–31; '[Q. 78] Do the bread and wine become the very body and blood of Christ? No, for as the

Keresszegi Herman in 1640 the elements of the sacrament were 'only signs and pledges' of the promise of salvation. In János Apáczai Csere's 1650 *Catechism* the elements in the sacrament were again merely 'signs and pledges' of salvation.[36]

The answers given to different questions about communion in Pál Kerestúri's examination of György and Zsigmond Rákóczi's understanding of their catechism provides further evidence about the explanations given by Reformed clergy of the sacrament. On the question as to whether Christ's body is actually eaten in services of communion, the response was given that 'we eat only with faith, because Christ's body is in heaven.' György Rákóczi replied that those who say that Christ's body is present in the form of bread, or in the bread, or with the bread, or under the bread, 'do not hold to Christ's words'. Keresztúri asked why God provided bread and not meat in the Lord's Supper, and elicited the response that it was because bread offers greater nourishment and has a closer resemblance to Christ's body. Meanwhile wine 'eases thirst, makes the heart joyful, and banishes fear', which are the spiritual benefits of partaking in Christ's blood. Pál Keresztúri clarified these explanations given about communion in a 1641 defence of his use of the Heidelberg *Catechism* against a Catholic writer. In *The Christian Adult*, Keresztúri insisted that the wine used in communion must remain wine, for if someone drank so much wine so that they became drunk, would they be drunk 'from Christ's blood, or only from the look and taste of the wine?' Keresztúri supported this position with a story he had recently heard from the Catholic Ciuc (Csík) region of eastern Transylvania. According to Keresztúri, one local Catholic was so drunk on leaving mass that he threw up the wafer outside the church, and Keresztúri asked his readers whether they were to believe that he could have 'thrown up Christ's body and blood?'. These sort of

---

water in baptism is not changed into the blood of Christ, nor becomes the washing away of sins by itself, but is only a divine sign and confirmation of it, so also in the Lord's Supper the sacred bread does not become the body of Christ itself, although, in accordance with the nature and usage of sacraments, it is called the body of Christ.' '[Q. 79] Christ called the bread his body] ... to assure us by this visible sign and pledge that we come to share in his true body and blood through the working of the Holy Spirit as surely as we receive with our mouth these holy tokens in remembrance of him, and that all his sufferings and his death are our own as certainly as if we had ourselves suffered and rendered satisfaction in our own persons.' '[Q. 80] ... the Mass teaches that the living and the dead do not have forgiveness of sins through the sufferings of Christ unless Christ is again offered for them daily by the priest ... Therefore the Mass is fundamentally a complete denial of the once for all sacrifice and passion of Jesus Christ (and as such an idolatry to be condemned).'

36 István Keresszegi Herman, *A keresztyén hitnek ágazatiról való prédikációknak tárháza* (Nagyvárad, 1640), 'tsak jele és zálaga'; János Apáczai Csere, *A keresztyéni vallasra rövid kérdésekben és feleletekben tanito Catechesis* (1650).

follow-up questions and stories, evidently used by Keresztúri as he taught the Rákóczi princes their catechism, and presumably used by other Reformed clergy to reinforce the meaning of crucial words found in the texts of catechisms, aimed clearly to establish that the elements of the sacrament were tokens of Christ's redeeming sacrifice by faith.[37]

The widespread and growing use of catechisms in the Hungarian Reformed Church during the early seventeenth century suggests that ordinary church-goers were increasingly being instructed and tested on knowledge about their religion, according to a set standard conveyed through the texts of catechisms. It suggests that Reformed congregations were expected to be able to repeat catechism answers which summarized core elements of basic Reformed religious beliefs, for example, ideas about communion and how they differed from rival churches. By the mid-seventeenth century some Reformed clergy expressed concern that although knowledge of catechism answers was spreading in their community, this knowledge was shallow and inflexible. Writers tried to adapt catechisms, providing follow-up questions to check on understanding, hoping that readers would internalize Reformed beliefs, perhaps even be able to orally rehearse such ideas in discussions and verbal contests over religious truth and error within their locality. Although there was an obvious danger of encouraging mere parrot-learning, key phrases in the most widely-used catechisms, the Heidelberg *Catechism* and Siderius' *Catechism*, expressed Reformed ideas in a powerful and condensed form. On the sacrament of communion, according to these catechisms, the elements were 'signs and pledges' of redemption by faith, and Christ's body 'could not be chewed' in the sacrament. These phrases conveyed simplified versions of abstract and complex theological issues, and could be backed up with further questions, examples and stories to reinforce the basic message. Such simple expressions, or 'clear words' according to Tamás Félegyházi, about Reformed beliefs in catechisms at least encapsulated key points where the church differed from its rivals, particularly on crucial questions such as the sacrament of communion.[38]

The phrases in memorized answers to a number of other key questions in catechisms were also likely to have been widely known. The words of the opening question in catechisms might well have been among the most immediately recognized form of language which marked out Hungarian Reformed religion. The first question in Bálint

---

[37] Pál Keresztúri, *Csecsemő keresztyén* (1638), pp. 65–6, 175; 'Eszszük, de csak hittel … '. Pál Keresztúri, *Fel-sördült keresztyén* (Nagyvárad, 1641), pp. 322–4, as a response to Mátyás Hajnal, *Kitett cégér* (Pozsony, 1640).

[38] Tamás Félegyházi, *Az keresztieni igaz hitnek reszeirol valo tanitas* (1583), p. 3.

Szikszai Hellopoeus' 1574 *Catechism* was 'For what ends did God create men? That they should recognise and respect their creator God.'[39] The first question of the Heidelberg *Catechism* as translated by Ferenc Szárászi, Albert Szenczi Molnár and others was phrased 'What is your only comfort, in life and in death?' With minor variations, all the Hungarian translations of the Heidelberg *Catechism* began with the same formula in response: 'that I belong – body and soul, in life and death – not to myself but to my faithful saviour, Jesus Christ'.[40] Although catechisms were probably not by any means entirely successful in transmitting detailed understanding of Reformed theology across Hungarian society, at least key phrases and sentences acted to advertise and confirm a sense of shared understanding between clergy and laity of what it meant to adhere to the Reformed Church.

What does the production and use of catechisms reveal about Hungarian Reformed identity in early modern Hungary and Transylvania? Reformed believers were attached to a system of belief entirely dominated by words, and very suspicious of the power of visual images. So while the spartan appearance of Reformed church buildings, with symbols perhaps only found on church spires, and the limited use of music in church services, were distinctive from confessional rivals and formed important aspects of Reformed identity, words were key expressions of Reformed religious life. The clergy's task of clearly establishing Reformed religious identity in a confessionally divided society in Hungary and Transylvania was influenced by the need to ensure that people knew what they were not supposed to believe as well as what they were supposed to believe. Formulas of words, phrases and slogans which summarized crucial points where Reformed beliefs

---

[39] Bálint Szikszai Hellopoeus, *Az egri keresztyén anyaszentegyháznak ... rövid catechismus* (1574); 'Mi vegre teremte Isten az emberec? Hog' az ö terömtö Istent megesmeric es tisztellic.'

[40] Albert Szenczi Molnár, *Kis katekizmus* (1607); '[Q. 1] Miczoda néked egyetlen egy vigasztalásod életedben és halálodban?'; János Siderius, *Kisded gyermekeknek való katechizmus* (1597); '[Q. 1] Micsoda te neked ember mind eletödben s-mind halalodban fü es kivaltkepen valo vigasztalasod?'; Johann Heinrich Alsted, *Catechismus* (1636); 'hogy mind testestöl lelkestöl, akar éllyek akar hallyak, de az én hüséges Uramnak és megvalto Jesus Christusomnak tulaydona vagyok ...' 'The Heidelberg Catechism, 1563' in Cochrane ed., *Reformed Confessions* (1966), p. 305 '[Q. 1] What is your only comfort, in life and in death? That I belong – body and soul, in life and death – not to myself but to my faithful saviour, Jesus Christ, who at the cost of his own blood has fully paid for all my sins and has completely freed me from the dominion of the devil; that he protects me so well that without the will of my Father in heaven not a hair can fall from my head; indeed, that everything must fit his purpose for my salvation. Therefore, by his Holy Spirit, he also assures me of eternal life, and makes me wholeheartedly willing and ready from now on to live for him.'

differed from those of rival churches were seen as vital in this endeavour. Catechisms were widely used both positively and negatively to define the confessional space occupied by the Reformed Church for its clergy and laity. Some Reformed ministers expressed anxiety about the power of some words within catechisms which might be seen by some in congregations as sacred, even magical, incantations. However, the power of those same words and phrases ensured the significance of catechisms in Reformed religious culture.

From an entirely different perspective, the Habsburg authorities paid a back-handed compliment to the social power of Reformed catechisms during the eighteenth century. As late as the 1760s they demanded the removal of certain questions from the Heidelberg *Catechism* which were deemed offensive to the Catholic Church, and prevented the full publication of the *Catechism*.[41] Within a political context of contested authority, and where legal rights had been granted to a variety of confessions, the coherence and clear transmission of religious ideas clearly mattered to the outcome of the Reformation in Hungary and Transylvania. Printed literature, and especially catechisms, proved vital in brokering the popular reception of Reformed religious ideas and to the development of Hungarian Reformed identity.

---

[41] József Pokoly, *Az Erdélyi református egyház története* (5 vols), (Budapest, 1904), vol. 3, pp. 111–12, 127.

CHAPTER SIX

Building a Romanian Reformed community in seventeenth-century Transylvania

Maria Crăciun

Hungarian Calvinists made a concerted effort to build a Romanian Reformed community in the Transylvanian principality during the seventeenth century. One part of this mission involved the production of a range of Romanian-language religious texts. Romanian historians have mostly been interested in these books merely as early examples of the development of Romanian as a literary language and as evidence of the emergence of print culture in Romania.[1] Despite obvious evidence to the contrary, the Calvinist initiative behind the emergence of these books has often been minimized, or understood as a purely commercial enterprise.[2] When the production of Romanian-language texts has been discussed in the context of Protestant efforts to initiate reform among the Orthodox Romanian population of Transylvania, it has been interpreted as part of a deliberate attempt to 'magyarize' Romanian communities.[3] The rejection of reform, at least by those outside the social elite, has therefore often been praised by Romanian historians as rightful resistance by Transylvanian Romanians to preserve their identity, and Hungarian Protestant missionary efforts have been seen as doomed to failure due to fundamental cultural incompatibilities between the two communities.[4] To some extent, this analysis is accepted in much Hungarian writing about attempts to reform Romanian Orthodoxy,

---

[1] Ion Gheţie, *Începuturile scrisului în limba română. Contribuţii filologice şi linguistice* (Bucharest: Editura Academiei, 1974); Cornelia Papacostea-Danielopolu, Lidia Demény, *Carte şi tipar în societatea românească şi sud est europeană secolele XVII–XIX* (Bucharest: Editura Eminescu, 1985).

[2] Eva Mârza, *Din istoria tiparului românesc. Tipografia de la Alba Iulia, 1577–1702* (Sibiu: Editura Imago, 1998), p. 14; Ioan Gheţie, Alexandru Mareş, *Originile scrisului în limba română* (Bucharest: Editura Ştiinţifică şi Enciclopedică, 1985), pp. 104–5.

[3] Alexandru Moraru, 'The Calvinist Catechism and the Orthodox Transylvanians of the xviith century', *Colloquia* 1/2 (1994), pp. 65–9.

[4] Zenovie Pâclişanu, 'Istoria Bisericii Române Unite Partea I, 1697–1751', *Perspective* 65–8 (1994–95), pp. 78–80.

which has also emphasized the futility of the Calvinist mission, insurmountable differences between the Latin and Orthodox worlds, and stressed the 'superstitious' responses of the 'illiterate' Romanian population. Hungarian writers deny that that there was any intention to transform Transylvania's Romanians into Hungarians by changing their religion. However, both historiographical traditions agree, if for different reasons, that attempts to create a Romanian Reformed community in seventeenth-century Transylvania were an inevitable failure.[5]

This chapter will look again at Hungarian Calvinist attempts to reform Transylvanian Orthodoxy during the seventeenth century. It aims to show that the Reformed mission, launched in Transylvania by its Calvinist princes and Reformed clergy hierarchy, resulted in the eventual emergence of a small Romanian Calvinist community, drawn not only from the ranks of the nobility. The confessional identity of these Romanian Calvinists was largely established in response to the production of confessional discourse by the Reformed Church elite. Leading Hungarian Reformed clergy sought to prepare the way for Romanians' conversion from Orthodoxy and to strengthen the beliefs of converted Romanian Reformed communities. In the context of a deliberate policy of Calvinist confessionalization pursued by the Hungarian Reformed political and ecclesiastical elite of the Transylvanian principality, religious books in Romanian, and especially catechisms, aimed to shape the religious identity of Protestant Romanians. Producing catechisms for Transylvania's Romanians formed a significant part of a mission led by princes and leading Reformed clergy to integrate the Orthodox population of the principality into the Reformed Church. The Transylvanian Reformed elite had to take into account the entirely different doctrinal and devotional traditions of the Orthodox community, and the focus here will be on the theological content of these catechisms rather than on assessing their linguistic achievement.

This seventeenth-century Calvinist mission to the Orthodox population of Transylvania was a distinct movement from previous efforts to convert Romanians undertaken during the sixteenth century

---

5 István Juhász, *A reformáció az erdélyi románok között* (Kolozsvár: Grafika, 1940); Antal Bitay, *Az erdélyi románok a protestáns fejedelmek alatt* (Dicsőszentmárton: Erzsébet Nyomda, 1925); Alexander Ungvary, *The Hungarian Protestant Reformation in the XVIth Century under Ottoman Impact. Essays and Profiles* (Lewiston, 1989), pp. 185–200; Ágnes Ritoók-Szalay, 'Il Ruolo mediatore del' Ungheria nella missione protestante orientale' in Robert Sauzet ed., *Les frontières religieuses en Europe du XV au XVII siècle* (Paris: Librairie Philosophique, 1992), pp. 291–9; Imre Révész, *La Réforme et les roumains de Transylvanie* (Budapest: Sárkány, 1937).

by both Lutherans and Calvinists. The German-speaking magistrates of Sibiu (Nagyszeben/Hermannstadt) and Braşov (Brassó/Kronstadt) had supported the production of catechisms and other religious literature in Romanian. They also introduced vague administrative measures meant to enforce reform on Orthodox Churches in the territories under their authority. Meanwhile, some Hungarian Calvinist nobles encouraged the Transylvanian diet to set up a separate bishopric for Calvinist Romanians, and some attempts to reform Orthodoxy were agreed by the diet. While these initiatives achieved only limited results, they supplied some precedents for strategies to convert Romanians to Protestantism which were pursued during the seventeenth century.[6]

There are a range of available sources which will be considered in this study of the seventeenth-century Calvinist mission to Transylvanian Orthodoxy. First, a series of conditions which were presented to the metropolitans of the Transylvanian Orthodox Church on their appointment to office. These were written by leading Reformed clergy and received the blessing of the ruling Transylvanian prince. If fully implemented, they would have gone a long way towards transforming the church of Transylvania's Romanians, and incorporated the Romanian-speaking Church within the Transylvanian Reformed Church. Relevant princely decrees, the results of church synods, and statements made by Orthodox metropolitans will also be considered. The degree to which the project of shaping a new confessional identity for Transylvanian Orthodoxy made an impact beyond the Romanian clergy hierarchy among local priests and their communities will be examined. Some visitation reports survive for the district of Făgăraş (Fogaras/Fogarasch) which allow discussion on how far key elements in the reform programme were actually being implemented in local Orthodox communities. Finally, surviving religious literature produced in Transylvania, and especially editions of catechisms translated into Romanian, will be analysed.

The Transylvanian principality was a Reformed state from the early decades of the seventeenth century led by Reformed princes, and with Calvinism as its ruling ideology.[7] Princes cooperated with the hierarchy of their Reformed Church on a range of educational projects, and on

---

6 Pâclişanu, 'Istoria Bisericii Române' (1994–95), pp. 20–46; A. Schullerus, 'Luthers catechismus und Agende in Rumänischen Sprache', *Korrespondenzblatt des Vereins für Siebenbürgische Landeskunde* 44 (1921), pp. 57–61.

7 The Transylvanian princes of this period were István Bocskai, elected in September 1605, Zsigmond Rákóczi (February 1607), Gábor Báthory (March 1608), Gábor Bethlen (October 1613), György I Rákóczi (December 1630), György II Rákóczi (February 1648) and Mihály Apafi (September 1661).

programmes to stimulate spiritual renewal and social discipline. Reformed princes were repeatedly idealized by Reformed ministers as the sole guarantors of true faith in the principality, and Reformed clergy tried to instil in princes a sense of mission to other religious communities as part of their duties as Christian sovereigns.[8] For example, István Geleji Katona, superintendent of the Transylvanian Reformed Church, wrote a letter in September 1640 to prince György I Rákóczi on the death of Orthodox metropolitan Ghenad:e of Alba Iulia (Gyulafehérvár/Weissenburg), arguing that it was the duty of the prince to care for the salvation of all the subjects in his realm. Geleji suggested that the prince should become directly involved in the appointment of a new Orthodox metropolitan. On the prospects for Ghenadie's replacement, Geleji wrote that 'so many souls cannot be entrusted to someone ignorant, because Romanians, although they are stupid, are still human beings and your Highness, as a Christian prince, has a duty to care for their souls.'[9] This attitude provided the context for the policies adopted by princes to integrate the Transylvanian Orthodox community within the Reformed Church. It was a mission conceived in religious terms to spread true faith. This effort to integrate a confessionally and linguistically distinct community within the Reformed Church had three key elements which will be discussed in turn here: institutional reform, the provision of schools, and the propagation of Calvinist doctrine.

As a result of institutional reforms undertaken as part of the Calvinist mission to Orthodoxy, the Romanian Orthodox Church technically became part of the Transylvanian Reformed Church. By the end of this process, the Romanian Orthodox Church only preserved some autonomy in the relationship between the clergy hierarchy and ordinary parish priests. The internal organization of the Romanian Orthodox Church also became increasingly similar to that of the Reformed Church during this period. The Orthodox hierarchy in Transylvania was led by a metropolitan at Alba Iulia, whose appointment was recognized by the state authorities on agreement to conditions laid down for each new

---

[8] Graeme Murdock, 'International Calvinism, Ethnic Allegiance and the Reformed Church of Transylvania in the Early Seventeenth Century' in Maria Crăciun, Ovidiu Ghitta eds, *Ethnicity and Religion in Central and Eastern Europe* (Cluj: University Press, 1995), pp. 92–100; Graeme Murdock, 'Between Confessional Absolutism and Toleration. Inter-Denominational Relations between the Hungarian Reformed and Romanian Orthodox Churches in Early Seventeenth-Century Transylvania', *Europa Balcanica Danubiana 2/A* (Budapest: Felelös, 1995), pp. 216–23.

[9] This letter from Geleji was published in *Új Magyar Múzeum* 1 (1859), pp. 203–204; Ioan Lupaş ed., *Documente istorice Transilvane, 1599–1699* (Cluj: Tipografia Cartea Românească, 1940), pp. 204–205.

appointment.[10] The Reformed hierarchy repeatedly tried to use this process to accept only pliant metropolitans who would enforce reforming measures and encourage use of newly-published Protestant texts. Regional clergy synods were introduced, with archdeacons supposed to be appointed by election in synods, and regular visitations of parishes became compulsory. All priests and archdeacons were also expected to attend annual meetings of the church's full synod. The decisions of these synods were made subordinate to the Reformed provincial superintendent, and had to be approved by the Reformed synod.[11] At the parish level, some Orthodox clergy had recently been released from the full weight of previously-imposed duties of serfdom in Transylvania. In 1603 the Transylvanian diet declared that Romanian priests, although living 'in the darkness of a false religion' were to be made exempt from taxation on their own lands in the 'hope that God would enlighten them to work hard for the salvation of their people'. However, if parish clergy were recruited from the ranks of the servile peasantry, taxation and labour duties remained in place unless removed as a privilege granted by the prince.[12]

The imposition of conditions on new Orthodox metropolitans in Transylvania continued throughout the seventeenth century. In 1639 a decree issued by György I Rákóczi stated that the Romanian metropolitan of Alba Iulia was under the authority of the Reformed superintendent, István Geleji Katona. When the office of metropolitan fell vacant on the death of Ghenadie in 1640, Geleji had an ambitious set of conditions drawn up for new candidates to accept. In 1640 Geleji wrote to the prince with twenty-four conditions which he wanted his favoured candidate, Meletie Macedoneanul, to accept. Meletie Macedoneanul was a cleric at the Wallachian court of Matei Basarab, with some background in using printing presses. Eventually, a further set of four less ambitious conditions was presented to the candidate, which focused on ending 'superstition' in the Romanian Orthodox Church. Appointed metropolitans in Alba Iulia thereafter tended to fall under the control of the Reformed Church, at least partially dependent on the advice and instructions issued by Reformed superintendents, who were also resident in the Transylvanian capital. In March 1643

[10] The Orthodox metropolitans in Alba Iulia during this period were Ghenadie II (1628–40), Ilie Iorest (1640–43), Simion Ștefan (1643–56), Sava Brancovici (1656–59, 1661–80), Ghenadie III (1659–60) and Iosif Budai de Pișchinți (1680–82).

[11] Timotei Cipariu, *Archiv pentru filologie și istorie* (Blaj: Tipografia Samuel Filtsch, 1867), pp. 575, 611–12; Păclișanu, 'Istoria Bisericii Române' (1994–95), pp. 70–71; A.A. Rusu, *Ctitori și biserici din Țara Hațegului până la 1700* (Satu Mare: Editura Muzeului Sătmărean, 1997), pp. 71–2, 76–7.

[12] Cipariu, *Archiv* (1867), pp. 573–4.

fifteen conditions were presented to the new Alba Iulia metropolitan, Simion Ştefan, which would if implemented, have propelled the Orthodox Church towards accepting Reformed religion.[13] A 1662 decree contained the conditions imposed on Sava Brancovici by Mihály Apafi, and in 1669 four new conditions were added to the previous regulations. These conditions stated that the Romanian metropolitan depended on the Calvinist superintendent for the right to call synods, for guidance on all issues regarding the ordination of priests, for permission to conduct parish visitations, and for any decisions on divorce cases. In 1674 the prince even announced that he had invested the Reformed superintendent, Gáspár Tiszabécsi, with the right to inspect all Romanian churches and to correct any mistakes he was able to find.[14]

When new metropolitans were confirmed in office, a decree clarified all the territory under their jurisdiction. Districts of the Orthodox Church in Transylvania which fell outside the control of the Alba Iulia metropolitan were then placed under the direct control of the Calvinist superintendent. Princes confirmed archdeacons to control these areas, such as the district of Haţeg (Hátszeg) and Bihor (Bihar) county. These archdeacons in Geleji's view effectively became vicars of the Calvinist superintendent in their areas.[15] Indeed when Avram Burdanfalvi was made superior of the Romanian Church in Bihor county in 1641, the conditions of his appointment confirmed his dependence on the Calvinist superintendent, and on the local Calvinist archdeacon and synod. Burdanfalvi was charged to teach the truth in Romanian and to administer the sacraments in their scriptural form.[16] There are also incidences of secular interference in the government of the Orthodox Church in this period, as ruling princes on occasion appointed some Orthodox archdeacons themselves in regions outside the territory given

---

[13] Conditions published in *Új Magyar Múzeum* 1 (1859), pp. 216–18; Zenovie Pâclişanu, 'Episcopul româno-calvin Avram Burdanfalvi din Bihor', *Cultura Creştină* 16 (1936), pp. 516–18; Lupaş, *Documente istorice* (1940), pp. 213–17; Cipariu, *Archiv* (1867), pp. 628–32; Juhász, *A Reformáció* (1940), pp. 246–51; Pâclişanu, 'Istoria Bisericii Române' (1994–95), pp. 5–6.

[14] This 1662 decree was published in Augustin Bunea, *Vechile episcopii româneşti* (Blaj: Tipografia Seminarului Arhidiecezan, 1902), pp. 120–22; Cipariu, *Archiv* (1870), pp. 611–12; Pâclişanu, 'Istoria Bisericii Române' (1994–95), pp. 46–76. The diploma appointing Sava Brancovici was published by Cipariu, *Archiv* (1870), pp. 648–50. Also new conditions of 1680 from Mihály Apafi in Timotei Cipariu, *Acte şi Fragmente latine româneşti pentru istoria Bisericii române, mai ales unite* (Blaj: Tipografia Seminarului Arhidiecezan, 1855), p. 60.

[15] Geleji's letter is published in *Erdélyi Protestáns Közlöny* 2 (1881), pp. 6–7.

[16] Pâclişanu, 'Episcopul româno-calvin Avram Burdanfalvi din Bihor' (1936), pp. 516–18.

to the Alba Iulia metropolitan.[17] In the territory of Făgăraş in southern Transylvania a presbyterian church structure was imposed on the region's Orthodox Church during the 1650s. Regular visitations were made of Romanian communities at the behest of the dowager princess, Zsuzsanna Lórántffy, and even the Reformed superintendent was discouraged from interfering in this area.[18] (See Figure 6.1.)

On educational reform, some Romanian schools had been set up in the sixteenth century as part of attempts to spread Protestantism and to help strengthen the faith of newly-converted Romanians. The Romanian Protestant bishop had been pressurized to promise to found Romanian schools, and schools at Lugoj (Lugos/Lugosch), Caransebeş (Karánszebes/Karansebesch), and then at Braşov and Sighetu Marmaţiei (Máramarossziget) were established. These schools provided a basic education for Romanian clergy, some of whom then studied in larger Hungarian Protestant colleges before returning to work within their communities. These attempts in the sixteenth century to support Romanian schools continued in the seventeenth century in parts of Transylvania where Reformed communities were established, most notably in south-western counties and in Făgăraş, where a joint Hungarian-Romanian school was founded by Zsuzsanna Lórántffy in the 1650s.[19]

A related element of the mission strategy adopted by the Reformed Church in Transylvania was the production of significant numbers of religious books. Orthodox religious literature had only ever been produced in Old Church Slavonic, and the Reformed mission supported the publication in Romanian of the New Testament, Psalters, hymn-books and catechisms. The Reformed Church enjoyed the full support of the state authorities to produce these books in Romanian.[20] Between 1648 and 1656 a Romanian printing press which used Cyrillic

---

[17] Pâclişanu, 'Istoria Bisericii Române' (1994-5), pp. 70–71; Cipariu, *Acte şi Fragmente* (1885), pp. 145–80; Lupaş, *Documente istorice* (1940), pp. 204–205, 238–41; *Új Magyar Múzeum* 1 (1859), pp. 203–204; Alexander Szűcs, *Hunyadmegyei történelmi és régiszeti társulat évkönyve* (Arad, 1884), p. 43; *Monumenta Comitialia Regni Tranyslvaniae. Erdélyi Országgyűlési Emlékek*, ed. Sándor Szilágyi, (21 vols) (Budapest: Akadémiai könyvkiadó, 1875–98), vol. 14 (1889), p. 267; Juhász, *A Reformácio* (1940), pp. 252–4; Ioan Lupaş, *Principele ardelean Acaţiu Barcsai şi Mitropolitul Sava Brancovici* (Bucharest, 1913), pp. 9–10.

[18] Zenovie Pâclişanu, 'Documente privitoare la istoria bisericii române aflate în arhiva parohiei reformate din Făgăraş', *Cultura Creştină* 1 (1911), p. 288. The text of this visitation is published in *Anuarul Institutului de Istorie Naţională* 7 (1936-8), pp. 582–619.

[19] Murdock, 'Between Confessional Absolutism and Toleration' (1995), pp. 216–23; Pâclişanu, 'Documente privitoare' (1911), no. 11, p. 289.

[20] Mârza, *Din istoria tiparului românesc* (1998), pp. 13–15.

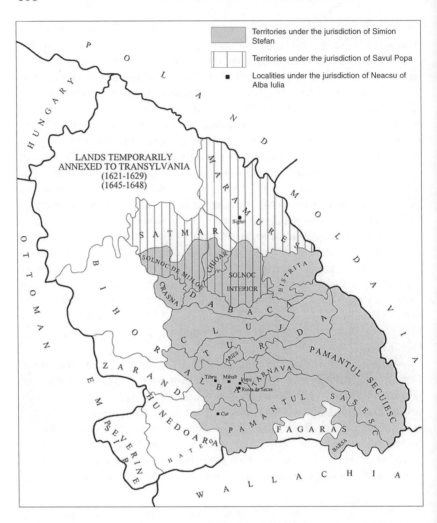

6.1   The territorial authority and jurisdiction of the metropolitan of Alba Iulia. Reproduced with kind permission of Radu Lupescu, Cartographer.

characters functioned as a section of the princely printing press at Alba Iulia, operating with its own editors and printers. The output of the Romanian press closely followed the programme set by the Reformed elite, with the cooperation of the Romanian metropolitan. Some of the Romanian books which were published were meant to prepare the Orthodox faithful for a new religious experience. Other books were intended to strengthen the faith of existing converts by transmitting the main tenets of Reformed doctrine. Supervising this work on behalf of the court was superintendent István Geleji Katona, György II Rákóczi's closest adviser on the progress of reform in the Orthodox Church. Geleji's enthusiasm for mission was matched by some other leading clergy and nobles including István Fogarasi, Márton Brassai, Ákos Barcsai and György Csulai, who later succeeded Geleji as Reformed superintendent.[21]

Before turning to assess some of the texts produced at Alba Iulia, it is important to establish the target audience for these books. Romanian Calvinist communities have never been studied in depth, because of the general assumption that attempts to spread Protestant ideas among Romanians was a complete failure.[22] Efforts to convert Romanians to Protestantism had been going on since the sixteenth century, and some historians have noted that the Reformation first spread among Romanians of noble status in south-western Transylvania, who had converted to Catholicism during the fourteenth and fifteenth centuries. These conversions to Catholicism, it has been argued, were part of an effort made by medieval Hungarian kings to integrate ethnically and confessionally distinct elites within their monarchy. Therefore, it has been assumed that even if Romanian Protestants did exist, they were part of a very small minority of previously Catholic nobles, and the possibility of direct conversion from Orthodoxy to Protestantism has been mostly discounted. For example, one historian has argued that Romanian nobles in the district of Haţeg first converted to Catholicism out of political expediency, and their subsequent receptivity to new Protestant ideas had in his opinion therefore more to do with 'fashion' and a quest for social acceptability than with any inner spiritual development. Romanian Protestantism has thus been mostly discussed as a shift from Catholicism to Calvinism, an analysis which saw as futile efforts to get converts to move directly from Orthodoxy to the Reformed Church.[23] (See Figure 6.2.)

Unfortunately we do not have any evidence from letters, diaries or personal reflections which discuss Romanians' experience of conversion. Consequently it is very difficult to make any grand assumptions concerning the motives of the Romanian elite in Transylvania who converted to Protestantism. Some historians have suggested that the Reformation may have made progress among

---

[21] Mârza, *Din istoria tiparului românesc* (1998), pp. 56–64; Marina Lupaş, *Mitropolitul Sava Brancovici* (Cluj: Tipografia Cartea Românească, 1939); Zenovie Pâclişanu, 'Cu privire la Sava Brancovici, în legătură cu cartea Mitropolitul Sava Brancovici de Marina Lupaş', *Cultura Creştină* (1939), p. 573.

[22] Pâclişanu, 'Istoria Bisericii Române' (1994–95), pp. 9–76.

[23] Ion Gheţie, 'Factori interni şi factori externi în problema începuturilor scrisului în limba română', *Limba Română* 19 (1980), pp. 123–6; Rusu, *Ctitori şi biserici din Ţara Haţegului până la 1700* (1997), pp. 141–333.

Counties and districts with Romanian protestants

● Localities with Romanian protestants

■ Archdeaconries with Romanian protestants

♦ Location of protestant synods

◢ Marghita Localities where calvinist ministers were appointed

6.2 Regions inhabited by Romanian Protestants. Reproduced with kind permission of Radu Lupescu, Cartographer.

Romanians in an urban context, especially in ethnically-mixed towns such as Hunedoara (Vajdahunyad/Eisenmarkt), Haţeg, Lugoj and Caransebeş.[24] Meanwhile it has been argued that Protestantism made little or no progress in rural areas because Romanian Reformed nobles did not attempt to persuade the servile peasantry to embrace Protestantism.[25] However, records from eastern Hungary show that

---

[24] Gheţie, 'Factori interni şi factori externi' (1980), pp. 123–6.

[25] Zenovie Pâclişanu, 'Câteva date despre preoţii româno-calvini', *Cultura Creştină* 1 (1911), p. 68.

several Romanian Calvinist priests were ordained and appointed to rural parishes in Bihor.[26] Available information shows that most Romanian peasant communities in Haţeg, despite often living under the authority of a Calvinist Romanian nobleman, remained faithful to Orthodoxy. However, Protestantism did make some progress in Romanian villages in Transylvania as well, and a number of Protestant congregations emerged around Haţeg, Hunedoara, Sibiu, Făgăraş, Lugoj and Caransebeş. Local church buildings were frequently used by both confessions in these areas. Whilst this practice was not unknown between other religions in Transylvania, it produced a particularly peculiar environment for worship and religious life in communities divided between Orthodoxy and Calvinism.[27]

The Calvinist programme to reform the Romanian Orthodox Church introduced institutional changes which placed the Church under the jurisdiction of the Reformed clergy hierarchy. A Romanian Reformed Church also required a new confessional identity around altered patterns of belief and forms of worship. Reformers faced the challenge of remodelling a completely different set of religious practices. Reformers normally resorted to describing Orthodoxy as 'corrupt' and 'superstitious', by which Calvinist clergy seemed to indicate almost all areas of traditional Orthodox religious life. The degree of difference between the two world views was such that the apophatic tradition in Orthodoxy made it difficult for people even to contemplate discussing doctrinal matters. One potential candidate for the office of metropolitan thus justified his evasiveness in discussing his conditions for appointment by saying that he had no experience of debating points of doctrine.[28]

Reformed clergy leading the mission to the Orthodox Church made clear through the conditions imposed upon the Alba Iulia metropolitans which elements of Orthodox belief, ritual and devotional life they

---

[26] Pâclişanu, 'Câteva date despre preoţii româno-calvini' (1911), p. 68. Romanian priests ordained in Bihor county include: in 1631 Mihail Tataroşi (Brusturi), in 1635 the Oradea synod ordained Petru Tataroşi, Petru Papafalvi and Ioan Csegeni, in 1671 the Debrecen synod ordained Ioan Tataroşi (Ciuteleac) and Petru Kövesdi (Petrea), in 1673 the Diosig synod ordained Callus Dedai (Uifalău), in 1675 the Csatar synod ordained Moise Tataroşi (Brusturi), George Varallyai, Mihail Szahegyi (Sărsig), and Demeter Totfalusi (Sârbi), in 1678 the Leta Mare synod ordained Mihail Sársegi (Sărsig), Ioan Tankanfalvi (Tăutufalva), Gabriel Király (Chiralău), Ioan Debreczeni, Peter Isopallagi (Isopalla) and George Buncskai (Furcska), in 1679 the Szoboszló synod ordained Gál Pop, and in 1680 the Almaş synod ordained Teodor Bologh (Marghita).

[27] Rusu, *Ctitori şi biserici din Ţara Haţegului până la 1700* (1997), pp. 192–203, 206–17.

[28] Lupaş, *Documente istorice* (1940), pp. 205–206.

wanted to change. Reformers targeted key points of difference between Calvinism and Orthodoxy, which had a completely different system of belief, of religious symbolism, and style of representing the sacred. First, these conditions imposed on metropolitans indicated that there was a concerted effort to lead Romanian Orthodox congregations towards a more personal experience of religion. It was hoped this would eventually prepare congregations for conversion, while also serving to strengthen the faith of those who had already converted to the Reformed Church. Thus, congregations were to be encouraged to participate in prayer and song during church services before and after a sermon from the priest, while children were supposed to learn from catechisms. Regulations also touched on the need for regular attendance at church services and on the appropriate standard of behaviour expected whilst at church. The conditions imposed upon metropolitans required the main tenets of Reformed belief to be clearly transmitted to local communities, primarily salvation through faith alone. The central role of Christ was stressed as the saviour and redeemer of mankind, while the intercessory power of saints and the role of good works in attaining salvation was discounted. Romanian priests were also encouraged to explain to their people the Reformed understanding of the sacrament of communion. The Reformed hierarchy also required church services to be held in the vernacular, and one of the conditions imposed by Geleji on the new Orthodox metropolitan in 1640 demanded that only Romanian be used in public worship. Priests were also advised not to offer communion to children, but only to adults who understood its meaning and could repent of their sins. These requirements aimed to develop an internalized system of belief among the Orthodox faithful, to prepare for the sacrament by acknowledging and repenting of their sin.[29]

Reforming patterns of Orthodox worship and ritual was often highlighted by Calvinist reformers as a means of accessing the realm of individual devotional life. Any understanding among Calvinists of the doctrinal points conveyed in traditional Orthodox religious practices was lost in general attacks on 'ignorance', 'superstition' and 'idolatry'. A broad range of Orthodox beliefs and ceremonies came under attack from Protestant reformers.[30] Conditions demanded that only water should be used in services of baptism, and that marriages should be

---

[29] *Új Magyar Múzeum* 1 (1859), pp. 216–18.

[30] For comparison with the reform of traditional religion in a Catholic context, see Robert Scribner, 'Introduction' and C. Scott Dixon, 'Popular Beliefs and the Reformation in Brandenburg-Ansbach' in Robert Scribner, Trevor Johnson eds, *Popular Religion in Germany and Central Europe, 1400–1800* (London: MacMillan, 1996), pp. 1–15, 119–39.

announced in church three times to discover any possible objections. They also stated that partners should exchange vows during marriage services, and allowed for divorce in cases of abandonment.[31] Conditions also insisted on introducing dramatic changes to the devotional life of Orthodox congregations, including abandoning belief in the intercessory power of saints, the role of good deeds in the process of salvation, the value of fasting, and the use of images in worship. Reformers attacked the liturgical cycle of communal celebrations which were central to the practice of Orthodoxy, and which often had pre-Christian roots. All customs related to the worship of saints came under attack, and emphasis on Christ as the sole mediator between God and mankind aimed significantly to modify the devotional patterns of the faithful. Part of the attack on traditional religion was also concerned with all customs related to care for the souls of the dead. The clergy were to persuade all Romanians to stop celebrating religious festivals on Fridays, enshrining Sunday alone as the day for services, and attacking traditional patterns of devotion such as the popular cult of Saint Friday (*Paraschiva Piatnica*).[32]

All available evidence suggests that this process of changing Orthodox religious practices was at best a very slow one. Instructions for parish visitations conducted among established Romanian Reformed communities continued to emphasize elements in need of reform. Some of the surviving reports from visitations in the Făgăraş region also allow us to assess the degree to which this reform programme had actually been implemented at a local level. The instructions for visitors in Făgăraş outlined some of the main requirements which parish clergy were expected to meet.[33] These concentrated on their ability to conduct church services using the Romanian language, and to be familiar with the Lord's Prayer, Apostles' Creed and the Ten Commandments. Parish priests were also expected to be able to read and write in Romanian, and those who could quote from catechisms were highly praised. A priest called Stoica from the village of Piatra (Kőfarka) was reported to have proved very willing to learn although he was an old man, while Toma

---

31 *Új Magyar Múzeum* 1 (1859), pp. 216–18; Graeme Murdock, 'Church Building and Discipline in early seventeenth-century Hungary and Transylvania' in Karin Maag ed., *The Reformation in Eastern and Central Europe* (Aldershot: Scolar Press, 1997), pp. 136–54.

32 Lupaş, *Documente istorice* (1940), pp. 206–209.

33 Romanian Calvinist priests in the Făgăraş district were: Dobre in Comana de Sus (Felsőkomana/ Oberkumanen), Neagoe in Comana de Jos (Alsókomana/ Unterkumanen), Sin in Vad (Vad), Oprea and Aldea in Şinca (Ósinka/Altschinka), Radu in Toderiţa (Todorica/Theodoren), Radul and Luca in Ludişor (Ludisor), and Mani in Voievodenii Mari (Nagyvajdafalva/Grosswoiwoden).

from Dridif (Dridiff) apparently surpassed all his colleagues in theological knowledge. The visitors also commended Stoica from Breaza (Suc) who had learned the Lord's Prayer, the Creed and the Ten Commandments. The visitors also recommended a number of younger people for study at the new school in Făgăraş.[34]

The moral life of the clergy in Făgăraş also came under scrutiny, with the visitation instructions emphasizing the function of priests in society as moral discipliners. Accusations against individual priests mainly focused on drunkenness, and on their violent or immoral behaviour. For example, the priest in the village of Ludişor (Ludisor) was criticized for living with his wife before getting married.[35] The way this issue was resolved suggests that some Reformed disciplinary mechanisms were also being implemented in the Făgăraş region. The offending priest and his wife had to ask forgiveness in front of the church community, following Reformed Church practices of exercising discipline through public shaming rituals.[36] During the early seventeenth century the Reformed Church in Transylvania in fact devoted increased enthusiasm to the cause of curbing immoral behaviour in their own community through imposing such public punishments on offenders.[37] However, this pressure on the moral behaviour of communities in Făgăraş was not mirrored elsewhere in Transylvania. There seemed to be no effort to enforce social discipline in the Haţeg district, where no penalties were imposed against priests or ordinary parishioners for continuing to follow traditional Orthodox practices.[38]

Creating a new institutional structure for a Romanian Reformed Church, attempting to introduce reforms through instructions to the Orthodox hierarchy, in some areas supported by parish visitations, were not the only means of attempting to shape a new confessional identity for a Romanian Reformed Church. Reformers spent much energy and efforts on producing texts which outlined basic theology and devotional

---

[34] *Anuarul Institutului de Istorie Naţională* 7 (1936–38), p. 597.

[35] Other results of the Făgăraş visitation included the priest Gherman in Veneţia de Jos (Alsóvenice) being accused of failing to give communion to the serf of Szegedi at the hour of his death. The priest at Cuciulata (Kucsulata) was accused of not delivering a sermon on Sundays. Two priests at Râuşor (Reusor) were reported to fight among themselves. Aldea was also accused of having failed to baptize the child of Ivan Frăţilă. The priest at Holban was accused of refusing to come and give communion to a dying man. The priest at Cuciulata (Kucsulata) was accused of frequenting the local tavern too often. The priest Comşa at Ileni (Illeny/Elisdorf) was accused of drunkenness. Two priests at Săsciori (Szeszcsor) were accused of drunkenness, violence and failing to hold Sunday services.

[36] *Anuarul Institutului de Istorie Naţională* 7 (1936–38), p. 599.

[37] Murdock, 'Church building and discipline' (1997), pp. 136–54.

[38] Rusu, *Ctitori şi biserici din Ţara Haţegului până la 1700* (1997), pp. 141–332.

literature to support their attempt to build a Romanian Reformed community.[39] Some of the books produced by the printing press in Alba Iulia were intended to encourage individual meditation on the scriptures, while others were meant to strengthen the faithful in their newly-acquired beliefs. One key element was the outlandish suggestion for Orthodox believers that they ought to be provided with a Bible which they could understand, either by reading it in their own language or by having it read to them. The Alba Iulia press produced a translation of the *New Testament* in 1648, thanks to the initiative and financial support provided by prince György I Rákóczi. Support from György II Rákóczi also allowed the publication of a *Psalter* in 1651, both to provide a focus for public worship and to encourage private devotion.[40]

Several other later Romanian language texts also aimed to encourage reform. An *Old Testament* may have been published in 1681, translated by the Reformed minister at Caransebeş, István Kezdivásárhelyi Matkó. A small collection of sermons for the dead, *The Golden Coffin*, printed in Sebeş (Szászsebes/Mühlbach) in 1683, was influenced by Reformed ideas.[41] Whilst concern for the dead was an obvious area of Orthodox piety, this particular book was edited by Ioan Zoba, whose introduction clearly stated that every sermon in the collection was based on the scriptures, and that he had used the 1590 Vizsoly *Bible* translated by Hungarian Reformed minister Gáspár Károlyi. At the behest of prince Mihály Apafi, Ioan Zoba also used the *New Testament* published at Alba Iulia in 1648 and the 1651 *Psalter* in this work. Another Protestant book was printed in Romanian in 1685 called the *Short Way to Good Deeds*. This devotional work was translated from English into Hungarian by István Kezdivásárhely Matkó, and then translated into Romanian.[42]

Catechisms were also published in Romanian during the seventeenth century, modelled on the 1563 Heidelberg *Catechism*. The first Romanian catechism was published in 1642. This was notionally on the initiative of metropolitan Ilie Iorest, but the catechism was in fact the project of István Geleji Katona with the support of György I Rákóczi.[43]

---

[39] Compare with Robert Scribner, 'Heterodoxy, literacy and print in the early German Reformation', in Peter Biller, Anne Hudson eds, *Heresy and Literacy, 1000–1530* (Cambridge: University Press, 1994), pp. 255–78.

[40] Mârza, *Din istoria tiparului românesc* (1998), pp. 34–55.

[41] Ioan Zoba de Vinţ, *Sicriul de Aur*, Anton Goţia ed. (Bucharest: Minerva, 1984); Ana Dumitran, 'Entre orthodoxie et réforme, l'appartenence confessionelle de l'archiprêtre Ioan Zoba de Vinţ' in Crăciun, Ghitta eds, *Ethnicity and Religion* (1995), pp. 136–49.

[42] Mihai Alin Gherman, 'O psaltire calvino-română necunoscută' in *Lucrări şi comunicări ştiinţifice* (Cluj: Bibl. Academiei, 1973).

[43] Lupaş, *Documente istorice* (1940), pp. 204–205; Mârza, *Din istoria tiparului românesc* (1998), p. 31.

The 1642 catechism was probably translated into Romanian by a priest called Gheorghe from Secu in south-western Transylvania, working under the supervision of the Reformed court chaplain, György Csulai.[44] A second catechism was then published in 1648, translated by the Reformed minister at Lugoj, István Fogarasi, from Latin-Hungarian versions of the Heidelberg *Catechism* earlier published in Transylvania. The introduction to Fogarasi's translation was dedicated to his patron, Ákos Barcsai, the leading noble around Lugoj and Caransebeş.[45] István Fogarasi had translated and published a Romanian *Hymn Book* in 1640, and in 1648 he had also translated part of the *Psalter*. A third catechism was printed in 1656, based on the 1642 catechism. This was probably published in response to a debate between Calvinists in Alba Iulia and the metropolitan of Iaşi in Moldavia, who had encouraged the publication of an Orthodox confession of faith in reaction to the previous catechisms which had appeared in Transylvania. (See Figure 6.3.)

The 1648 *Catechism* published by István Fogarasi clearly indicates the nature of the reforms proposed for Transylvanian Orthodoxy, and how far they were presented to a wider audience beyond the Orthodox hierarchy.[46] Fogarasi defined his *Catechism* as a manual to strengthen the faith of newly-converted Protestants which conveyed the main tenets of their new faith in simple, accessible terms. The questions and answers are based on discussion of the Apostles' Creed, the Ten Commandments and the Lord's Prayer. Fogarasi's *Catechism* first explains the route to salvation for the true believer. Salvation can only be achieved through justification by faith alone, and emphasis is placed throughout on the role of Christ's sacrifice in offering salvation to man. The joy of life comes from knowledge of the saving action of Christ and the promise of redemption through him. In order to achieve happiness, man has to be aware of his need for divine grace, which requires familiarity with the law of God. The law of God arouses awareness of sin, and of the need for a saving faith. Man is incapable of making peace with God by adhering to the law of God, and righteousness is only possible through God's offer of grace and through the mediating sacrifice of Christ.

---

[44] Mârza, *Din istoria tiparului românesc* (1998), pp. 34–55.

[45] *Fogarasi István kátéja. Fejezet a Bánsági és Hunyadmegyei rumeneség művelődéstörténetéből*, ed. Tamás Lajos (Cluj: Minerva, 1942), pp. 8–10: Gheorghe Bariţiu ed., *Catehismulu calvinescu impusu clerului şi poporului românescu sub domnia principilor Georgio Rakoczy I şi II* (Sibiu, 1879).

[46] *Fogarasi István kátéja* (1942). Pál Hunfalvy, 'Az oláh Káte', *Századok* 15 (1886), pp. 475-89; András Mózes, *Az erdélyi román reformáció káteirodalma* (Kolozsvár: Orient, 1942). I would like to thank Carmen Florea for assistance with the Hungarian bibliography concerning this text.

6.3   Ioan Zoba, *The Golden Coffin* (Sebeş, 1683)

Man cannot abide by the law of God through his own efforts, because man's nature is inherently sinful from the fall of Adam. As sin will not go unpunished, man is facing divine judgement and eternal punishment. The redemptive sacrifice of Christ is the only source of freedom for man from sin.[47]

The 1648 *Catechism* time and again emphasizes that Christ's sacrifice alone brings salvation from the consequences of sin. Christ was judged and sentenced to death so that he could save mankind from God's judgement. A number of questions and answers in the *Catechism* concern the crucial issues related to the events around Christ's passion, crucifixion, death, entombment and resurrection. It is clearly stated that Christ was buried so that it would be obvious that he had truly died, and was then resurrected from the dead so that mankind could receive the gift of grace. Christ's death was offered in exchange for mankind's salvation, and his resurrection provides proof that mankind can be saved. Man should expect to enter into heaven, just as Christ was taken to heaven in the sight of the Apostles. Christ, seated at the right of the Father, is the head of the Church and will return to judge the living and the dead. This emphasis on the role of Christ alone in the scheme of salvation, pursued through supporting Bible passages, was a radical departure from traditional Orthodox representations of salvation through good works and the intercession of Mary and the saints. Rather than concentrate on attacking these elements of Orthodox belief directly, the catechism offered believers a redirected concentration on Christ's life, death and saving power.[48] (See Figure 6.4.)

Treatment of the Apostles' Creed in the 1648 *Catechism* was structured into three parts, dealing with God the Father, God the Son, and the Holy Spirit, but all were intended to emphasize the unitary nature of God. God the Father is presented as the almighty creator of mankind. Emphasis is placed on the eternal and ubiquitous qualities of God. The section on Christ is much longer than the section on God the Father, and most of the ideas in this section concerning Christ's role in the salvation of the world have already been discussed above. Christ is described as both human and divine, which raises a brief consideration of the immaculate conception, through which Christ was born of the body of Mary by the action of the Holy Spirit. The Holy Spirit is then carefully described as part of the Trinity, one with the Father and the Son. The Holy Spirit transforms man through faith and enables him to make contact with the sacred. This concentration in the catechism on explaining doctrine about the Trinity very clearly, was partly related to

---

[47] *Fogarasi István kátéja* (1942), pp. 49–52.
[48] *Fogarasi István kátéja* (1942), pp. 53–4.

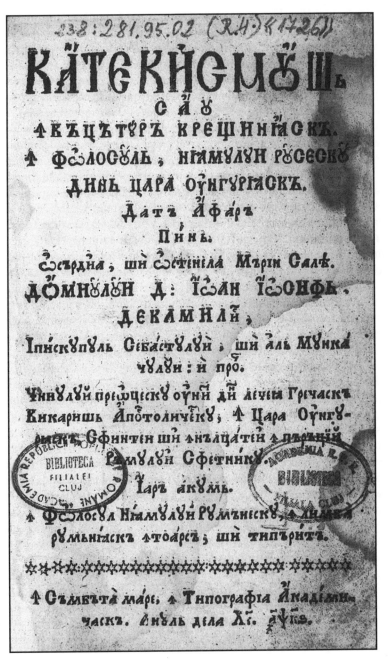

6.4 Istuán Fogarasi, *Catechism* (Alba Iulia, 1648)

the presence of a large anti-Trinitarian Church in the Transylvanian principality, and was also of particular significance to an audience familiar with the Orthodox Church's different understanding of the place of the Holy Spirit within the Trinity.[49]

The frequent references throughout the *Catechism* to the role of Christ's death and sacrifice in effecting salvation raises the question of how Fogarasi's work presented the concept of predestination. The *Catechism* explained that Christ selected a string of pearls from mankind who, through the action of the Holy Spirit, are predestined for eternal life. Each man should believe that he is a living part of this string of pearls and that he has been chosen for salvation. Man must believe that ultimately, by the will of Christ, he will find complete happiness in heaven. The importance of good deeds is again minimized, since heavenly rewards stem from God's mercy alone. However, Fogarasi's *Catechism* attempted to prove that good deeds are still necessary as men must show that they have faith, and provide continuous proof of the fruits of God's grace in their daily lives. The *Catechism* then sets out the role in strengthening faith of the two remaining sacraments of baptism and the Eucharist. These sacraments are described as seals of the promise of salvation and the forgiveness of sins. Baptism is associated with the cleansing sacrifice of Christ. Man enters the Church through baptism and individually receives the promise of salvation, as Christ promised that he would wash mankind with his blood. The *Catechism* defends infant baptism on the grounds that only through baptism can one enter membership of the Church. The Eucharist meanwhile is explained as only commemorating Christ's sacrifice and acting as assurance to mankind of its salvation, and is only available to those who repent sincerely of their sins.[50]

The 1648 *Catechism* also outlines the law of God through the Ten Commandments, which are explained as the living, breathing faith of mankind. Man must know only one God and must believe that it is possible to be saved by God, but be aware of his inclination to sin and to break the law. While man should strive to adhere to God's law and live a sober, disciplined life, again the reminder is offered that Christ alone can reconcile man to God. The interpretation of the fifth commandment is broadened from respect for parents to include deference to all those in positions of authority. The importance of moral conduct, ranging from sexual propriety to respect for property, is also emphasized. Finally, the *Catechism* placed a significant emphasis on prayer, especially the Lord's Prayer, as the centre piece of dialogue

---

[49] *Fogarasi István kátéja* (1942), pp. 52–3.
[50] *Fogarasi István kátéja* (1942), pp. 54–7.

between man and God. God is a righteous judge and a benevolent father who will not refuse requests sought in true faith. The *Catechism* highlights the danger of idolatry, and man is urged not to make any representations of the face of God. However, given the significant role of icons in Orthodox worship, there is no particular concentration on the issue of idolatry, and no encouragement to iconoclasm.[51]

Transylvanian Calvinists who embarked on a mission to integrate Romanian Orthodox communities into their church during the seventeenth century introduced a programme of institutional reforms and educational initiatives, made efforts to monitor the quality of priests, and produced religious texts to explain doctrine to parish clergy and the laity. Institutional changes attempted to turn the Romanian Orthodox Church into a branch of the Transylvanian Reformed Church. There were attempts to use schools to form a new band of priests able to transmit Reformed religion to the Romanian laity of the principality. Parish visitations were used in Făgăraş to check whether the clergy were familiar with the main tenets of faith and able to hold church services in the vernacular. Reformers were faced with the task of initiating major changes to the traditional system of Orthodox belief, and tried to begin the process of acculturation of Romanians to different patterns of behaviour from those which marked out traditional Orthodox religion. Through the conditions imposed on metropolitans at Alba Iulia and through the religious texts published in Romanian, above all the catechisms, reformers identified key areas which they wanted to change, including understanding of the intercessory role of saints and 'superstitious' devotional practices. Fogarasi's 1648 *Catechism* outlined an entirely changed world of theological doctrine and religious practices, which Romanian Reformed communities were encouraged to study and adhere to.

The efforts of seventeenth-century Calvinist reformers in Transylvania can often come across as a full-scale attack on traditional religion, and to modern eyes may seem to display a lack of sensitivity for systems of representation different from their own. However, where Romanians accepted Reformed religion, the process of forging a new system of belief and confessional identity through catechisms and other religious books did not focus on polemical attacks against the old religion, but rather attempted to offer a coherent alternative system of belief. The religious texts published in Romanian stressed the importance of internalized religious experience, that salvation comes through faith alone, the central role of Christ as the saviour of mankind,

---

[51] *Fogarasi István kátéja* (1942), pp. 58–61.

and focused on explaining the meaning of the sacraments, especially communion. The importance of scripture was also consistently highlighted as the basis of true faith. The conditions imposed upon Orthodox metropolitans also insisted on the scriptural foundation for all religious ritual, while catechism answers were always illustrated by Bible quotations. Vernacular catechisms were thus perceived by the Reformed clergy hierarchy of Transylvania to be the key instruments by which Romanian Reformed clergy could decode the Bible and guide their congregations to true faith.

CHAPTER SEVEN

Catholic devotional literature in seventeenth-century Transylvania

Csilla Gábor

Ideas about religious reform spread right across the Continent from the 1520s and made a significant impact in the Hungarian kingdom from the 1540s. In Transylvania, Luther's teachings were first introduced into the German-speaking towns of Transylvania largely thanks to the preaching of Johannes Honterus, a priest from Braşov (Kronstadt/Brassó). From the 1550s a second, Calvinist wave of reform also began to affect the counties of western Hungary still held by the Habsburgs, but found particularly strong support in the eastern counties of the Hungarian plain and in Transylvania, by then under the rule of a series of native princes. In the wake of Reformed religion, anti-Trinitarianism also gained support in some of Transylvania's towns and in the Szekler areas of eastern Transylvania, with only much smaller pockets of support for anti-Trinitarian belief emerging elsewhere in Hungary.

By the early decades of the seventeenth century, this varied pattern of reception of Reformation ideas had established distinct confessional and cultural environments for the two non-Ottoman states of the former Hungarian kingdom. To the west, Catholic interests were solidly promoted by the Habsburg rulers of Royal Hungary while, to the east, a series of seventeenth-century Reformed rulers of Transylvania upheld the multi-confessional constitutional settlement agreed by the diet of the principality during the 1560s. However, this broadly-drawn context of the impact of the Reformation across Hungarian society hardly does justice to the complicated reality of the confessional environment in either Habsburg Royal Hungary or in the Transylvanian principality. The aristocracy and towns of Royal Hungary never entirely reverted to embrace Catholicism in the seventeenth century, nor was there a homogenous pattern of Protestant domination of the so-called *Partium* of the eastern Hungarian plain nor in Transylvania proper.[1]

---

[1] Ludwig Binder, *Grundlagen und Formen der Toleranz in Siebenbürgen bis zur Mitte des 17. Jahrhunderts* (Cologne-Vienna: Böhlau Verlag, 1976); Gábor Barta, 'The Principality of Transylvania' in Béla Köpeczi ed., *A History of Transylvania* (Budapest: Akadémiai Kiadó, 1994), pp. 287–90; István Bitskey, 'Spiritual Life in the Early Modern

By the turn of the seventeenth century the Catholic Church in Transylvania was largely limited to the estates of some noble supporters and to pockets of support in the eastern Szekler region. Throughout the seventeenth century the Transylvanian diet continued to uphold laws which ensured the constitutional status of the Catholic Church as one of the principality's four 'received religions'. While Catholics in Transylvania retained legal rights to practise their religion freely, in reality the Catholic Church, as a small confessional minority, had a far less privileged status compared to its Protestant rivals. Catholic property had been appropriated by the state in 1556 and the Church's administrative structures had collapsed in Transylvania during the middle decades of the sixteenth century. Despite repeated attempts to re-establish a clergy hierarchy, Transylvanian Catholics had to survive without the leadership and authority of a resident bishop during the seventeenth century, only able to elect a bishop's vicar who was not empowered to ordain priests. Consequently, the shortage of Catholic priests in Transylvania increased over time, causing ever greater difficulties in providing effective pastoral care for the principality's Catholic believers. Jesuits, so prominent in teaching, preaching and missionary work elsewhere, were mostly prevented from settling in Transylvania, and even when they were permitted access to the principality their activities were strictly limited.[2]

Despite these difficult circumstances for any recovery of support for the Catholic Church in Transylvania, some missionary efforts were undertaken during this period. In the second decade of the seventeenth century a Jesuit priest, István Szini, sent a report from Cluj (Kolozsvár/Klausenburg) to his superior in Rome, Muzio Vitelleschi, on attempts to bolster Catholic religion in the principality. Szini wrote that he had successfully travelled to the extreme east of Transylvania to visit the mountainous Ciuc (Csík) region, where the majority of the population remained faithful to Rome. Szini's report claimed that he had succeeded in convincing two local Catholic priests who were married to leave their wives. He also wrote that he had brought some order to the public worship and spiritual life of six parishes, where he had heard confessions, conducted baptisms, and converted the wife of a local noble. Szini also urged the need for the Catholic Church to produce a

---

Age' in László Kovács ed., *A Cultural History of Hungary. From the Beginnings to the Eighteenth Century* (Budapest: Corvina–Osiris, 1999), pp. 244–7; Völkl Ekkehard, 'Möglichkeiten und Grenzen der konfessionellen Toleranz dargestellt am Beispiel Siebenbürgens im 16. Jahrhundert', *Ungarn-Jahrbuch* (1972), pp. 46–60.

   2 Konrád Szántó, *A katolikus egyház története* (3 vols), (Budapest: Szent István Társulat, 1983) vol. 2, p. 169.

refutation of the work of György Enyedi, a local anti-Trinitarian writer and former superintendent of the anti-Trinitarian (or Unitarian) Church. A summary of Enyedi's ideas had been published in 1598 at Cluj, and was widely known both in Transylvania and beyond during the first half of the seventeenth century. Thanks to Szini's suggestion, a response to Enyedi's ideas was indeed later produced by Ambrosius Penalosa at Vienna in 1635.[3]

The position of the Catholic community in Transylvania during the early decades of the seventeenth century improved somewhat, thanks to aspects of the relatively tolerant religious policies pursued by the Calvinist prince, Gábor Bethlen. Bethlen sanctioned the activity of Jesuits in several towns and allowed them to open schools. The prince was sufficiently impressed by the quality of Jesuit schooling to cite their methods when attempting to develop local Reformed centres of education in the principality. When Bethlen established the regulations for a new princely academy at his capital of Alba Iulia (Gyulafehérvár/Weissenburg), he commanded his teachers, 'do not teach by the mistaken customs of Hungarian schools', but 'in the style of the Jesuits'.[4] Bethlen also offered financial support of 100 forints for the publication of a Hungarian translation of the Bible by the Jesuit priest, György Káldi. This support was intended to reward Káldi's diplomatic endeavours for the Transylvanian prince at the imperial court in Vienna.[5] Káldi, referring in one of his sermons to a meeting with Bethlen, mentioned the warm reception which he and fellow Jesuits had received from the prince:

> The world knows how Gábor Bethlen, the prince of Transylvania, treated us, who, had he known about any of our sins, [or listened] to the many intriguers against us who surrounded him, would never have received us in a golden carriage in front of all of his men, nor shown good will and honour towards us, which has since been a source of resentment for our many enemies.[6]

Nevertheless, Catholic services and sermons, especially in Protestant-dominated towns, were still on occasion disturbed by unwanted interruptions. Káldi himself recalled one such episode when his

---

3 Mihály Balázs, István Monok et al. eds, Erdélyi és hódoltsági jezsuita missziók (2 vols), (Szeged: Attila József University, 1990), vol. 1, pp. 277–81.

4 Zsigmond Jakó, 'Négy évszázad a művelődés szolgálatában. A kolozsvári Báthori István iskola jubileuma' in Jakó, Társadalom, egyház, művelődés (Budapest: Magyar Egyháztörténeti Enciklopédia, 1997), p. 270.

5 István Bitskey, 'Bethlen, Pázmány és a Káldi-Biblia' in Bitskey, Eszmék, művek, hagyományok (Debrecen: Csokonai Könyvkiadó, 1996), pp. 201–203.

6 György Káldi, Az vasarnapokra-valo predikatzioknak elsö resze (Pozsony, 1631), p. 615.

preaching had been disrupted by Protestants at Cluj: 'I remember in the year 1605, when I was complaining in my daily sermon at Cluj about innovators in religion who disapproved of fasting and condemned such practices, a [Protestant] preacher became quite enraged about this.'[7]

Alongside the work of Jesuits in Transylvania to support remaining Catholic communities, Franciscans also played an important role in the survival of Catholic religion in the principality, especially in the eastern Szekler region. Reports produced by Franciscan missionaries in Transylvania which were sent to Rome during the first half of the seventeenth century detailed the difficult circumstances of Catholic communities in this area. These Franciscan reports highlighted the shortage of priests, and low standards of personal morality among remaining priests, as well as ongoing internal conflicts between Catholics. The Franciscans offered the suggestion that the situation in Transylvania required the foundation of missionary centres in the principality, and requested that foreign priests who spoke Hungarian, Romanian or German be sent into the region.[8]

Despite the Catholic Church's official status as a constitutional confession, the practice of Catholic religion in Transylvania was therefore limited in several significant regards during the seventeenth century. Partly as a result of the church's marginal position in seventeenth-century Transylvanian society, there are many difficulties in reconstructing an accurate picture of the spiritual life of Catholic communities in the principality during this period. However, there is a range of surviving Catholic literature from the seventeenth century, although much derives from works published outside the principality and was not published in the vernacular. The assessment in this chapter of the role of printed literature in sustaining Catholic worship and spirituality within Transylvania's Protestant-dominated environment considers texts, often translated from western languages, which were produced in Royal Hungary during this period. In particular I assess the contribution made by Gergely Vásárhelyi in producing devotional literature for the Transylvanian Catholic community. This Jesuit author and translator was originally from Târgu-Mureş (Marosvásárhely/ Neumarkt) in Transylvania, and was active in both Translyvania and Ottoman-occupied Hungary. Finally, I summarize the contribution made

---

7 Mihály Balázs ed., *Jezsuita okmánytár. Erdélyt és Magyarországot érintő iratok, 1601–1606* (Szeged: Attila József University, 1995), 1/xix, 2/353. Thanks to Mihály Balázs for drawing my attention to this.

8 István György Tóth ed., *Relationes missionariorum de Hungaria et Transylvania (1627–1707)* (Rome-Budapest: Bibliotheca Academiae Hungariae, 1994), pp. 241, 247, 258–9, 278.

to Transylvanian Catholicism by the first Catholic press of the seventeenth century in the principality, founded in the 1670s by the Observant Franciscans at Şumuleu Ciuc (Csíksomlyó) in the Szekler region.

Evidence from Transylvania about the extent to which printed devotional literature spread across the Catholic communities of the principality during this period is very difficult to obtain. However, some progress can be made from studying the surviving stock of books in the Catholic, Reformed and Unitarian college libraries of Cluj. It is striking that various Catholic texts from the seventeenth century appear quite frequently in the contemporary catalogues of the Reformed and Unitarian college libraries. A good number of Protestant works are also to be found in the Catholic school's stock of books. Each confession might well have decided to acquire such texts if directed against their own system of belief but, in addition to polemical literature, there are also a considerable number of Catholic books on prayer and meditation in these collections.

Attempts to inspire readers to meditate on the truth of the Gospel and to reflect upon their own moral conduct and daily lives seems to be at the heart of surviving Catholic devotional literature in Transylvania from this period. The basic aims of meditation as an individual devotional practice and religious activity are to develop skills of contemplative reflection and to apply lessons from this contemplation to daily life. Meditative thought carries the implication of engaging the whole personality in reflection, and an attempt to foster moral and charitable attitudes not just in the mind but also in the heart. As a literary genre, meditative texts incorporate elements both of dogmatic theology and of mystical approaches to religion, attempting to make relevant to each individual otherwise impersonal propositions about doctrinal truth. The structure of much meditative literature first seeks to encourage readers to recognize their own sinfulness, and then directs them to turn towards God to experience divine mercy.[9] Some work on the role of meditative literature in Catholic spirituality has suggested a relationship between the popularity of such work and periods of religious crisis. While any such suggestion might be questioned in many ways, it certainly provides one potential explanation for the strong interest shown in meditative works among Catholics in Hungary and Transylvania during the seventeenth century.[10]

---

[9] Klára Erdei, *Auf dem Wege zu sich selbst: die Meditation im 16. Jahrhundert. Eine funktionsanalytische Gattungsbeschreibung* (Wiesbaden: Otto Harrasowitz, 1990), pp. 3–27.

[10] Erdei, *Die Meditation im 16. Jahrhundert* (1990), pp. 48–53.

Returning to examine the context in which this literature was produced and read, around the turn of the seventeenth century Transylvanian politics descended into chaos amidst the destruction caused by renewed war against the Ottomans. During this Fifteen Years' War, Transylvania was ruled by Catholic princes up to the 1604 revolt of the Calvinist noble, István Bocskai. Bocskai received widespread support from the nobles and towns of eastern Hungary and Transylvania for his rebellion against Habsburg attempts to recover control over the Transylvanian principality and to promote the interests of the Catholic Church. Against the background of these turbulent years of warfare, some indication of the fortunes of Transylvania's different confessions can be gauged from the output of the Protestant-run Heltai press in Cluj, a town dominated by anti-Trinitarians from the 1560s. In 1599 the Heltai press produced an anti-Trinitarian theological work entitled *Explanationes*, edited by Máté Toroczkai from the writings of György Enyedi.[11] However, the Catholic prince, András Báthory, prevented the circulation of this work, and many copies were publicly burned. This was in keeping with previous censorship laws imposed by István Báthory in the 1570s, according to which books dealing with themes on religion were only allowed to be published with the permission of the prince. Then in 1599 the Heltai press published a translation of Peter Canisius' *Catechism*, and editions of this work in Hungarian were also produced in Vienna in 1604, 1615 and 1617.[12] This publication of Canisius' *Catechism* at Cluj is of interest within the changeable politics of Transylvania during the Fifteen Years' War, but it is also significant to this discussion of the printed sources of Transylvanian Catholic spirituality in the seventeenth century. Alongside the questions and answers of Canisius' *Catechism*, which explained the Apostles' Creed and Lord's Prayer, sections were included which detailed the ceremonies and liturgical traditions of the church. Church music was also included in the text, with Latin versions of psalms and hymns published in the first edition which were subsequently translated into Hungarian in later editions. This perhaps was intended to respond to the

---

11 György Enyedi, *Explicationes locorum Veteris et Novi Testamenti, ex quibus Trinitatis dogma stabiliri solet. Avctore Georgio Eniedino superintendente ecclesiarum in Transyluania, unum Patrem Deum et eius Filium Iesum Christum per Spiritum Sanctum profitentium* (Kolozsvár, 1598).

12 Peter Canisius, *Catechismus. Canisius Petertöl irattatot kereztyeni tudomanynak summáya magyar kalendáriummal és az egy igaz hitnek bizonyos ismeretevel. Az Anya sz. egyhazba valo caeremoniaknac rövid ertelmeröl valo tanusag. Az üdvözülendö leleknec tüköre. Hetedszaki imadsagoc es lelki elmelkedesec* (Kolozsvár, 1599); from Peter Canisius, *Summa Doctrinae Christianae per quaestiones tradita et ad capitum rudiorum accomodata* (1555).

success of recent editions of hymnals for the Reformed Church in the region. Prayers and meditations also appeared within Canisius' *Catechism* including 'Seven devotional prayers as spiritual meditations', which offered an account of the main elements of salvation from the creation of the world, the Fall of man, to Christ's life, death and resurrection. These meditations began with an introductory prayer followed by an examination of the subject for meditation, then moving to further prayer, a second meditation, and then a final prayer.[13]

A similar structure was followed by Gergely Vásárhelyi in his published compilation of prayers and meditations for each Sunday of the year and for the major festivals of the Catholic calendar. Vásárhelyi's book of meditations, published at Vienna in 1618, was a collection of Bible passages followed by paragraphs of sources for meditation. These sections ended by urging the reader to further prayer, but without giving any specific examples of prayers for readers to use. Vásárhelyi also included additional relevant biblical references in the margins of his text, which 'can be of great help to simple preachers, who mostly are in want of books'. Vásárhelyi's work may indeed have been primarily intended to be used by priests. However, the text followed normal patterns of meditative literature, personally addressing the 'Christian reader', either clerical or lay, and appealing to them to respond to their sense of sin. Differences between these potential audiences were reflected within the text and in the tone which Vásárhelyi adopted even within single passages. This allowed for a priest to use the book while addressing the common problems of their community, or for an individual believer to read the text independently and apply moral lessons to his own life.[14]

Vásárhelyi dedicated his 1618 work to Zsigmond Forgách, lord-lieutenant of the Hungarian counties of Sáros, Szabolcs and Nógrád. Vásárhelyi's preface suggested that the cause of Hungary and Transylvania's many miseries was that the people had turned away from God. However, he chose not to become embroiled in any specific controversy between Catholics and Protestants. This was against the background of a series of public debates between the confessions during these decades, such as a 1602 dispute between István Magyari, a Lutheran preacher from Sárvár, and Péter Pázmány, the leading Hungarian Catholic cleric of the early seventeenth century. Vásárhelyi's preface did not dwell on any polemical issues or on any particular innovations in religion which were to blame for invoking divine wrath

---

13 Canisius, *Catechismus* (1599).

14 Gergely Vásárhelyi, *Esztendö altal; az anyaszentegyhaztól rendeltetet vasarnapokra és innepekre evangeliomok es ezekre való lelki elmélkedések* (Vienna, 1618); Ferenc Jenei, 'Vásárhelyi Gergely Kempis-fordítása', *Irodalomtörténeti Közlemények* 65 (1961), p. 598.

against Hungary and Transylvania, nor did he spend much time reflecting upon the collective moral faults of the Hungarian community, but concentrated instead on personal weaknesses not necessarily linked with belief in any particular confession. Vásárhelyi's preface also commented on the purpose of meditation, with a series of rules and explanations to guide personal and prayerful reflection. First, Vásárhelyi established the importance to meditation of external conditions to set the appropriate environment for calm and thoughtful reading, so that 'all things or actions brought before you to think about, should be in front of your inner eyes as if you saw them with your real eyes or heard them with your ears.'[15] The methods and structure which Vásárhelyi used in his text were heavily influenced by the *Spiritual Exercises* of Ignatius Loyola. Loyola had stressed the importance of using the imagination alongside the intellect to aid devotion and engage reflection, and had urged that meditation be punctuated with prayer and always end in prayer. Gergely Vásárhelyi's work therefore marked an early example of Hungarian Catholic reception of Jesuit spirituality and application of the methodology of Loyola's *Spiritual Exercises*.[16]

Another well-known western Catholic work by Thomas Kempis, *De imitatione Christi*, was translated by Péter Pázmány into Hungarian and published in 1624 at Vienna.[17] Pázmány was not the first to attempt to translate Kempis' book into Hungarian, and some fragments of Kempis' text survive in six medieval manuscripts. Two years before Pázmány's edition appeared, another translation by Gergely Vásárhelyi had already been published by Heltai's press in Cluj, a work which was long thought not to have any surviving copies.[18] The dedication of Vásárhelyi's translation was written to Zsigmond Haller, lord-lieutenant of Inner-Szolnok county in Transylvania. Completed one year before Gergely Vásárhelyi's death, the translator called himself 'the sickly minister of your Highness'. Vásárhelyi's preface commented that across the entire Christian world Kempis' work had been translated into 'every language, for spiritual testimony and consolation'. Vásárhelyi revealed that he had in fact completed a translation of the work some twenty-eight years

---

[15] Vásárhelyi, *Esztendö altal: lelki elmélkedések* (1618).

[16] Ignatius Loyola, *Exercitationes Spirituales* (Rome, 1548); see later pub. (Trnava, 1698), 'Quintum exercitium de inferno', and 'Contemplatio secunda de Nativitate'; Erdei, *Die Meditation im 16. Jahrhundert* (1990), p. 100.

[17] Péter Pázmány tr., *Kempis Tamásnak Christus követésérül négy könyvei* (Vienna, 1624).

[18] Gergely Vásárhelyi tr., *Christus Jesus követéséröl való könyvek* (Kolozsvár, 1622); Jenei, 'Vásárhelyi Gergely Kempis-fordítása', pp. 594–8. A copy without a title-page, but with the complete text, can be found in the library of the former Unitarian college in Kolozsvár, and a second copy is in the possession of the Franciscan library at Esztergom.

earlier, but the manuscript had been lost, and thus he repeated the work for the 'spiritual consolation of many'. It is unknown why Péter Pázmány, who was personally acquainted with Vásárhelyi, had no knowledge of the 1622 Cluj edition of *De imitatione Christi*. While Pázmány and Vásárhelyi might have met at Vágsellye at the beginning of the 1600s, Vásárhelyi did not return to Royal Hungary after 1612, and perhaps news of his work had failed to reach the archbishop of Esztergom before he started his own translation. Certainly analysis of the two texts clearly demonstrates that the two translations were made independently from one another. The two prefaces also expressed different perspectives on the nature of the task of translation, with Pázmány much more anxious to establish a form of written Hungarian which was close to the spoken vernacular.[19]

Vásárhelyi continued to dedicate himself to produce material to bolster the spiritual life of the Transylvanian Catholic community, and before his death completed a further moral tract.[20] Vásárhelyi also engaged in discussions with the principality's Protestant political elite and with leading Reformed ministers. Despite this polemical edge to his activity, there were claims that when prince Gábor Bethlen was sent some works on Catholic belief by Vásárhelyi he apparently read them with 'wonderful delight'.[21] Vásárhelyi's political manoeuvres at the Transylvanian court primarily aimed to ensure the continued presence of Jesuits within the principality. Records from the Jesuit mission in Transylvania and from Ottoman-occupied Hungary indicate that Vásárhelyi supported direct action to gain conversions. However, towards the end of his life Vásárhelyi seemingly had come to realize that a less aggressive approach, as had been attempted by István Szini, might prove more effective in ensuring the continued presence of, and some success for, the small Jesuit mission in Transylvania.[22]

Another example of Catholic devotional literature which was well-known in seventeenth-century Hungary and Transylvania was Robert Bellarmine's work, *De ascensione mentis in Deum per scalas rerum creaturarum opusculum*. Bellarmine's book on meditation described the

---

19 Vásárhelyi, *Christus Jesus követéséröl való könyvek* (1622); Jenei, 'Vásárhelyi Gergely Kempis-fordítása' (1961), p. 595.

20 Gergely Vásárhelyi, *Vilag kezdetitöl fogva, iosagos, es gonosz czelekedeteknek példáinak summái* (Kassa, 1623).

21 'Dedi libellos illustrissimi cardinalis Bellarmini principi, mira delectatione perlegit de ascensu mentis in Deum ... Dicit se nunquam similem libellum legisse'; Béla Holl, 'Vásárhelyi Gergely pályája (1560–1623)', *Irodalomtudományi Közlemények* 87 (1983), p. 159.

22 Balázs, Monok et al. eds, *Erdélyi és hódoltsági jezsuita missziók* (1990) vol. 1, p. 20; Holl, 'Vásárhelyi Gergely pályája (1560–1623)' (1983), pp. 150–62.

soul responding to the beauty of the world and rising towards God, drawing out themes on man's sin, the world, and celestial bodies, and then set out a stairway of knowledge leading to God. Bellarmine, best known for his polemical theology, applied himself in this text to a contemplative and intimate discourse about personal religiosity. Just over three decades after this work's initial publication, it was translated into Hungarian by Gáspár Tasi and published at Bardejov (Bártfa/Bartfeld) in Upper Hungary in 1639.[23] Tasi, then secretary to the palatine of Royal Hungary, Miklós Eszterházy, had been educated at a Jesuit school. His translation demonstrates the importance to the Catholic community of such schools, and the contribution which Hungarian lay Catholics made to the development of devotional literature during this period. The descriptions of the natural world in Bellarmine's text which Tasi had to attempt to translate into Hungarian also meant that his work was a considerable linguistic achievement. In this regard it stands alongside the developments made in Protestant vernacular texts from the latter decades of the sixteenth century, and alongside the forms of language used in works on personal piety translated by Reformed ministers in Transylvania during the 1630s and 1640s.[24]

In the dedication of his work to Miklós Eszterházy, Tasi revealed the care which he had taken over this work to make it as useful as possible for readers. Tasi outlined some of the difficulties of translating Latin into Hungarian, and set out why he had left marginal notes in Latin of new Hungarian words or expressions which he had included. Tasi explained that if the reader 'could not make sense out of it [the text], he would not have to look up the Latin [words], but could find them in the margin of the book.' Tasi also noted the limitations of word-by-word translation into Hungarian, not because the resulting phrases would 'not sound Hungarian', but rather because it would render the overall text entirely meaningless. Tasi illustrated his point in the following terms:

> Among these Latin words and terms there are ones which, if one
> said them in Hungarian as the meaning of the words were in
> themselves, it would be very far from their [original] meaning:

23 Gáspár Tasi, *Elménknek Istenben föl-menetelérül a teremtett állatok garádichin. Robertus Bellarminus Jesuiták rendiböl való Cardinal könyvechkéje* (Bártfa, 1639). Original copies are preserved in the Academic and University Libraries of Cluj. Gábor Tüskés, *A xvii. századi egyházi irodalom európai kapcsolatai (Nádasi János)* (Budapest: Universitas Kiadó, 1997), pp. 47–8; Gábor Tüskés, Éva Knapp eds, *Johannes Nádasi 1614–1679. Leben und Werk (Archivum Historicum Societatis Jesu. Extractum e vol. lxii)* (Rome, 1993).

24 Márton Tarnóc, 'Bevezetés' in Tarnóc ed., *Laskai János válogatott művei* (Budapest: Akadémiai Kiadó, 1970), pp. 15–16.

'*Deus est actus purus*', if I wrote this word by word [in Hungarian]
... you would not find the tiniest of meanings in it.[25]

A range of devotional literature was therefore available within the
Catholic community in Transylvania during the first half of the
seventeenth century. However, a dedicated Catholic press was only
founded in Transylvania in 1676 by the Observant Franciscans at
Şumuleu Ciuc in the Szekler region. This press was established by János
Kájoni, and according to its charter was primarily intended to satisfy the
spiritual needs of local Catholics.[26] Some of the first books produced by
the press included calendars, Cicero's letters, and Latin grammar-books
by Aelius Donatus and Emmanuel Alvarez. Since it was the only
functioning Catholic printing-press in Transylvania, these books were
essential to the work of Catholic schools in the Szekler region which were
otherwise forced to resort to use editions produced by the Lutheran press
at Braşov.[27] János Kájoni was one of the most effective and versatile of
the Franciscans who served in the Szekler region during this period.
Alongside his work at the Şumuleu Ciuc press, he played the organ, and
rebuilt the Şumuleu Ciuc organ after it was destroyed by invading Tartars
in 1664.[28] Kájoni combined his interests in music and books in 1676
when he produced a *Cantionale Catholicum*, a collection of over 800
songs in both Latin and Hungarian. This collection, which has preserved
traditional forms of language used in the Szekler region, marked an
outstanding accomplishment in the field of sacred music. Another of the
most important devotional works produced by the printing-press was
János Haller's 1682 translation of *The Shield of Endurance*. Haller was
not a priest, but the one-time lord-lieutenant of Turda (Torda) county in
central Transylvania. He worked on this book while in prison, and
applied to his own situation this work of consolation for those who suffer
because of the inconstancy of the world.[29]

---

[25] Tasi, *Elménknek Istenben föl-menetelérül a teremtett állatok garádichin* (1639),
p. 5.

[26] ' ... pro necessitate Missionis Apostolicae et Catholicorum huius regni'; János
Kájoni, *Fekete könyv. Az erdélyi ferences kusztódia története*, ed. Edit Madas (Szeged:
Attila József University, 1991), p. 60.

[27] Aelius Donatus, *De Octo Partibus Orationis Methodus, Questiunculis puerilibus ...*
(Csíksomlyó, n.d.); Emmanuel Alvarez, *De Institutione Grammatica Libri tres, quarum
secunda nuper est ad Veterem fere Grammaticorum rationum revocatus* (Csíksomlyó, n.d.);
János Karácsonyi, *Szent Ferencz rendjének története Magyarországon, 1711-ig* (2 vols),
(Budapest: Magyar Tudományos Akadémia, 1924), vol. 2, pp. 245–6; Vasile Mocanu, *Ioan
Căian* (Bucharest: Editura muzicală a Uniunii Compozitorilor, 1973), p. 108.

[28] *Codex Caioni*, Saviana Diamandi ed. (Bucharest: Editura muzicală a Uniunii
Compozitorilor, 1993), pp. 81–4.

[29] János Kájoni, *Cantionale Catholicum* (Csíksomlyó, 1682); János Haller, *Pais, a
békességes türésnek paisa* (Csíksomlyó, 1682).

Other devotional and meditative books which were produced by the Şumuleu Ciuc press were new editions of earlier works. For example, a collection of prayers and meditations written by the Jesuit Péter Ágoston, from Sânzieni (Szentlélek) in the Szekler region, was published at Şumuleu Ciuc in 1685. This work, *Treasure of the heart: a little book of earnest prayers on the suffering and death of Our Lord Christ*, had been originally published at Trnava (Nagyszombat) in Hungary in 1671. The new Şumuleu Ciuc edition appeared without the name of the original author, but included a dedication by Kájoni to István Apor, his noble patron from Turia (Altorja).[30] Ágoston's work set out poetic dialogues between the soul of the reader and the suffering Christ, structured into short passages for daily use. It included reflections on the Last Supper, Christ's crucifixion and burial, all of which were supported by quotations from relevant Bible passages. As with other similar devotional works, the reader was invited to consider how the lessons learned from these meditations could be applied to their own personal circumstances. Devotional literature by Transylvanian clerics also continued to be published outside the principality during these decades, such as the collection of meditations published in Vienna and Trnava by András Illyés.[31]

While the Catholic Church retained its constitutional status as a 'received religion' in Transylvania during the seventeenth century, Catholics remained a small minority in the principality with limited patronage from the nobility and little support in many towns. While the Reformed Church received the active backing of a series of co-religionist princes during the seventeenth century, the Transylvanian Catholic Church was heavily reliant on external support for survival. The devotional literature available within the Transylvanian Catholic community during the seventeenth century was thus mostly made up of works published in Royal Hungary. Despite these circumstances, some of the most important Catholic devotional works of the period did circulate in Transylvania. Examination of the notes made by readers in the margins of surviving copies of devotional literature from this period confirms ready engagement by local Catholics with this material. The

---

30 Péter Ágoston, *Szívek kincse. Avagy Kristus Urunk szenvedésén, és halálán fohászkodó könyvecske: mely nagy lelki buzgóságra gerjeszti, és Istenhez emeli, az áhítatos szíveket* (Csíksomlyó, 1685).

31 András Illyés, *A kerestyeni jossagos cselekedeteknek és a tekelletessegnek gyakorlatossaga, mely a Jesus Tartsasagabeli tisztelendő Rodericus Alfonsus Spanyól Pap-által Spanyólúl megirattatott; annak-utánna külömb-külömb-féle nyelvekre; mostan pedig Olaszból, es Deákból, szorgalmatossan meg-magyaráztatott Illyes Andras-által, A Tekéntetes, és Tiszteletes Posoni Káptolom Anyaszentegyházának Lectora-által* (Nagyszombat, 1688).

translation of many of these works into the vernacular was significant in trying to address the needs of Transylvanian lay Catholics, although the role of priests remained central even in the use of literature on meditation. While books published in Royal Hungary were transported to Transylvania, and Catholic works had earlier been produced by the press at Cluj, the development of a domestic Catholic press in the 1670s was of great significance for Catholic education and spiritual life in the principality. Once Transylvania had been incorporated into the Habsburg monarchy at the end of the seventeenth century, the Catholic Church could look forward to cooperation with the state to promote its interests. However, for much of the century, Catholic spirituality was only sustained in Transylvania by the efforts of isolated clergy and lay activists who worked to provide their community with printed devotional literature.

CHAPTER EIGHT

Catholic identity and ecclesiastical politics in early modern Transylvania

Joachim Bahlcke

Early modern Transylvania provides abundant material for a wider discussion on the construction and nature of religious identity in east-central Europe.[1] This eastern region of the former kingdom of the Holy Crown of St Stephen was transformed into an autonomous principality by the Ottomans in the middle of the sixteenth century. Subsequently, it took various Protestant confessions only three decades to emerge as newly formed and distinct groups. This added a multi-confessional structure to, and thereby strengthened still further, the 'state of estates' (*Ständestaat*) which had developed in Transylvania from the later middle ages. From the late 1560s three Protestant denominations positioned themselves alongside the Catholic Church in the principality. Each of these was accompanied by a specific form of culture which was in turn rooted within the respective denomination. This was also true for the fourth alternative confession to Catholicism in Transylvania, the Orthodox Church. From the middle of the sixteenth century, alongside the corporate rights of the estates and prerogatives of the prince, a religious tolerance was established based on a consensus which both the prince and the estates agreed to honour. The notion of four 'received religions' within the principality, which was first used in the Transylvanian diet's decisions of 1568, comprised the Roman Catholic

---

[1] This article was translated from German by Ulrich von Sanden. N. Bocşan, I. Lumperdean, Ion-Aurel Pop eds, *Ethnie et confession en Transylvanie du xiiie au xixe siècles* (Cluj: Fundaţia Culturală Română, 1996); Graeme Murdock, 'Church building and discipline in early seventeenth-century Hungary and Transylvania' in Karin Maag ed., *The Reformation in Eastern and Central Europe* (Aldershot: Scolar, 1997), pp. 136–54; Krista Zach, 'Stände, Grundherrschaft und Konfessionalisierung in Siebenbürgen. Überlegungen zur Sozialdisziplinierung (1550–1650)' in Joachim Bahlcke, Arno Strohmeyer eds, *Konfessionalisierung in Ostmitteleuropa. Wirkungen des religiösen Wandels im 16. und 17. Jahrhundert in Staat, Gesellschaft und Kultur* (Stuttgart: Steiner, 1999), pp. 367–91; Krista Zach, 'Zur Geschichte der Konfessionen in Siebenbürgen im 16. bis 18. Jahrhundert', *Südostdeutsches Archiv* 24/5 (1981–82), pp. 40–89.

Church, the Reformed Church, the Lutheran Church and the anti-Trinitarian Church. This resolution was also confirmed in the first codification of the principality's laws in 1653 (*Approbatae Constitutiones Regni Transsylvaniae et Partium eidem annexae*), which remained effective as law in Transylvania until 1848.[2] In addition some sectarian movements, including Sabbatarians, Hutterite Brethren and Anabaptists, could rely on a certain degree of tolerance in Transylvania during the seventeenth century.

Although this almost perfect model of a multi-confessional 'state of estates' holds a particular fascination, detailed knowledge about Transylvanian religion remains partial and unsatisfactory. Transylvania's ecclesiastical and religious history has not yet found adequate treatment, either in historiography produced in Hungary and Romania, which has largely tried to stake respective claims to the territory, or by the purely regional approach centred on ethnic groups and denominations which the older historiography of Transylvania's German Saxons followed. Ludwig Binder's 1982 contribution to the ecclesiastical history of Transylvania may serve as a telling example of a historiography limited by denominational and regional assumptions.[3] Far from treating the topic in its entirety, he merely outlined the German viewpoint of the Saxons' ecclesiastical history. Since the various religious communities in Transylvania have largely only recorded their own history, it becomes evident why no historian has been particularly inclined to deal with Catholic Church history up to 1716, when a Catholic hierarchy was missing, or the history of the ensuing years, when this hierarchy was painstakingly being reconstructed. It is therefore hardly surprising that Károly Veszely's two volumes of primary sources on Catholic ecclesiastical history in Transylvania published in 1860 and 1893 have remained the main basis for early modern case studies, regardless of their systematic shortcomings and multiplicity of errors.[4] Moreover, research on the Catholic Church in

---

[2] A. Csizmadia, 'Az erdélyi jog fejlődése a fejedelmi korban. Kodifikációs munka a xvii. századi Erdélyben' in Csizmadia, *Jogi emlékek és hagyományok. Esszék és tanulmányok* (Budapest: Közgazdasági és Jogi Könykiadó, 1981), pp. 141–71.

[3] Ludwig Binder, 'Tendenzen und Aufgaben der siebenbürgischen Kirchengeschichtsschreibung', *Zeitschrift für Siebenbürgische Landeskunde* 5 (1982), pp. 188–95. An exception is Georg Daniel Teutsch, 'Die kirchlichen Verhältnisse Siebenbürgens', *Deutsch-evangelische Blätter. Zeitschrift für den gesamten Bereich des deutschen Protestantismus* 31 (1906), pp. 483–502, 535–54, 614–35.

[4] Károly Veszely, *Erdélyi egyháztörténelmi adatok* (Kolozsvár, 1860); Károly Veszely, *Az erdélyi róm. kath. püspöki megye autonomiája, vagy is az 1711-től 1892-ig tartott erdélyi római katholikus status gyülések nevezetesebb tárgyalásainak, határozatainak, felterjesztéseinek és más ezekre vonatkozó okmányoknak gyüjteménye* (Gyulafehérvár, 1893).

Transylvania, especially on its legal position and autonomy, has been seriously distorted by more recent political history. Most studies on the Catholic Church were published around 1930, at a time when the diocese of Transylvania was subordinated to the Catholic archbishopric of Bucharest, which disrupted its historical affiliation to the Hungarian Church province of Kalocsa.[5]

However, some complimentary remarks are necessary on the achievements of previous scholars working on Transylvanian Catholic history. The significance of the *Status Romano-Catholicus Transilvaniensis* (hereafter *Status Catholicus*) was recognized from the period when the Romanian state negotiated a concordat with the Catholic Church between 1921 and 1927. As both a Hungarian and Catholic institution, this representative board attracted the attention of both Romanian churches and the Romanian state in several respects. Not only did the *Status Catholicus* control considerable ecclesiastical assets, but also enjoyed full autonomy with regard to schooling and managed the Transylvanian diocese's endowments and funds available for educational purposes.[6] Elemér Gyárfás, a Transylvanian lawyer and politician who was also a member of the *Status Catholicus* directorate assessed the basic problem as follows:

> Les grands changements politiques, survenus au cours de ces dernières années, nous ont apporté de grands problèmes à résoudre dans les différents domaines de la vie publique. L'un des plus graves est la question religieuse, et particulièrement l'adaptation au nouveaux régime des autonomies ecclésiastiques, qui existent en Transsylvanie depuis des siècles ... Les plus grandes difficultés résident, à mon avis, dans le fait, que l'opinion publique roumaine ne connait pas suffisamment ni les bases et le développement historiques, ni l'organisation actuelle des institutions transylvaines, dont le *Status Catholicus* (l'organisation autonome des Catholiques de Transylvanie) est une des plus importantes, des plus anciennes et des plus considérables.[7]

After interventions by the Papacy, the threatened dissolution of the

---

5 O. Ghibu, *Catolicismul unguresc în Transilvania şi politica religioasă a Statului român* (Cluj, 1924); I. Kosutány, *A római katholikus egyház Erdélyben* (Szeged, 1925); A. Vorbuchner, *Az erdélyi püspökség* (Brassó, 1925); Á. Bitay, *Erdély jeles katholikus papjai* (Kolozsvár, 1926); A. Balázs, *Az erdélyi katholikus autonómia* (Budapest, 1930); O. Ghibu, *Un anahronism şi o sfidare: Statul romano-catolic ardelean. Studiu istoric-juridic* (Cluj, 1931); Zoltán Szász, 'Az erdélyi római katholikus "státus"', *Magyar Szemle* 17 (1933), pp. 193–200, 290–96; 18 (1933), pp. 97–104; F. Csorba, *Az erdélyi katholikus autonómiáról* (Budapest, 1897); M. Bochkor, *Az erdélyi katholikus autonómia* (Kolozsvár, 1911).

6 Elemér Gyárfás, *Erdélyi problémák 1903–1923* (Kolozsvár, 1923).

7 Elemér Gyárfás, *L'Église catholique en Transylvanie* (Dicsőszentmárton, 1923), p. 3.

Status Catholicus by the Romanian Ministry of Education, which had been looming since the autumn of 1931, was eventually prevented. In return, the Papal court complied with the wishes of the Romanian government and gave the new Romanian name of Alba Iulia to the bishopric of Transylvania. The Vatican accord signed in Rome on 30 May 1932 ratified the 1929 concordat and explicitly safeguarded the position of the *Status Catholicus*. Simultaneously, however, the committee was converted into a diocesan council which was only to act with the bishop's approval as a consultative body.[8] In the years to come, the role of the *Status Catholicus* provoked heated discussion in the Romanian press and politics. In 1940, the Bucharest government confirmed the institution's existence by law, but eight years later the Communists dissolved it.

A tendency to understand the Transylvanian *Status Catholicus* as 'Roman Catholicism's defensive bulwark against the east' can often be observed in works published in Hungary.[9] Until now these have often been the only available material when addressing questions about Transylvania's confessional and religious history during the early modern period. A volume of essays about Transylvanian Catholicism by leading Hungarian church historians from 1925 remains the only book attempting to analyse both secondary and original sources. Its thirty articles add up to the only study which devotes a considerable amount of attention to the Catholic Church in Transylvania after it ceased to be an autonomous principality.[10] Scholarship in the field has hardly deepened since then. This becomes obvious when considering a recent short compendium on the ecclesiastical history of the bishopric of Transylvania, which merely sums up familiar landmarks and deprives the reader of any notation.[11] It goes without saying that my brief essay can only attempt to outline a picture which has previously remained indistinct in many regards. Questions regarding the interaction between clergy and politics are posed here to gain insights into the development

---

[8] *Ştatusul catolic ardelean şi acordul de la Roma. Recursul episcopiei catolice de rit latin de Alba-Iulia în contra sentinţei Nr. 51/1932 din 4 iulie 1933 a tribunalului Cluj* (Cluj, 1933); Elemér Gyárfás, A. Jánossy eds, *Explanatio iuridico-historica documentorum de fundis dioecesis Albaiuliensis ritus Latini* (Cluj, 1937); *De Institutione Catholica: 'Status Romano-Catholicus Transsylvaniensis'. De evolutione historico-juridica. De legalitate juxta leges civiles. De jure personalitas. De canonica institutione* (Cluj, 1932).

[9] F. Vild, *Geschichte der Autonomie der Katholiken Siebenbürgens* (University of Vienna diss., 1934), p. ii.

[10] *Az Erdélyi Katholicizmus múltja és jelene* (Dicsőszentmárton, 1925).

[11] J. Marton ed., *Az erdélyi/gyulafehérvári egyházmegye története* (Gyulafehérvár: Gloria, 1993).

of Catholic identity in Transylvania. With the Habsburg recovery of the principality, tensions emerged between the desire of the church hierarchy for ecclesiastical autonomy and the demands imposed upon the church by the political authorities.

Scholarly opinion has remained divided on when the Latin bishopric of Transylvania was actually founded. Situated at the eastern periphery of the kingdom of Hungary, the suffragan diocese to the Hungarian archbishopric of Kalocsa may have been set up together with the bishoprics of Győr (Raab), Pécs (Fünfkirchen) and Eger (Erlau) in 1009 by St Stephen, or, almost a century later by Ladislas I. It remains equally doubtful whether bishop Franco can be claimed as the first bishop. In 1075 he is referred to as *episcopus Bellegradiensis*, the Slavonic name for Alba Iulia (Gyulafehérvár/Weissenburg), whereas bishop Simon, recorded as late as 1111, was explicitly titled *episcopatus Ultrasilvanus*.[12] The complexity of Transylvania's autonomous administrative structure was also reflected in the bishopric's judicial authority, which was linked to the archbishops of Esztergom (Gran) and Kalocsa, as well as to the bishops of Oradea (Nagyvárad/Wardein) and Csanád.

The legal position of the Transylvanian residential bishop was restricted when Béla III raised the *eccclesia Theutonicorum* to become the free provostship of St Ladislas in 1191, in reaction to far-reaching social changes within the Alba Iulia diocese. Exempted areas were subordinated directly to the primate of Hungary, or rather, to the Holy See. The autonomous provostships of Sibiu (Nagyszeben/Hermannstadt) and Țara Bârsei (Burzenland) which the Teutonic Order had been granted under feudal tenure, caused long-standing conflicts between the individual dignitaries, the Papal curia and the Hungarian king.[13] Even though popes twice declined to raise the provostship of Sibiu to a bishopric at the beginning of the thirteenth and at the end of the fifteenth century, the unique position of this Catholic *hospites*-church became increasingly stable. The process of establishing an ecclesiastical organization of its own was promoted by the antagonism shown

---

12 J. Temesváry, *Erdély középkori püspökei* (Kolozsvár, 1922) begins his collection of 32 bishops with Simon (1111–13); J. Temesváry, 'Series episcoporum Transylvaniensium emendata et correcta', *Erdélyi Történelmi Értesítő* 1 (1912), pp. 45–8; Georg Daniel Teutsch, F. Firnhaber eds, *Urkundenbuch zur Geschichte Siebenbürgens. Erster Theil, enthaltend Urkunden und Regesten bis zum Ausgang des arpadischen Mannsstammes (1301)* (Vienna, 1857), no. 1, p. xiii.

13 Krista Zach, 'Die katholische Kirche in Siebenbürgen vom 12. bis zum 20. Jahrhundert', *Siebenbürgische Semesterblätter* 12 (1998), pp. 43–67, here 53–8; Krista Zach, 'Anmerkungen zur Konfessions- und Religionsgeschichte Siebenbürgens', *Siebenbürgische Semesterblätter* 12 (1998), pp. 15–42.

towards it by the bishop of Alba Iulia, and, at the turn of the fifteenth century, this process led to the formation of the so-called German Saxons' *Geistliche Universität* in Transylvania. After the Reformation this organization became an umbrella for the Saxons' two *hospites*-deaneries and the rural chapters, which proved able to shelter their church during numerous subsequent conflicts.[14]

Roman Catholic Church organization in Transylvania fell apart from the middle of the sixteenth century as the forces of Reformation flourished in the principality. The Catholic clergy hierarchy lost their power in political conflicts which broke out during the struggle for supremacy within the principality. Having briefly occupied Transylvania, Ferdinand I appointed Pál Bornemisza as bishop in May 1553. During his episcopacy a quarrel concerning episcopal revenues finally reached its peak, after smouldering for more than two decades. Faced with the secularization of his episcopal revenues and properties, which to a large extent had already taken place, in March 1556 Bornemisza demanded permission from the archbishop of Esztergom to leave his see.[15] In December 1556 the Transylvanian diet legally sanctioned the sequestration of episcopal property. Shortly after, the cathedral chapter also dissolved itself and the episcopal palace in Alba Iulia became the princely residence.[16]

From the Papal curia's point of view, Transylvania after 1556 had thus turned into a country in need of mission. This further fuelled a re-emerging controversy between Rome and Vienna about who had the right to appoint bishops. While the Congregation for the Propagation of Faith, which Gregory XV created in 1622, regarded the principality as being within its sphere of jurisdiction and consequently demanded the right to appoint the bishop there, the Habsburgs insisted on their rights of presentation and nominated their own candidates for the Alba Iulia see.[17] Vienna's motives were mostly political; by demanding this right, the *Corona Regni Hungariae* first supported its legal claim to the lost

---

[14] K. G. Gündisch, 'Zur Entstehung der Sächsischen Nationsuniversität' in W. Kessler ed., *Gruppenautonomie in Siebenbürgen. 500 Jahre siebenbürgisch-sächsische Nationsuniversität* (Cologne-Vienna: Böhlau, 1990), pp. 45–60.

[15] Zach, 'Konfessionen in Siebenbürgen' (1981–82), pp. 57, 60–64.

[16] H. Fassel, 'Der Fürstenhof von Weissenburg (Alba Iulia) und seine Bedeutung für Wissenschaft und Kunst in Siebenbürgen zur Zeit Gabriel Bethlens' in A. Buck et al. eds, *Europäische Hofkultur im 16. und 17. Jahrhundert* (Hamburg: Hauswedell, 1981), pp. 637–45.

[17] D. Kokša, 'L'organizzazione periferica delle Missioni in Ungheria e in Croazia' in J. Metzler ed., *Sacrae Congregationis de Propaganda Fide Memoria Rerum 1622–1972, vol. 1/2: 1622–1700* (Rome-Vienna: Herder, 1972), pp. 274–91; J. Temesváry, *Erdély választott püspökei (1618–1695)* (2 vols), (Szamosújvár, 1913–14).

territory of the Transylvanian principality, and secondly strengthened the royal party at the Hungarian diet.[18] The bishops of Transylvania appointed by Vienna must not be confused with the *episcopi electi*, who were also frequently appointed at this time. Since their powers were not recognized by Rome, they remained merely titular bishops lacking proper episcopal consecration.[19]

Although Transylvania's four 'received religions' formally enjoyed equal rights, the Catholic Church in the principality faced certain restrictions.[20] Religious matters were subject to the autonomous powers of each estate in the principality from the middle of the sixteenth century. Even the mere appointment of a curate to head the administration of the Catholic Church posed considerable problems. The curate, elected by church boards, had to be confirmed in office by the prince.[21] In this exceptional situation for the Catholic Church, by then largely confined to the eastern Szekler lands, to the areas of influence of a few noble families like the Báthorys, and to Franciscan monasteries, during the mid-seventeenth century an institution came into existence which took over the administration of Catholic property, revenues, and education, and defended the church's interests within the principality.[22]

Comprising both Catholic clergy and laity, the *Status Catholicus* board first appeared during the Transylvanian diet of 1615. Its self-governing status, the breadth and depth of its powers and lay participation in the administration of the church, were all features which were a product of a Catholic Church pushed to the very edge of

---

18 Vencel Bíró, *Püspökjelölés az erdélyi római katholikus egyházmegyében* (Kolozsvár, 1930); Vilmos Fraknói, *A magyar királyi kegyúri jog Szent Istvántól Mária Teréziáig. Történeti tanulmány* (Budapest, 1895); Vilmos Fraknói ed., *Oklevéltár a magyar királyi kegyúri jog történetéhez* (Budapest, 1899); Jozef Tomko, *Zriadenie Spišskej, Banskobystrickej a Rožňavskej diecézy a kráľovské patronátne právo v Uhorsku* (Spišské Podhradie, 1995).

19 R. Ritzler, 'Die Bischöfe der ungarischen Krone', *Römische Historische Mitteilungen* 13 (1971), pp. 137–64.

20 W. Daugsch, 'Toleranz im Fürstentum Siebenbürgen. Politische und gesellschaftliche Voraussetzungen der Religionsgesetzgebung im 16. und 17. Jahrhundert', *Kirche im Osten. Studien zur osteuropäischen Kirchengeschichte und Kirchenkunde* 26 (1983), pp. 35–72.

21 Marton ed., *Az erdélyi egyházmegye története* (1993), p. 204. Transylvanian curates from the beginning of the seventeenth century were Márton Fehérdi (1618–26), Miklós Fejér (1626–34), György Ferenczi (1634–41), István P. Szalinai (1641–53), János Sükösd (1654–59), János László (1659–69), Kázmér P. Domokos (1669–77), János Kászoni (1677–78), Bertalan Szebelébi (1678–1707) and János Antalfi (1707–12); Veszely, *Erdélyi egyháztörténelmi adatok* (1860), vol. 1, pp. 40–51, 54–7, 296–301.

22 Zach, 'Konfessionen in Siebenbürgen' (1981–82), pp. 49, 58, 61, 77; Zach, 'Katholische Kirche' (1998), pp. 59–60.

existence and fighting for survival. When Alba Iulia was re-established as an episcopal see a century later, these powers became the source of numerous conflicts with the residential bishop, the Hungarian Church hierarchy, the Papacy and the Viennese court. The sphere of influence of the *Status Catholicus* was formalized in 1653 by the *Approbatae Constitutiones Regni Transsylvaniae*. After the *Approbatae* laws had been drawn up, the *Status Catholicus* assembled regularly, usually in its entirety during a diet, or sometimes the clergy met as a body called the *communis congegratio*. A detailed form of organization to determine the chairmanship, the number of participants (with two-thirds lay membership), as well as the *Status Catholicus'* precise functions, was only eventually established with the statutes accepted under bishop Mihály Fogarasy after Transylvania was united with Hungary in 1868.[23] However, the *Status Catholicus* had long since become an important partner and ally for both Vienna and the Papacy in promoting Catholic interests in Transylvania. Its authority was acknowledged by granting the right to submit propositions to the court regarding ecclesiastical appointments, and the *Status Catholicus* assumed the height of its influence during the first decades of Habsburg rule.[24]

The confessional variety characteristic of Transylvania since the Reformation remained unaffected by the political changes which took place after 1687.[25] There were no alterations to the Transylvanian constitution, nor to the privileged status of its three 'nations', nor to the equality of the four 'received religions'. The right to worship freely, granted in several Transylvanian constitutional statutes, proved to be a successful barrier against a violent Counter-Reformation, for which Royal Hungary had set the example from the late seventeenth century.[26] The Habsburgs were hardly inclined to return all claimed Catholic property. Lengthy negotiations conducted during the diets of 1691 and

---

23 M. Fogarasy, *Az erdélyi püspökökről polgári tekintetben* (Vienna, 1837).

24 Elemér Gyárfás, 'Der katholische 'Status' von Siebenbürgen und seine Kämpfe', *Nation und Staat. Deutsche Zeitschrift für das europäische Minoritätenproblem* 8 (1935), pp. 513–22.

25 L. de Ferdinandy, 'Das Verhältnis des Fürstentums Siebenbürgen zu Ungarns Heiliger Krone' in J. G. Farkas ed., *Überlieferung und Auftrag. Festschrift für Michael de Ferdinandy zum sechzigsten Geburtstag* (Wiesbaden: Pressler, 1972), pp. 337–52.

26 M. Endes, *Erdély három nemzete és négy vallása autonómiájának története* (Budapest, 1935), pp. 267–371; Krista Zach, 'Fürst, Landtag und Stände. Die verfassungsrechtliche Frage in Siebenbürgen im 16. und 17. Jahrhundert', *Ungarn-Jahrbuch* 11 (1980–81), pp. 63–90; P. Philippi, 'Staatliche Einheit und gesellschaftliche Pluralität in der Religionsgesetzgebung des Fürstentums Siebenbürgen', *Heidelberger Jahrbücher* 18 (1974), pp. 50–65; F. Müller ed., 'Materialien zur Kirchengeschichte Siebenbürgens und Ungarns im siebzehnten Jahrhundert', *Archiv des Vereines für siebenbürgische Landeskunde* 19 (1884), pp. 579–750.

1692 showed how the *Status Catholicus* hoped to consolidate its position in this new political and confessional environment. A Catholic bishop was appointed, and preliminary steps taken to secure the return to Transylvania of the Jesuits, who had been driven out in the early seventeenth century.[27] According to a Roman record compiled in 1714, Catholics still only accounted for 30,000 souls in Transylvania. However, by establishing a Greek Catholic, or Uniate, Church from among Transylvania's Romanian Orthodox population, Catholic interests were strengthened considerably.[28]

In January 1696 the emperor appointed András Illyés as the new bishop of Transylvania at the behest of the archbishop of Esztergom, cardinal Leopold Kollonich.[29] However, initial euphoria over the appointment of Kollonich's canon proved to be short-lived. Although the choice had prudently fallen on a native Transylvanian (Illyés stemmed from Sfîntu-Gheorghe (Sepsiszentgyörgy)), the *Status Catholicus* had been completely ignored in the election process. Faced with an apparent violation of the Transylvanian legal system, the provincial government (*Gubernium*) of Transylvania was forced to take action. This was also in response to Illyés' memorandum to Rome in which he claimed that the time had come to bring Transylvania back into the general political and ecclesiastical structures of the Hungarian kingdom.[30] Before the end of 1697, Illyés was ordered to leave Transylvania, even though the bishop had just received Papal confirmation in January 1697, had begun to make local visitations, and had called for a synod of the *Status Catholicus* in July. Like the bishops appointed before him, Illyés was thus not able to take over his see in Alba Iulia.[31]

After the failed anti-Habsburg rising headed by Ferenc II Rákóczi, questions about the Catholic Church hierarchy were addressed at the *Status Catholicus* synod held at Mediaş (Megyes/Mediasch) in 1712. The *Status Catholicus* achieved the return of all church property, including the episcopal residence, the cathedral and attached buildings

---

27 K. Fabritius, 'Der Religionsstreit auf den siebenbürgischen Landtagen von 1691 und 1692', *Archiv des Vereines für siebenbürgische Landeskunde* 6 (1863), pp. 107–51.

28 Octavian Bârlea, *Ostkirchliche Tradition und westlicher Katholizismus. Die Rumänische Unierte Kirche zwischen 1713–1727* (Munich: Academy of the Socialist Republic of Romania, 1966), pp. 34f.

29 A. Szeredai de Szent-Háromság, *Series Antiquorum, et recentiorum Episcoporum Transilvaniae* (A. Carolinae, 1790), pp. 220–23; F. Kollányi, *Esztergomi kanonokok 1100–1900* (Esztergom, 1900), pp. 314–17.

30 Béla Köpeczi ed., *Kurze Geschichte Siebenbürgens* (Budapest: Akadémiai Kiadó, 1990), p. 371.

31 Veszely, *Erdélyi egyháztörténelmi adatok* (1860), vol. 1, pp. 51–4.

in Alba Iulia. However, when Charles VI appointed György Mártonfi bishop of Alba Iulia in February 1713, the *Status Catholicus* was passed over once more. That Mártonfi also came from the Szekler region of eastern Transylvania could at least be seen to indicate a certain willingness to oblige local sensitivities. The Habsburg court certainly did not want to risk further undermining the power of the *Status Catholicus* at this stage, because of the reputation and the authority of the institution and because Vienna still regarded the situation of Catholics in Transylvania as perilous.[32] Mártonfi, who was not installed in his diocese before Papal confirmation was granted in August 1714, had so far not been able to take possession of his property in Transylvania. His position was bolstered when the emperor prepared for a new war against the Turks in 1715, transforming Alba Iulia into a modern fortress, after which the city was renamed Karlsburg. The new blueprint for the city had at its centre the princely castle and the cathedral, which up to then had been in the hands of the Calvinists. Beyond the reach of the estates, and under military protection, the Catholic bishop was finally able to take back his residence in Alba Iulia. The city renewed its role as the base of the Transylvanian Catholic hierarchy, while the Greek Catholic bishopric was transferred to Făgăraş (Fogaras/Fogarasch) by imperial edict.[33]

The circumstances under which this transfer took place require a brief review of the situation of the Romanian Greek Catholic Church after the death of its bishop Atanasie in 1713. The issues emanating from the question of his succession provide insights not only into the policies embraced by Transylvania's Catholic authorities, but also its identity and self-conception. For the first time it had to face the difficult situation of having to combine its ecclesiastical claims with the reality of its political environment.[34] The Romanian Greek Catholic synod had repeatedly refused to add Ioan Pataki, the court's candidate, to the list of proposed candidates, which had been mandatory since Leopold's Second Diploma of 1701. The Greek Catholic bishopric's vacancy lasted for ten years during which time the various conflicting interests were clearly revealed. The archbishop of Esztergom attempted to secure the rights of the Romanian synod, whereas the governor of Transylvania,

---

32 V. Bíró, 'Az impériumváltozás kora (1690–1716)' and 'A katholikus restauráció kora (III. Károly, Mária Terézia, II. József)' in *Az Erdélyi Katholicizmus* (1925), pp. 104–24, 147–73.

33 F. Teutsch, *Geschichte der ev. Kirche in Siebenbürgen*, vol. 2: *1700–1917* (Hermannstadt: Krafft, 1922), pp. 3–72.

34 Bârlea, *Ostkirchliche Tradition und westlicher Katholizismus* (1966), pp. 21, 33, 40, 72.

Sigismund Kornis, and the Transylvanian court chancellery in Vienna, upheld imperial authority. In December 1714 the Romanian clergy finally bowed to secular pressure and voted, in a dubious election, for the imperial candidate. With Mártonfi installed as Latin bishop of Transylvania, a new endowment for the bishopric was a logical demand and, surprisingly, Rome also extended this demand to the vacant Greek Catholic bishopric. Charles VI offered donations simultaneously for both bishoprics in December 1715. The Latin bishopric received a new annual endowment of 13,000 guilders, obtained from the public purse of Alba Iulia and from taxes on Saxon towns.[35] Additionally, the bishop was awarded half of Alba Iulia's castle for his residence and 4,000 guilders for the alteration and reconstruction of the building. Remarkably, the twofold endowment was applied 'per modum novae fundationis', as the imperial decree put it.[36] The court of Vienna thus attempted to indicate that both bishoprics were completely new foundations, thereby, in one clever move, also legitimizing the royal right of presentation in Transylvania, which the Holy See had long accepted for Hungarian bishoprics.

Vienna's quest for power, however, collided with the interests of various parties in Transylvania, above all the bishop of Alba Iulia and the *Status Catholicus*. The latter sought to extend its rights regarding the nomination of the Latin bishop in Transylvania to the Greek Catholic Church. We find evidence for this in a formal request the *Status Catholicus* wrote in January 1715 on behalf of all Catholics, both of western and eastern rite. Addressing the emperor as well as the archbishop of Esztergom and the primate of Hungary, the *Status Catholicus* requested the reappointment of Pataki as bishop, since he was the most likely to prepare the ground for a conversion of the Romanian nation to the western rite. At the end of 1715, the Transylvanian governor told Gábor Hevenesi, a Hungarian Jesuit priest and headmaster of the Hungarian seminary in Vienna, the *Pazmaneum*, that the entire *Status Catholicus* had unanimously passed a vote for Pataki's confirmation as the Romanian Greek Catholic bishop in Transylvania.[37]

The bishop of Alba Iulia also attempted to extend the reach of his jurisdictional power and to establish Catholic episcopal power in areas held by the Greek Catholic and the Orthodox churches.[38] Mártonfi did

---

[35] Bârlea, *Ostkirchliche Tradition und westlicher Katholizismus* (1966), pp. 34–5; Zach, 'Konfessionen in Siebenbürgen' (1981–82), p. 75.

[36] Bârlea, *Ostkirchliche Tradition und westlicher Katholizismus* (1966), pp. 100–101.

[37] Bârlea, *Ostkirchliche Tradition und westlicher Katholizismus* (1966), pp. 14, 30.

[38] Bârlea, *Ostkirchliche Tradition und westlicher Katholizismus* (1966), pp. 78–82.

not content himself with the assertion that his sphere of jurisdiction was not restricted by the newly founded Greek Catholic bishopric, but strove for Pataki's subordination under his own jurisdiction. He supported his claims by citing the 1215 Fourth Lateran Council, which granted easterners living with westerners a ritual bishop, but only as a curate to the Latin bishop. Addressing the Congregation for the Propagation of Faith assembled in October 1718, Mártonfi cited the legal position of the Greek Catholic bishop of Mukačevo (Munkács), whom he claimed was subordinate to the Latin bishop of Eger.[39] A few weeks on, Mártonfi requested Pataki to consider himself as his curate for worshippers by the eastern rite. Only the Papal nuncio himself and the Congregation of Faith were finally able to convince Mártonfi of the special privileges which the Romanian Church possessed, and of the equal rights enjoyed in the principality by both rites.[40]

Once a Latin Catholic bishop was re-established and endowed in Transylvania, the ecclesiastical situation of Catholics rapidly stabilized in the principality. There were no conflicts between the bishop in residence and the *Status Catholicus*, which further consolidated its internal organization from 1711. This is clear from the number of meetings held in the following decades by the *Status Catholicus*, attended by up to 100 people. This included the bishop, Jesuit superiors, Franciscan wardens, capitulars, archdeacons and district deans. The *Status Catholicus* often exercised an even more important function than the local diocesan bishop in its contacts with the Habsburg court. Moreover, the *Status Catholicus* and bishop normally cooperated well, which became especially evident in struggles for formal religious equality in Transylvania. For decades, Transylvanian Catholics sought a cancellation of 1699 laws disadvantaging the Catholic Church, the so-called 'five points of Mikes'.[41] The *Status Catholicus* continued to press the court for action on these laws, which led to a first success in 1729, when the emperor asked the provincial government to submit an expert opinion. A government proposition to revoke the laws was indeed presented to the Transylvanian

---

[39] Bârlea, *Ostkirchliche Tradition und westlicher Katholizismus* (1966), pp. 37–8, 48–50.

[40] 'Eapropter etiam ego quà Sanctae Romanae Ecclesiae subjectus et obedientissimus Filius eandem Fundationem ultra non controverto, sed me dispositioni Sacrae Congregationis subjicio, et quantocius pro magna animarum necessitate et salute a Sede Apostolica nominati Domini Episcopi confirmationem ex Gratia Eminentiae Vestrae per secretam viam fiendam devotissime recommendo et efflagito, firmiter sperando eandem cum modis et formis Bullae Pij Papae IV de data 16 Februarij Anni 1564 expediendam fore'; Bârlea, *Ostkirchliche Tradition und westlicher Katholizismus* (1966), p. 152, see also pp. 38, 49–50, 106–108.

[41] Veszely, *Erdélyi egyháztörténelmi adatok* (1860).

diet in the following year but was defeated. A significant breakthrough was only finally achieved in 1744, when all earlier laws limiting the work of the Catholic bishop, canons or religious orders were declared invalid. Jesuit properties were removed from the treasury and transferred to the *Status Catholicus*, who immediately entrusted them back to the Jesuits.[42]

The political influence wielded by the *Status Catholicus* during this period also becomes evident with regard to nominations for both clerical and lay offices. Immediately after the accession of Charles VI in 1714, it proved possible to push through the appointment of the *Status Catholicus'* suggested candidate as Transylvanian governor. Sigismund Kornis, who had been the leading lay member of the *Status Catholicus* for many years, became the first Catholic to hold this office.[43] Questions concerning the appointment of the bishop proved far more complex. The emperor had made unrestricted use of his right of presentation in the cases of Illyés, Mártonfi, and Mártonfi's successor, Ferenc Mednyánszky, who was appointed in 1722. From then on, however, the *Status Catholicus* insisted more vigorously on its rights. At the end of December 1722 on the death of Mednyánszky, it proposed the canon of Esztergom, Mihály Olász, or native Transylvanians, János Antalfi or István Letai, as candidates to the emperor. Charles VI's decision to nominate Olász and Antalfi re-established the right of the *Status Catholicus* to present candidates for the Alba Iulia see. The *Status Catholicus* indeed exercised this right of proposition up to the nomination of József Antal Bajtay in October 1760. Then Vienna put an end to Transylvania's special status, after problems erupted with the Transylvanian chancellery, which also claimed the right to choose episcopal candidates.[44] Maria Theresa's decision in 1760 entirely corresponded with her new absolutist ecclesiastical policy, and her Council of State aimed at resolutely curbing all privileges of the Catholic clergy and at regulating clerical power.[45] The Transylvanian *Status*

---

[42] Zsolt Trócsányi, 'Az ellenreformáció Erdélyben 1711-től a felvilágosult abszolutizmus kezdeteiig', *Theologiai Szemle* 22 (1979), pp. 219–26.

[43] J. Höchsmann, 'Studien zur Geschichte Siebenbürgens aus der ersten Hälfte des 18. Jahrhunderts', *Archiv des Vereines für siebenbürgische Landeskunde* 11 (1873/4), pp. 253–310, here 265.

[44] J. Temesváry, *Öt erdélyi püspök rangemelése* (Kolozsvár, 1910); J. Temesváry, *Az erdélyi püspöki szék betöltése (1696–1897)* (Kolozsvár, 1932); F. Eckhart, *A püspöki székek és a káptalani javadalmak betöltése Mária Terézia korától 1918-ig* (Budapest, 1935), pp. 14–15.

[45] R. Reinhardt, 'Zur Kirchenreform in Österreich unter Maria Theresia', *Zeitschrift für Kirchengeschichte* 77 (1966), pp. 105–19; A. H. Benna, 'Zur Situation von Religion und Kirche in Österreich in den Fünfzigerjahren des 18. Jahrhunderts – eine Denkschrift Bartensteins zum Kronprinzenunterricht Josefs II' in *Sacerdos et pastor semper ubique. Festschrift zum 40-jährigen Priesterjubiläum ... Franz Loidl* (Vienna: Dom-Verlag, 1972), pp. 193–224.

Catholicus had at first been supported by the Habsburg authorities, but it had come to be regarded as an impediment to modernization and even as a potential adversary to the policies of enlightened absolutism. The *caesura* of the year 1760 was also indicated by the sudden cessation of all *Status Catholicus*' synods, which did not resume again until 1790.[46]

A decline in Transylvanian regional authority is also clear from the bishops appointed during this period. The social origins and conception of ecclesiastical politics of bishops in Transylvania changed across the eighteenth century, in parallel with developments in Hungary. However, the bishopric of Alba Iulia held a small annual income. Consequently, its importance and prestige was certainly smaller than the Hungarian sees, in which the court drew nominees from the ranks of leading magnates in the Empire from the beginning of the eighteenth century.[47] The three Transylvanian-born bishops nominated by the emperor, Illyés, Mártonfi and Mednyánszky, were followed by János Antalfi (1724–28), the candidate of the *Status Catholicus*.[48] For later bishops, Gergely Zorger (1729–39), Ferenc Klobusiczky (1741–48), Zsigmond Antal Sztoyka de Szala (1749–59), József Batthyány (1759–60), József Antal Bajtay (1760–72), Pius Manzador (1772–74), Ladislaus Kollonich (1774–80) and Ignác Batthyány (1780–98), the Transylvanian bishopric was a first step into the ranks of the Hungarian church hierarchy. From Klobusiczky's appointment, individual candidates' familiarity with Transylvanian politics continuously declined.[49] In contrast to the period before 1750, when Transylvanians were nominated in the first place, members of the Hungarian aristocracy were mostly appointed in the latter decades of the century. Among them were József and Ignác Batthyány, Ladislaus Kollonich or clerics like Pius Manzador, the provincial of Austria's Barnabites, who was actually working in Vienna and was also, as a member of the *Religionshofkommission*, a close confident of Maria Theresa.[50]

Transylvania's Catholic hierarchy had to be self-reliant to a

---

[46] Vencel Bíró, F. Boros eds, *Erdélyi katolikus nagyok* (Kolozsvár, 1941), pp. 93–4, 109–19.

[47] Joachim Bahlcke, 'Aristokraten aus dem Reich auf ungarischen Bischofsstühlen in der frühen Neuzeit. Zur Instrumentalisierung einer geistlichen Elite', *Ungarn-Jahrbuch* 23 (1997), pp. 81–103.

[48] Bârlea, *Ostkirchliche Tradition und westlicher Katholizismus* (1966), pp. 40–41, 100–101, 111, 113–14.

[49] Zsolt Trócsányi, 'Die ständische Bewegung in Siebenbürgen 1741–1742' in Kálmán Benda et al. eds, *Forschungen über Siebenbürgen und seine Nachbarn. Festschrift für Attila T. Szabó und Zsigmond Jakó* (2 vols), (Munich: Trofenik, 1988), vol. 2, pp. 31–58.

[50] J. Temesváry, *Manzador Pius erdélyi püspök élete és irodalmi működése* (Budapest, 1931).

considerably greater extent than their Hungarian colleagues throughout the eighteenth century. Even though the Catholic bishop was first councillor and deputy governor of Transylvania, by virtue of his office after an imperial edict of March 1721, he could still only attend the diet as an individual, and the Catholic clergy were not represented at the diet.[51] Under these circumstances, the greatest influence was wielded by bishop Sztoyka, who set up a seminary in 1753. During the vacancy of the governor's office from 1755 to 1759, Sztoyka became the nominal head of the provincial government.[52] However, even then he could not confront the majority Protestant estates in Transylvania with a straightforward Catholic policy, regardless of the *Status Catholicus*' authority, the power of the army, or the influence of the Jesuits. The estates complained to the court more than once about the bishop's double role in church and politics, pointing out that he could not fulfil both functions without breaking either his own ecclesiastical oath or his oath sworn on the Transylvanian laws to defend the rights of the four 'received religions'.[53] They also protested against the Latin bishop always calling himself simply 'bishop of Transylvania'.[54]

Bishop Bajtay made several attempts to enlarge his power in the 1760s. As the former teacher of the heir to the throne, Joseph, he could rely on close relations with the court. During his time in office from 1760 to 1772, elements of jurisdiction originally subordinated to the archbishop of Esztergom were again put under the control of the bishop of Alba Iulia.[55] Bajtay also succeeded in preventing a project for a Protestant university in Sibiu, which had been suggested by Samuel von Brukenthal and had already gained Maria Theresa's approval in 1765.[56] And finally, in 1766, supported by the commanding general of the army in Transylvania, Andreas von Hadik, he tried to gain more influence on the nomination of offices in powerful local administrative bodies. Arguing that Catholic bishops were the largest landowners around Alba Iulia, he aimed to gain the office of lord-lieutenant in Alba county. His suggestion that the Transylvanian bishops had been '*perpetui supremi*

[51] R. Kutschera, *Landtag und Gubernium in Siebenbürgen 1688–1869* (Cologne-Vienna: Böhlau, 1985), p. 52.

[52] J. Marton, *Papnevelés az erdélyi egyházmegyében 1753-tól 1918-ig* (Budapest, 1993).

[53] István Juhász, 'Das Edictum tolerantiae und das siebenbürgische Fürstentum', *Zeitschrift für Siebenbürgische Landeskunde* 7 (1984), pp. 1–17, here 3.

[54] Teutsch, 'Kirchliche Verhältnisse Siebenbürgens' (1906), pp. 548–9.

[55] I. Miskolczy, *Bajtay J. Antal* (Budapest, 1914); I. Miskolczy, 'Bajtay Antal szerepe Erdély közéletében', *Századok* 47 (1913), pp. 656–69, 736–52.

[56] G. A. Schuller, *Samuel von Brukenthal* (2 vols), (Munich: Oldenbourg, 1967–69), vol. 1, pp. 150–53.

Comites Albenses' in the past was, however, rather spurious.[57] In fact, with the exception of bishop Mártonfi, only secular dignitaries had held this office.[58]

Bajtay's conception of his role in church and politics, and his participation in reorganizing the Catholic Church, his pastoral activities in the entire diocese, his claims of autonomy, his numerous attempts to gain more political influence and his constant conflicts with leading Saxon representatives, must be seen in the context of a transitional period for Transylvania around the middle of the eighteenth century. In those years the forms in which the classic piety of the Baroque era had expressed itself were increasingly disintegrating and being replaced by ideas of religious tolerance and Enlightenment. They resulted in new principles of cooperation and coexistence between the various confessions and between the state and the Catholic Church.[59] Thus, while the court had long taken a completely different course on religious policy, Bajtay kept trying to muster all Catholic forces against local Protestants in order to cause the collapse of the '*sacrum Diploma*', as he deprecatingly called Transylvania's constitution.[60] While Bajtay was trying to abolish the equal rights of the 'received religions' guaranteed by the Transylvanian constitution, the court was steering away from confessional polarization and promoting religious peace. Bajtay's support for a combative Catholic identity in Transylvania was as anachronistic as the activities of Padányi Bíró in Veszprém. The fate of both bishops bear strong similarities. After the publication of Bíró's *Enchiridion de fide* in 1750 supporting the harsh treatment of heretics in the seventeenth century, he fell into disgrace with Maria Theresa. Bajtay chose a different course and resigned from his office in October 1772.[61]

This reversal of court ecclesiastical policy is highlighted by its

---

57 Georg Daniel Teutsch, 'Actenmäßige Beiträge zur Geschichte Siebenbürgens im xviii. Jahrhundert, 1. Gutachten des römisch-katholischen Bischofs in Siebenbürgen, Freiherrn Joseph Bajtay, wie die katholische Religion hier in größere Aufnahme zu bringen sei', *Archiv des Vereines für siebenbürgische Landeskunde* 11 (1873/4), pp. 469–84, here 481.

58 M. Lázár, *Erdély főispánjai (1540–1711)* (Budapest, 1889); Zoltán Fallenbüchl, *Magyarország főispánjai. Die Obergespane Ungarns, 1526–1848* (Budapest: Argumentum, 1994), p. 142.

59 Kálmán Benda, 'Politische Strömungen in Siebenbürgen während der zweiten Hälfte des 18. Jahrhunderts', *Zeitschrift für Siebenbürgische Landeskunde* 2 (1979), pp. 185–96, here 185.

60 Teutsch, 'Actenmäßige Beiträge' (1873/4), p. 473.

61 Joachim Bahlcke, 'Frederick II of Prussia, Austria and the Hungarian Protestants: Bishop Márton Padányi Bíró of Veszprém and the *Enchiridion de fide*', *Austrian History Yearbook* 31 (2000), pp. 15–32.

approach to appointing county lord-lieutenants, which Bajtay had claimed in Alba county in 1766. Step by step all clergy were being removed from these offices across Hungary and Transylvania from the beginning of the 1770s.[62] In Transylvania the privileges of the bishop and special rights of the *Status Catholicus* were also being questioned.[63] Since Bajtay's resignation in 1772, the bishop of Alba Iulia was merely an ordinary member of the governing council, and in 1786 Joseph II had the bishop dismissed from the province's government altogether. The influence of the *Status Catholicus* was also limited by the foundation of the '*Commissio in publico-ecclesiasticis*', a state authority composed of Catholic councillors which had the right to issue decrees bypassing the government, the *Status Catholicus*, and sometimes even the bishop. Faced with the power of this Catholic commission, the Saxon Brukenthal spoke of the existence of a 'second provincial government' and in 1777 he succeeded in having it at least put under the supervision of the governor.[64] Four years on, Joseph II had the commission incorporated into the provincial government and set up an independent commission for education.[65] The *Status Catholicus* never formally acknowledged the existence and activities of this commission which competed with its own responsibilities. Several of its tasks were transferred to the commission, including administration of the assets of the Catholic Church, among them the orphanage founded in Sibiu in 1768.[66]

Joseph intended his Edict of Toleration, issued for Transylvania in November 1781, to check the dominance of the Catholic Church in his monarchy. However, in a province in which four religions enjoyed equal rights, bitter feelings resulted. The grant of freedoms to the other confessions assumed that Catholicism had been dominant in the first place. To the court's surprise, the Catholic Church in Transylvania was left under considerable pressure after the edict. According to a report by the Alba Iulia bishop, Ignác Batthyány, within two months of the Edict of Toleration, 168 adherents had already withdrawn from the church. Joseph II therefore felt obliged to issue a new regulation in May 1782, which made leaving the Catholic Church more complicated through the imposition of several conditions.[67] The ecclesiastical measures of

---

62 Fallenbüchl, *Magyarország főispánjai* (1994), pp. 41–7.

63 Kutschera, *Landtag und Gubernium* (1985), p. 154.

64 Schuller, *Samuel von Brukenthal* (1969), vol. 2, p. 8.

65 E. Josupeit-Neitzel, *Die Reformen Josephs II. in Siebenbürgen* (Munich, 1986), pp. 84–8; Kutschera, *Landtag und Gubernium* (1985), p. 150.

66 Veszely, *Erdélyi egyháztörténelmi adatok* (1860), vol. 2, pp. 119–20.

67 I. Lungu, 'Les Lumières en Transylvanie et le joséphisme', *Cahiers roumains d'études littéraires* 2 (1977), pp. 70–86; Juhász, 'Edictum tolerantiae' (1984), pp. 11–15.

Joseph's reforms met with resistance in Transylvania, but on a far smaller scale than in Hungary. In Hungary, the clergy had already positioned themselves as spokesmen for the opposition and defenders of the '*natio Hungarica*' after the diet of Bratislava (Pozsony/Pressburg) of 1764/5. Adopting aggressive tactics, the clergy had taken to a bold form of Ultramontanism, of which there are only a few examples in Transylvania. Perhaps this was partly because the programme of the Hungarian clergy also included Transylvania's closer integration into the Hungarian Church.[68]

Similar reorientations of the Transylvanian clergy occurred during Ignác Batthyány's period of office. He was open to scientific methods and experiments as well as to recent developments in art.[69] Taking part in regular interchanges with leading enlightened philosophers and scholars like György Pray, Daniel Cornides, Adam Ferenc Kollár, István Katona and István Kaprinai, Batthyány intended to found a Transylvanian literary society in 1781.[70] Even though he managed to acquire and transfer archbishop Migazzi's collection of more than 8,000 books and manuscripts by 1782, his plan could not be put into operation.[71] At the same time Batthyány defended the autonomy of his church. From 1785 Batthyány published his monumental three-volume study, *Leges ecclesiasticae regni Hungariae*, the most important ecclesiastical answer to Joseph's church reforms in Transylvania.[72] The

---

68 Joachim Bahlcke, "'*Vexatio dat intellectum*". Klerus, Ständeverfassung und Staatskirchentum in Ungarn zur Zeit Maria Theresias', *Historické štúdie* 40 (1999), pp. 35–50.

69 Vencel Biró, *Gr. Batthyány Ignác. 1741–1798. Emlékezés születésének kétszázéves évfordulóján* (Kolozsvár, 1941); Zsigmond Jakó, 'Batthyány Ignác, a tudós és a tudományszervező' [1991] in Jakó, *Társadalom, egyház, művelődés. Tanulmányok Erdély történelméhez* (Budapest: Metem, 1997), pp. 359–82.

70 H. Stănescu, 'Eine geplante Siebenbürgisch Literarische Gesellschaft', *Südost-Forschungen* 31 (1972), pp. 335–7; H. Stănescu, 'Deutschsprachige wissenschaftliche und Lesegesellschaften der achtziger Jahre des 18. Jahrhunderts in Siebenbürgen und im Banat' in E. Amburger, M. Cieśla and L. Sziklay eds, *Wissenschaftspolitik in Mittel- und Osteuropa. Wissenschaftliche Gesellschaften, Akademien und Hochschulen im 18. und beginnenden 19. Jahrhundert* (Berlin: Camen, 1976), pp. 187–94; C. Göllner, 'Aspekte der Aufklärung in Siebenbürgen im 18. Jahrhundert' in É. H. Balázs et al. eds, *Beförderer der Aufklärung in Mittel- und Osteuropa. Freimaurer, Gesellschaften, Clubs* (Essen: Hobbing, 1987), pp. 153–60.

71 T. A. Vanyó, *Püspöki jelentések a magyar szent korona országainak egyházmegyéiről 1600–1850* (Pannonhalma, 1933), pp. 91–123; T. A. Vanyó, *A bécsi pápai követség levéltárának iratai Magyarországról 1611–1786* (Budapest, 1986), pp. 187–91.

72 Ignác Batthyány, *Leges ecclesiasticae regni Hungariae, et provinciarum adiacentium, opera, et studio Ignatii Comitis de Batthyán episcopi transilvaniae collectae, et illustratae* (3 vols), (Alba Iulia-Claudiopolis, 1785–1827).

close of the Josephine decade was marked by the diet of Cluj (Kolozsvár/Klausenburg) in 1790–91, which passed a number of important laws concerning religious matters, but in particular confronted the problems originating from the Romanian national movement.[73] This topic has been dealt with in many studies and goes beyond the scope of this paper, but marks a significant break with previous conflicts in ecclesiastical politics.[74]

The identity of the Transylvanian Catholic Church was established through political conflict and social antagonism during the eighteenth century. The Catholic Church hierarchy was only re-established comparatively slowly in Habsburg Transylvania, and competition between rival Catholic institutions squandered the potential of the *Status Catholicus*, in which lay Catholics had played a prominent role in the struggle to maintain the Church through the period of Protestant dominance of the principality. The alliance between the Transylvanian clergy hierarchy and the Habsburg court only broke down in the latter decades of the century. Meanwhile the Catholic hierarchy had maintained a problematic relationship with the political authorities in Transylvania, and the clergy hierarchy remained in some ways integrated to a lesser extent into Transylvania's political life than were the representatives of the other denominations. Struggles to establish clerical power and arguments over rights of jurisdiction and appointment marked the ecclesiastical policy of the Catholic clergy hierarchy across much of the century. Such internal conflicts, and the determination of the Protestant estates to defend their traditional liberties, helped to ensure that Catholicism remained a minority church in Transylvania during the eighteenth century.

---

[73] F. v. Zieglauer, *Die politische Reformbewegung in Siebenbürgen in der Zeit Joseph's II. und Leopold's II* (Vienna, 1881).

[74] Keith Hitchins, *The Rumanian national movement in Transylvania, 1780–1849* (Cambridge [MA], 1969); David Prodan, *Supplex Libellus Valachorum. On the Political Struggle of the Romanians in Transylvania during the 18th century* (Bucharest: Academy of the Socialist Republic of Romania, 1971); E. Turczynski, *Konfession und Nation. Zur Frühgeschichte der serbischen und rumänischen Nationsbildung* (Düsseldorf: Schwann, 1976); Mathias Bernath, *Habsburg und die Anfänge der rumänischen Nationsbildung* (Leiden: Brill, 1972).

CHAPTER NINE

The first Greek Catholic catechisms in Hungary and Transylvania

Ovidiu Ghitta

In 1681 the printing-press at Trnava (Nagyszombat) acquired a set of Cyrillic characters.[1] The initiative to allow this printing-press, in a citadel of Catholicism in Royal Hungary, to be able to produce books in languages using Cyrillic characters was taken by Leopold Kollonich, bishop of Wiener Neustadt and president of the Hungarian Chamber at Bratislava (Pozsony/Pressburg).[2] Kollonich intended the press to publish texts in the languages of Ruthenians and Serbs in Hungary, to lift them from their religious ignorance and to improve their moral standards. An arch-promoter of Catholic interests, Kollonich focused his attention on these two communities in the light of progress made towards union between Orthodoxy and the Roman Catholic Church in the Habsburg monarchy during the seventeenth century.[3] This move towards union also had earlier antecedents from the results of the late-sixteenth century synods of the Ruthenian Church held at Brest in the Polish-Lithuanian commonwealth.[4]

The timing of the unions between the Catholic Church and the Serbian and Ruthenian clergy highlights two crucial elements of the process. Firstly, the interests of each of the parties involved, and secondly their different views concerning the path towards reconciliation. The Catholic party comprised the House of Austria, the

---

[1] This article would not have been possible without the valuable information and suggestions offered by Simona Floruțău from the Institute of Social Studies in Târgu Mureş. Károly Szabó ed., *Régi magyar könyvtár* (3 vols), (Budapest: MTA, 1885) vol. 2, p. 527.

[2] Jozeph Maurer, *Cardinal L. Kollonitsh Primas von Ungarn. Sein Leben und Wirken* (Innsbruck: Rauch, 1888).

[3] Michael Lacko, 'Die Union in Kroatien (1611)' in Wilhelm de Vries ed., *Rom und die Patriarchate des Ostens* (Freiburg in Breisgau: Alber, 1963), pp. 108–13; Michael Lacko, *Unio Užhorodensis Ruthenorum Carpaticorum cum Ecclesia Catholica* (Rome: Institutum Orientalium Studiorum, 1955), pp. 91–151.

[4] Oscar Halecki, *From Florence to Brest* (Rome: Sacrum Poloniae Millenium, 1958), pp. 287–392; Borys Gudziak, *Crisis and Reform. The Kyivan Metropolinate, the Patriarchate of Constantinople and the Genesis of the Union of Brest* (Cambridge [MA]: Harvard University Press, 1998), pp. 209–45.

Latin episcopal hierarchy of the Hungarian kingdom, and the Jesuits. From the reign of Ferdinand II, the Habsburgs had shown increasing signs of their wish to turn Catholicism into the spiritual and ideological means by which to unify and control the conglomerate of kingdoms, hereditary provinces and dukedoms placed under their authority.[5] The Habsburg monarchy included a wide range of ethnic, religious and cultural groups in various areas. The court's desire to achieve religious uniformity involved working with the Roman Catholic hierarchy, also directly interested in regaining authority lost during the sixteenth century as a consequence of Protestant progress. In Royal Hungary the diets of 1608 and 1647 proclaimed and reiterated the right of Lutherans and Calvinists to freely exercise their religion, which seriously hampered Catholic ambitions.[6]

Through the activity of Jesuits and the Latin hierarchy at Zagreb (Zágráb/Agram) and Eger (Erlau), a path opened to integrate numerous 'schismatics' who lived within the confines of the Habsburg monarchy into the Catholic Church. These Orthodox Christians had also been targeted by Protestant missionary activity. Such attempts were not encumbered by any constitutional barriers, since Orthodox religion did not have any legal status. On the Orthodox side, clergy led the negotiations for unions with a bishop speaking for the Serbs from Croatia-Slavonia, and archdeacons, parish clergy and Basilian monks representing Ruthenians from Upper Hungary. They were above all concerned to raise the impoverished and underprivileged Orthodox clergy to a better social and legal status. They aimed to achieve parity with Roman Catholic clergy, and secure clergy income, tax exemptions and ecclesiastical immunities.

This brief survey of the objectives of the parties involved in the negotiations for union offers clues to decipher their views on the nature and consequences of ecclesiastical union. It would seem that from the perspective of the Catholic party, Orthodox Serb or Ruthenian Christians would become a part of the Roman Church through a 'union in faith'. They would be integrated into the Catholic Church as practitioners of a distinct rite, a principle which had been accepted by

---

[5] On territorial states' efforts to achieve confessional uniformity and enhance the loyalty of subjects, see Wolfgang Reinhard, 'État et Église dans l'Empire entre Réforme et Absolutisme' in Jean Philippe Genet, Bernard Vincent eds, *État et Église dans la genèse de l'état moderne* (Madrid: Biblioteque de La Casa de Velazquez, 1986), pp. 175–85. On Habsburg confessional policy, see Robert Evans, *The making of the Habsburg Monarchy: an interpretation* (Oxford: Clarendon, 1991), pp. 41–80.

[6] Erich Zöllner, *Istoria Austriei de la începuturi până în prezent, vol. I* (Bucharest: Editura Enciclopedică, 1997), p. 253; Béla Köpeczi, *La France et la Hongrie au debut du XVIII-e siècle* (Budapest: Akádemiai Kiadó, 1971), p. 21.

the Papacy at the end of the sixteenth century.[7] However, this integration also implied that the union had to be followed by a process of unification and adoption of the elements which defined the post-Tridentine church.[8] Thus, the bishop of Eger and Jesuits tried to impose Catholic standards of moral discipline and devotional practices on the Ruthenian clergy shortly after the 1646 Union of Užhorod (Ungvár).[9] From the point of view of the Roman Catholic party, the union in faith opened a new chapter in the religious life of the 'easterners' who had come under the pastoral care of the Pope. They had to gradually receive a new Catholic confessional identity. From the perspective of the Greek-rite clergy who attended union negotiations, they were following the spirit of the Council of Ferrara-Florence of 1438–39. Orthodox clergy saw moves towards unions as an inter-ecclesiastical process which would not be followed by a loss of autonomy for their church or by any renunciation of their religious traditions.[10] According to this attitude, union would not lead to any form of innovation, except in the social and legal position of their church.

The year that Leopold Kollonich ensured that the Trnava press received a set of Cyrillic characters was not promising for the Catholic cause in Royal Hungary. In 1681 the Hungarian diet at Sopron resisted Habsburg absolutist and Counter-Reformation policies, instead confirming freedom for Calvinists and Lutherans to practise their religion.[11] Catholic attention turned to rebuilding the support which had previously been established among Serbian and Ruthenian Orthodox clergy for union with Rome. After 1681 Kollonich tried to bolster those Orthodox communities who had already more or less accepted union with the Catholic Church, and attempted to promote negotiations for further unions. By printing religious texts in Serbian and Ruthenian, Kollonich did not hope to further negotiations or prepare for union, but wished to make sure that the process of union, once started, would be

---

7 Vittorio Peri, *Chiesa Romana e 'rito greco'* (Brescia: Paideia Editrice, 1975).

8 On the concepts of union and unification, see Joseph Macha, *Ecclesiastical Unification. A Theoretical Framework together with Case Studies from the History of Latin-Byzantine Relations* (Rome: Institutum Orientalium Studiorum, 1974), pp. 1–4, 11–12.

9 Lacko, *Unio Užhorodensis* (1955), p. 139; Athanasius Pekar, *The History of the Church in Carpathian Rus'* (New York: Columbia University Press, 1992), p. 28.

10 Cesare Alzati, 'L'Ortodossia' in G. Filoramo, D. Menozzi eds, *Storia del Cristianesimo. L'eta moderna* (Roma: Editori Laterza, 1997), pp. 350–51.

11 Jean Bérenger, *Histoire de L'Empire des Habsbourg, 1273–1918* (Paris: Fayard, 1990), p. 346; Robert Kann, *A History of the Habsburg Empire 1526–1918* (Berkeley [CA]: University of California Press, 1977), pp. 114–15; János Varga, 'Berendezési tervezetek magyarországon a török kiüzésének idöszakában. Az 'Einrichtungswerk'', *Századok* 5–6 (1991), p. 451.

irreversible. However, all these plans were frustrated by conflict between royal troops and Hungarian rebels led by Imre Thököly in Upper Hungary. Fighting started again shortly after an armistice imposed by the Sopron diet in 1681, and only came to a conclusion in 1688. After 1683 Habsburg armies were also engaged in conflict in central Hungary against the Ottomans.[12]

Plans for negotiations about ecclesiastical union were entirely overshadowed by these events, and the Trnava printing-press did not publish any texts in Serbian or Ruthenian in the first fifteen years of its existence. However, programmes to facilitate and strengthen Orthodox union with Rome were gradually resuscitated from the late 1680s. This partly resulted from the expanding frontiers of the Habsburg monarchy during the last decades of the century, which brought much larger numbers of Orthodox Serbs and Romanians within the Habsburg monarchy. By 1688 the Habsburgs had wrested control over the central part of the former medieval Hungarian kingdom from the Ottomans and had also gained the principality of Transylvania.[13] While efforts to encourage union with the Serbian Church failed, Catholic efforts to bring Orthodox priests and believers under the authority of the Pope were relaunched with spectacular success in the Ruthenian Church of Upper Hungary. This was partly due to the zeal of Joseph de Camellis, a former student of the Greek College in Rome who was appointed by Pope Alexander VIII in 1689 as apostolic vicar to the 'Greeks' of the diocese of Mukačevo (Munkács) and to 'other territories and places gained in Hungary'.[14] A decree from Leopold I of August 1692 supported this move, and guaranteed new legal privileges for all Orthodox clergy who embraced union with Rome. During the 1690s, Romanian clergy from the *Partium* of eastern Hungary were drawn towards union for the first time, a decision to unite with the Catholic Church which probably had an impact on developments in Transylvania. In 1697 Romanian clergy from Transylvania led by metropolitan Teofil agreed to union, a decision which was confirmed in 1698 and 1700 under metropolitan Atanasie.[15]

---

[12] Bérenger, *Histoire de L'Empire* (1990), pp. 347–8, 364; Mathias Bernath, *Habsburgii şi începuturile formarii natiunii române* (Cluj: Dacia, 1994), pp. 49–56.

[13] J. Fiedler, *Beiträge zur Union der Valachen in Slavonien und Syrmien* (Vienna, 1867), pp. 3–12; Wilhelm Ploechl, 'The Church Laws for Orientals of the Austrian Monarchy in the Age of the Enlightenment', *Quarterly Bulletin of the Polish Institute of Arts and Sciences in America* (1944), p. 8.

[14] Athanasius Pekar, 'Tribute to Bishop Joseph J. de Camellis OSBM (1641–1706)', *Analecta OSBM* (1985), pp. 376–90.

[15] Ernst Suttner, 'Unirea bisericeasca din Transilvania 1697–1761. Straduinta pentru comuniune sacramentala între Bisericile surori degenereaza în convertirea crestinilor

Leopold Kollonich, who had become a cardinal and the primate of Hungary and archbishop of Esztergom (Gran), then revived his old project to promote printing using Cyrillic characters. Kollonich's wider intentions quickly became clear: by producing religious books, he aimed to strengthen Catholicism across the territories of the former Hungarian kingdom. In 1696 catechisms were printed in several languages of the region, aimed at Catholics in Latin, Hungarian and Slovak, and at Greek Catholics in Romanian. Unfortunately, there are no surviving copies of the Greek Catholic catechisms published at this time. However, from information provided by the historian István Katona, one work was apparently printed in Romanian using Cyrillic characters in 1696 and again in 1726, and printed with Latin characters at Sibiu (Nagyszeben/Hermannstadt) in 1709 under the supervision of the Jesuit Ferenc Szunyog. There were some suggestions that this was a Romanian version of the famous catechism by Peter Canisius, but surviving copies of the 1726 edition do not confirm this.[16] Assuming that the association made between these three editions of this catechism is correct, the 1696 catechism was written by bishop Joseph de Camellis for the priests and faithful under his ecclesiastical authority.[17] Two years later, the same printing press started to circulate a version in Ruthenian of the same

---

ortodocsi la catolicism', *Teologia*, 1 (1997), pp. 46–9; Ovidiu Ghitta, 'Episcopul Iosif de Camellis si românii din "Partile unguresti"', *Studia Universitatis Babes-Bolyai. Historia* 42 (1997), pp. 66–70; Zenovie Pâclişanu, 'Istoria Bisericii Române Unite I (1697–1744)', *Buna Vestire* 1–2 (1976), pp. 20–27; Octavian Bârlea, 'Unirea Românilor (1697–1701)', *Îndreptar* 49–50 (1990), pp. 7–39.

[16] 'Edidit Catechismum Valachicum maiorem Romano catholicum, typo Valachico Tirnaviae 1696, 1726, typo Latino Cibinii 1709': Stephano Katona, *Historia critica Regum Hungariae stirpis Austriacae, XIX, ordine XXXVIII* (Buda, 1806), pp. 890–91; Peter Canisius, *Summa Doctrinae Christianae per quaestiones tradita et ad capitum rudiorum accomodata* (1555).

[17] Work on the catechism was finished before August 1691, when the Ruthenian monk Ivan Kornyčkyi started translation of the Latin manuscript. Two years later, de Camellis announced to the Congregation for the Propagation of Faith that he had written a 'catechism for the needs of this people, which I have translated into Ruthenian, preparing it for printing and in order to disseminate it in the diocese, because the books printed by the schismatics are full of errors'; Kálmán Zsatkovics, 'De Camellis Jozsef munkácsi püspök naplója', *Történelmi Tár* (1895), p. 718; A. Hodinka, *A munkácsi gör. szert. püspökség okmánytára, vol. 1* (Ungvár, 1911), p. 364. The text was probably then translated into Romanian, and printed before the translation of Kornyčkyi; *Catechismuş sau învăţătură creştinească în folosul neamului rusesc din Ţara Ungurească. Dat afară prin osîrdia şi osteneala Mării Sale D: Ioan Iosif De Camilis, ipiscupul Sebastului şi al Muncaciului i proci. Cinului preoţesc unit din legea grecească vicariş apostolicescu, în Ţara Ungurească sfintei şi înălţatei împărăţii Rîmului sfetnicu. Iară acum, în folosul neamului rumânescu, în limba rumânească întoarsă şi tipărită* (Sîmbăta Mare, 1726).

work.[18] The production of this text in both Ruthenian and Romanian represents a significant move from discussion of the principles of union and negotiations about the adherence of Orthodox clergy to formulas of union with the Catholic Church, to the actual building of a Greek Catholic Church in Upper Hungary and the *Partium*.

The application of Kollonich's strategy in Transylvania to use books to spread Catholic interests in the principality produced similar results. The negotiations for union were more or less completed by the visit of the metropolitan Atanasie to Vienna in 1701. On this occasion, Atanasie promised to share with his clergy and the laity of Transylvania 'a catechism of just laws', which was supposed to be produced with the support of the Hungarian primate.[19] One year later the work was printed in Alba Iulia (Gyulafehérvár/Weissenburg) under the title *Bread of the Innocents*.[20] This catechism was compiled by the Hungarian Jesuit László Bárányi, and was translated into Romanian by János Duma from Borobanți.[21]

Thus, the first printed texts which were produced for the Greek Catholics of Upper Hungary, the *Partium* and Transylvania were catechisms, instruments which were seen as fundamental in advancing reformed Catholicism. Catechisms were intended to be used to establish a sound and uniform religious education at parish level, and to lead to improvements in public morality. They were supposed to educate communities by disseminating fundamental elements of the system of belief promoted by the ecclesiastical hierarchy.[22] The publication of catechisms in the wake of union with Orthodox churches was also meant to aid the remodelling of Greek Catholics to the spiritual, cultural and moral ideals of the Roman Church, and to spread a Catholic

---

18 Szabo ed., *Régi magyar könyvtár* (1885), vol. 2, pp. 526–7; P.R. Magocsi, Bohdan Strumins'kyi, 'The First Carpatho-Ruthenian Printed Book', *Harvard Library Bulletin* 25 (1977), pp. 296–309.

19 Two documents were drawn up on this occasion; Samuil Micu, *Istoria Românilor* (Bucharest: Editura Viitorul Românesc, 1995), vol. 2, p. 275; Ştefan Lupşa, 'Biserica ardeleană şi "unirea" în anii 1697–1701', *Biserica Ortodoxă Română* 1–2 (1949), p. 51.

20 On the printing-press in Alba Iulia see Eva Mârza, *Din istoria tiparului românesc. Tipografia de la Alba Iulia 1577–1702* (Sibiu: Editura Imago, 1998).

21 *Pîinea pruncilor, sau învăţătura credinţii creştineşti strânsă în mică şumă. Care o au scris în mici întrebăciuni şi răspunsuri ungureşti cinstitul pater Boroneai Laslo parohuşul besearicii catoliceşti de la Bălgrad. Şi s-au întors în limba românească de Duma Janeşu din Borbanţi. In anul Domnului 1702*; Ion Muşlea, "Pîinea Pruncilor' (Bălgrad, 1702). Din istoria unei cărţi vechi româneşti' in *Omagiu lui Ioan Lupaş la împlinirea vîrstei de 60 de ani* (Bucharest, 1943), pp. 617–31.

22 Geoffrey Dickens, *La Contre Réforme* (Paris: Flammarion, 1969); Jean Delumeau, *Le catholicisme entre Luther et Voltaire* (Paris: Presses Universitaires de France, 1971), p. 288.

confessional identity among 'easterners' who had only recently come under the authority of the Pope.

Neither Joseph de Camellis nor László Bárányi had risen from the ranks of the Ruthenian or Romanian clergy who had accepted union. However, de Camellis, as Greek Catholic bishop of Mukačevo, followed the eastern rites of the Church, while László Bárányi, a Jesuit, did not. Nevertheless, the structure of their two catechisms is almost identical, and de Camellis and Bárányi closely followed the model offered by Peter Canisius' *Summa Doctrinae Christianae*. The two catechisms explained true faith, prayer, the law, the sacraments and sin. However, de Camellis introduced a third component of the 'priest's voice' alongside the other two sections of questions and answers. This was intended to assist priests in leading catechism classes to find clarification of points of doctrine and detailed explanations of answers, as well as provide essential scriptural and patristic references. De Camellis seems to have been concerned to bolster the learning and authority of badly-educated priests by providing all the information needed to enable them to transmit the contents of the catechism to their congregations. By choosing this particular method, the Greek Catholic bishop proved that he had been inspired not just by Canisius' catechism, but also by a work which set out to assist post-Tridentine Catholic clergy.[23]

These two catechisms reveal much about the nature of the ecclesiastical union between the Catholic and Orthodox churches, and about Greek Catholic religion. The two authors approach the subject of union in radically different ways. Bárányi's *Bread of the Innocents* simply does not address the issue of union, seek to justify it or to explain its significance. Since he conceived of union as a union of faith, Bárányi did not believe that any additional explanations were necessary about the position of the external church. Bárányi merely intended his catechism to be used by Catholics who acknowledged the authority of the Pope and accepted all points of Catholic doctrine. Thus, *Bread of the Innocents* does not include any indication that Bárányi was addressing Romanian Greek Catholics with any separate confessional history or identity. Indeed Bárányi did not wish to highlight any particular features of the new subjects of Rome which distinguished them from Latin Catholics.[24] The main objective of his catechism was the spiritual and moral edification of Catholic Christians in conformity with the imperatives of Tridentine reform.

---

23 *Catechismus ex decreto concilii Tridentini ad parochos* (Lugduni, 1569).

24 Simona Floruţău, 'Aspecte ale mesajului catehetic la începutul secolului XVIII. Pâinea Pruncilor (Balgrad, 1702)', *Anuarul Institutului de Cercetări Socio-Umane 'Gh. Şincai'* 2 (1999), p. 87.

De Camellis' catechism took a completely different perspective on this issue, and deemed it necessary to instruct his flock as to the meaning and purpose of the recent ecclesiastical union. While explaining articles of the Apostles' Creed, de Camellis introduced the decisions reached by 'Greek and Latin Fathers' at the 1439 Council of Florence.[25] This mention of a Church council as the basis for union invoked a body which was held in the highest authority in the Orthodox world. De Camellis explained the institutional framework of the Florentine debates and then detailed the four 'articles of Catholic faith' accepted by the members of the eastern delegation present at the Council. First, recognition of 'the Pope from Rome as the true and lawful heir of St Peter, who was the first apostle and vicar of Our Lord Christ on earth, and, [that] the church of Rome, catholic and orthodox is the head and the first chair and unmovable pillar of the Christian and catholic faith'. Second, acceptance of the origins of the Holy Spirit in both the Father and the Son; third, agreement that unleavened bread could be used in the sacrament of communion, and fourth, acknowledgement of the existence of purgatory as a place between hell and heaven where people are cleansed of their sin. These statements were presented as the theological basis for reconciliation between the churches. De Camellis insisted that union had to be accomplished only in such 'matters of faith', and not in 'other matters which are not faith but rather ornaments' of the churches and in which 'those from the west and those from the east differ'.[26] De Camellis informed Greek Catholic clergy that while union meant that they accepted the four Florentine articles, reconciliation with the Roman Catholic Church did not imply abandoning or modifying traditional eastern rites. Union merely aimed to reconstruct Christian unity under the spiritual authority of the heir of St Peter. De Camellis viewed that this explanation of the legitimacy of the Greek Catholic community was essential to bolster those who had chosen union, and to provide answers to those who questioned their choice and their new confessional identity.

Continuing this examination of the discourse which was intended to shape the confessional identity of Greek Catholics, the two catechisms contain significant references to other confessions as a means to establish what a Greek Catholic was and what he was not. Both the catechisms of László Bárányi and Joseph de Camellis are clear that the status of a 'true Christian' does not only stem from receiving baptism, nor only from respecting the teachings of Christ, but also from

---

25 De Camellis, *Catechismuş* (1726), p. 393.
26 De Camellis, *Catechismuş* (1726), pp. 70, 389, 393–5.

belonging to the 'true Church'.[27] Both catechisms repeat that the faithful must belong to the 'orthodox or catholic' Church, that is, to the Church of Rome. Bárányi's catechism commented that 'the Church of Rome teaches the true teaching of Christ', while bishop de Camellis explicitly stated that 'the true Christians are the Latins ... because they guard the law and believe in the teachings that have been given by the Apostles, the synods, and the Holy Fathers from the west and east.'[28] Romanian and Ruthenian Greek Catholics were to understand that only members of the true Church, who benefited from the guidance of the Pope, could follow true Christian teachings and thus attain salvation. Joseph de Camellis added that a follower of eastern rites could be a true Christian if he shared with the same faith as Catholics. For de Camellis, ritual differences and rival ecclesiastical traditions should not prevent *rapprochement* between the new and the old subjects of the Pope. Greek Catholics had entered sacramental communion with the Roman Church, and 'papists' must now be perceived as 'brothers unto faith', or, as Camellis put it, 'those whom you must love with all of your heart'.[29]

Attitudes in the catechisms to those outside the Catholic Church are combative, but the extent and degree of polemic attacks against Protestants and the Orthodox Church vary between the two texts. Bárányi concentrated his fire against Lutheran and Calvinist heresies, while de Camellis was preoccupied with attacking eastern 'schismatics'. In *Bread of the Innocents*, Bárányi focused on the need to destroy any influences which Protestants in Transylvania might have exerted over Romanians.[30] Bárányi highlighted points of theological difference between the Catholic Church and Protestant Churches, and indicated the appropriate attitude to be taken towards Protestants. For Bárányi, Protestant 'heresy is a great sin ... because it breaks with faith, which is a gift from God', and he concluded that 'the heretics together with the pagans would lose the Church of God' and not attain salvation.[31]

De Camellis meanwhile devoted a section of his catechism to consider 'heretics, pagans and schismatics', and stated that heretics were those:

> ... who believe in Christ and are baptized but do not believe in all the articles of faith which have been given by the holy Catholic Church; some of these are Arians, Lutherans, Calvinists, Nestorians and many others, who for a long time have broken away from the

---

[27] Bárányi, *Pîineá Pruncilor* (1702), ff. 1r–2r; De Camellis, *Catechismuş* (1726), pp. 21, 24.

[28] De Camellis, *Catechismuş* (1726), pp. 364–5; Bárányi, *Pîinea Pruncilor* (1702), f. 28r.

[29] De Camellis, *Catechismuş* (1726), p. 13.

[30] Floruţău, 'Aspecte ale mesajului catehetic' (1999), pp. 88–9.

[31] Bárányi, *Pîinea Pruncilor* (1702), ff. 3v, 7r–v.

> holy Church, and break away now, who misrepresent the words of
> the holy Gospels and interpret them at their will, do not hold to all
> the sacraments of the Church and do not believe in all the
> achievements of the great holy synods, the Church Fathers and the
> Church of Rome.[32]

De Camellis distinguished clearly between a 'true Christian' who is
'orthodox and catholic', and a 'heretic' who disregards church tradition
and most of the sacraments. However, de Camellis also mentioned that
Protestants and Catholics share faith in baptism and belief in Christ. He
even stated that, in emergencies, baptisms performed by 'heretics and
the unfaithful' could be accepted. De Camellis also suggested that people
should accept the idea of Catholic godparents for 'sons of heretics', since
even if they were baptized as 'heretics', there was hope that they might
eventually be drawn to true faith by the example of their godparents.[33]
De Camellis' catechism was straightforward and forthright in attacking
his perception of heresy, but also made acknowledgement of the multi-
confessional environment of his region and dealt with the practical
issues facing his community.

While Bárányi limited himself to combating the threat posed by
Protestants, de Camellis also set out his view of the Orthodox Church.
De Camellis was intent on providing Romanian and Ruthenian clergy
with arguments against eastern 'schismatics', perhaps the most sensitive
issue facing the Greek Catholic community. It was very difficult to
present attacks on former co-religionists in a catechism, identifying the
sins which those who studied the catechism had committed until
recently and the faults of their fathers and ancestors. De Camellis
carefully argued that:

> A schismatic is one who is baptized and believes all that he is meant
> to believe and holds all that he is meant to hold, but does not know
> the Pope in Rome as the head of all the Church and vicar of Christ.
> These are called the Greeks and they hold the faith and law of the
> Church Fathers and respect the Pope of Rome no more than one of
> the Patriarchs. Since they are cut off from the head [of the Church],
> they are like rotting parts cut off from a body.[34]

For de Camellis, 'schismatics' stand closer to the status of 'orthodox or
catholic' Christians, because unlike 'heretics' they respect the teachings
of the Church. Thus, to enter the ranks of 'true Christians', former
'schismatics' did not have to abandon 'the holy rite of the Greek Church,
approved by the holy Church of Rome'. The Greeks are schismatic

---

32 De Camellis, *Catechismuş* (1726), pp. 366–7.
33 De Camellis, *Catechismuş* (1726), pp. 197, 200.
34 De Camellis, *Catechismuş* (1726), p. 367.

because they failed to recognize the primacy of the papacy. Here, de Camellis proved once again his profound attachment to the Florentine model of ecclesiastical union, which only required 'easterners' to recognize the primacy of the Roman See and specific teachings on the Holy Spirit, purgatory and use of the host in the Eucharist.

De Camellis went on to establish that responsibility for the rupture within the Church was not shared equally by all of eastern Christendom. One people were particularly to blame, who had led the others into ignorance. De Camellis, himself a Greek, suggested that the 'entire Ruthene people' should cleanse their minds 'of stubbornness and disobedience', and forsake the 'Greeks who bear the flag of the break from the true holy Church', instead bowing 'with great humility and respect to the head of the Catholic Church in Rome'.[35] The Greeks were given particular blame for their stubborn opposition to union and reaction to the Council of Florence. De Camellis asked why Ruthenes should persist in schism for the sake of these Greek foreigners, especially when the road to the true Church was so short and smooth? His arguments were intended to allow those in his diocese to divide themselves from those Orthodox culprits who had sustained schism, and to establish the necessary distance between the Greek Catholic community and 'schismatics' without neglecting entirely their ancient solidarity with common heirs of the eastern religious tradition. The text of de Camellis' catechism suggests that a Greek Catholic was a Catholic through his faith, but not a 'Latin', an 'easterner' through the rite but not a 'schismatic'.

There were further ways in which these catechisms sought to establish Greek Catholic identity. As 'true Christians', Greek Catholics were now required to show solidarity and brotherly love only to Roman Catholics, who also recognized the supreme spiritual authority of the Pope. Remaining loyal to post-Tridentine ecclesiology, László Bárányi's catechism portrayed union as the integration of Greek-rite communities within the body of the universal Church, and suggested that the Romanian Greek Catholic Church was not a distinct ecclesiastical entity. However, de Camellis' catechism presented the situation of the Greek Catholic Church in a more detailed and complicated way. De Camellis agreed that ecclesiastical union had turned easterners into members of the great Christian community of the 'orthodox and catholic' Church led by the Pope. However, once again showing his loyalty to the Florentine model of inter-ecclesiastical reconciliation, de Camellis considered that, although under the authority of the Pope, Greek

---

35 De Camellis, *Catechismuş* (1726), p. 77.

Catholics formed a distinct 'branch' of the universal Church. For de Camellis, this 'branch' had institutional autonomy, and his catechism referred to 'our eastern Church' and 'our Greek Church'. This view matched the vision of the relationship with the Latin Church taken during negotiations for union by both the Ruthenian and Romanian clergy hierarchy. The easterners wished to preserve their local framework of ecclesiastical organization and to maintain their distinct confessional traditions and ceremonies.

These significantly diverging opinions on the position of the new Greek Catholic confession in part reflected the differences between the Jesuit László Bárányi and the Greek Catholic bishop Joseph de Camellis. They also in part reflect the different nature of the audiences they were addressing. Bárányi's text potentially addressed all Transylvanian Catholics, including the substantial Hungarian Catholic community, when it presented the defining elements of a Roman Church to the Romanian community of the principality. Consequently, his catechism appears much more to serve Greek Catholic communities in need of acculturation to their new Catholic context. De Camellis produced the first truly Greek Catholic manual of catechetical instruction printed within the Habsburg monarchy which aimed to define a Catholic identity for Greek Catholics, stressing the specific circumstances, particular eastern heritage and autonomous ecclesiastical hierarchy of the Greek Catholic Church.

Despite the significant differences between the ways in which these two writers conceived of Greek Catholic identity, both authors strongly advanced the devotional, moral and disciplinary requirements of reformed Catholic religious life.[36] Both Bárányi and de Camellis were convinced of the need for thorough and uniform instruction of Greek Catholics in the truth of their faith. Both catechisms demanded a new type of internalized and reflective individual piety. For example, they insisted that prayers should only be recited after a serious examination of conscience, after freeing the mind from 'the turmoil of the heart', and with complete faith in God. Similarly, a true Christian should welcome confession as an ideal occasion to monitor his life and behaviour in a responsible and systematic way. A true son of the Church also had the supreme duty to attend church services on Sundays and on major feast days throughout the year, to observe fasts and to take communion regularly. Another part of shaping the religious behaviour of Greek Catholic parishioners in accordance with reformed

---

[36] Ronald Po-chia Hsia, *Social Discipline in the Reformation: Central Europe 1550–1750* (London: Routledge, 1992), pp. 129–73; Ronald Po-chia Hsia, *The World of Catholic Renewal 1540–1770* (Cambridge: University Press, 1998), pp. 197–206.

Catholic standards pursued by both authors was the aim to establish firm boundaries between the sacred and the profane, between faith and superstition, between canonical and non-canonical ceremonies and rituals. Both catechisms attack 'spells, incantations and superstitions', the cult of 'idols', 'worship of foreign Gods' and magical 'blessing of vessels before eating'. Bárányi was particularly concerned by these elements of traditional religious life, and in the final part of *Bread of the Innocents* attacked superstitious beliefs and practices, showing greater intolerance than de Camellis for such manifestations of popular religiosity.[37]

The two catechisms also established the expected conduct of a pious Christian within their family and local society. In sections of the catechisms which dealt with the Ten Commandments, both Bárányi and de Camellis detailed and condemned any lapses from expected standards of moral conduct. The range of immoral behaviour which was described extended from showing disobedience to parents, making false oaths, physical violence, suicide, abortion, rape, sodomy, theft and slander. Both texts used the presentation of the law as the basis for forceful and lengthy demands for high moral standards within Greek Catholic communities. Bárányi dedicated a paragraph on the seven deadly sins to stimulate introspection and self-disciplining among all social groups predisposed to sin, from 'kings, gentlemen, judges', to 'ladies, servants, fools and children'. All members of Greek Catholic congregations had the duty unswervingly to follow a strict model of ethical conduct, and catechizing by parish priests was supposed to help achieve these disciplinary ambitions.

These two catechisms compiled by László Bárányi and Joseph de Camellis were the first to be printed for use among Greek Catholics in Hungary and Transylvania. Both texts indicate the beginning of a process of establishing Greek Catholic churches in these territories beyond the formal acceptance of formulas of union. The fact that neither author was from the ranks of local clergy highlights the lack of a domestic Greek Catholic elite able to produce such texts. The two catechisms reveal that beyond the apparently common interests of advocates of union there were fundamentally distinct views about the nature of the act of union. László Bárányi understood union as the birth of new Catholic denomination, while Joseph de Camellis stressed some elements of continuity in the liturgical traditions and institutional autonomy of the Greek Catholic Church. These two currents of thought were present both in the negotiations about union, and in the first

---

[37] Bárányi, *Pîinea Pruncilor* (1702), pp. 145–52.

articulations of the identity of the Greek Catholic Church, and marked a fundamental tension about the nature of the church which continued throughout the eighteenth century and beyond.

CHAPTER TEN

The confessional identity of the Transylvanian Greek Catholic Church

Pompiliu Teodor

The agreement made by Transylvanian Orthodox clergy to unite with Rome at the end of the seventeenth century has provoked much heated debate among Romanian historians. Studies have focused on the negotiations for union, the acts of union and the pressure placed on the Transylvanian Orthodox Church hierarchy to agree to unite with the Catholic Church.[1] Traditional writing on this subject has been heavily coloured by partisan confessional loyalties, or by a tendency in Romania to view the emergence of the Greek Catholic Church from a nationalist perspective. These limitations are to some extent being rectified by current research, which assesses the union with Rome within the broader context of the political and cultural history of the period. In this light, the union agreed between the Transylvanian Orthodox Church and Rome was one part of the political and religious agenda of the Catholic Habsburg court within their newly acquired principality. Union also led to the construction and development of a new Greek Catholic confessional identity in Transylvania which brought Transylvania's Romanian community into closer contact with the world of Latin Christendom.[2]

---

[1] Keith Hitchins, *A Nation Discovered. Romanian Intellectuals and the Idea of Nation 1700–1848* (Bucharest: Editura Enciclopedică, 1999), pp. 11–41; Mathias Bernath, *Habsburgii şi începuturile formării naţiunii române (Cluj: Dacia, 1994)*; Silviu Dragomir, *Românii din Transilvania şi Unirea cu Biserica Romei. Documente apocrife privitoare la începuturile Unirii cu catolicismul roman (1697–1701)* (Bucharest: Institutul Ortodox, 1963).

[2] David Prodan, *Supplex Libellus Valachorum* (Bucharest: Editura Enciclopedică, 1984); Francisc Pall, *Inochentie Micu-Klein. Exilul la Roma 1745–1748* (3 vols) (Cluj: Fundaţia Culturală, 1997); Pompiliu Teodor, *Interferenţe Iluministe Europene* (Cluj: Dacia, 1984); Ovidiu Ghitta, 'Consideraţii privind Unirea rutenilor şi românilor cu Biserica Romei' in Nicolae Bocşan, Nicolae Edroiu and Aurel Răduţiu eds, *Convergenţe europene. Istorie şi societate în epoca modernă* (Cluj: Dacia, 1993), pp. 149–57; Ovidiu Ghitta, 'Schiţă pentru o istoriografie a Unirii religioase în nord-vestul Transilvaniei' in Sorin Mitu, Florin Gogâltan eds, *Studii de istorie a Transilvaniei* (Cluj: Asociaţia istoricilor

This chapter focuses on the stages of development of this Greek Catholic identity in the eighteenth century. This process reached beyond the ecclesiastical sphere and even beyond the realms of religious experience, as Catholicism and Habsburg expansion in the region proved significant in shaping Romanian ethnic and even 'national' awareness. This chapter also highlights the role played by printed religious literature in articulating the position of the Transylvanian Greek Catholic Church 'between' Latin Catholicism and Orthodoxy. In order to fully understand how Greek Catholic identity was forged in Transylvania, it is necessary to clarify two concepts which are widely used in the historiography on this subject, ecclesiastical union and religious union. Institutional change is emphasized in the first case, while spiritual and doctrinal elements are prominent in the second. Religious union could only be accomplished when Greek Catholic clergy had integrated Catholic doctrine into their belief system, while maintaining the practice of their distinctive church rites.

Greek Catholic (or Uniate) Churches initially emerged in east-central Europe from a series of agreements between representatives of the Catholic Church and local Orthodox clergy hierarchies. At the end of the sixteenth century clergy from the Ruthenian Church in the Polish-Lithuanian commonwealth agreed to unite with Rome at Brest, and in 1646 agreement was reached with the Ruthenian Church of Upper Hungary.[3] In the 1690s Catholic leaders in the Habsburg monarchy launched plans for union which drew in both Ruthenians and Romanians in Hungary. These agreements about union took place between representatives of the Roman Catholic hierarchy, and metropolitans and archdeacons of the Ruthenian and Romanian Orthodox Churches. By an agreement of 1697, which was confirmed in 1700, the Romanian Church in the Transylvanian principality also decided to unite with Rome, and again the local metropolitan and archdeacons played a decisive role in negotiations.[4]

The acts of union agreed in 1697 with metropolitan Teofil and the protopopes of the Transylvanian Orthodox Church recognized the Pope

din Transilvania, 1994), pp. 88–96; Pompiliu Teodor, 'Unirea rutenilor şi românilor cu Biserica Romei' in Dennis Deletant, Keith Hitchins, Pompiliu Teodor et al. eds, *Istoria României* (Bucharest: Editura Enciclopedică, 1998), pp. 285–90.

    3 Oskar Halecki, *From Florence to Brest* (Rome: Sacrum Poloniae Millenium, 1958); Ghitta, 'Consideraţii privind Unirea' (1993), pp. 149–57.

    4 Teodor, 'Unirea rutenilor şi românilor cu Biserica Romei' (1998), pp. 285–90; Joseph Macha, *Ecclesiastical Unification. A Theoretical Framework together with Case Studies from the History of Latin-Byzantine relations* (Rome: Institutum Orientalium, 1974), pp. 145–6.

as the supreme head of the Church. The Orthodox participants also accepted several points of Catholic doctrine, which had first been agreed by the Council of Florence in 1439. The Transylvanian clergy acknowledged that unleavened bread could be used for the host in the Eucharist, alongside the continued use of leavened bread which was customary in the Orthodox Church. They also accepted the existence of purgatory as a place between heaven and hell, and that the Holy Spirit originated in both God the Father and the Son. This agreement was confirmed by the Catholic primate of Hungary, cardinal Leopold Kollonich. However, during further negotiations in 1698 the Orthodox party, under the new metropolitan Atanasie, withdrew acceptance of these points of doctrine and were only prepared to acknowledge Papal supremacy. By 1700 the Transylvanian Orthodox synod had returned to the original position held in 1697, and 'received, confessed and believed that [all] four points seem to have kept us [Catholic and Orthodox] apart'. Unlike previous efforts made by Protestants in the region to reform elements of Orthodox religious practices, including the use of icons and veneration of saints, the acts of union with the Transylvanian Church assured the Orthodox party that they could retain their traditional liturgy, ceremonies, rites and church calendar, and that priests would still be allowed to be married. The 'Pravila' Orthodox canon law book was also retained, although all elements deemed adverse to the new union were carefully excised.[5]

In March 1701 union was sealed by the consecration of Atanasie as bishop of the Greek Catholic Church in Transylvania. This agreement between the Catholic Church and the Orthodox clergy served Habsburg aims of trying to establish Catholic dominance over the Protestant estates of Transylvania. Leopold I had issued diplomas in 1692 and 1699, which offered Greek Catholic clergy the prospect of equal legal status with Catholic clergy, which they had previously been denied in the constitution of the Transylvanian principality.[6] The Papacy was also satisfied that union in Transylvania had established the primacy of Papal authority and the integration of previously Orthodox Churches within the Catholic fold. Essential points of Catholic doctrine had been agreed, and the Papacy was willing to see the Eastern Churches maintain their traditional rites. Indeed, instructions issued by the Congregation for the Propagation of Faith in 1669 on conditions for union with Orthodoxy referred to the absolute need for the legitimacy of the Roman bishop as the only vicar of Christ and true successor of St Peter to be

[5] Dragomir, *Românii din Transilvania* (1963), pp. 6–34; Ion Micu Moldovan, *Actele Sinodale* (2 vols) (Blaj: Tipografia Seminarialǎ, 1872), vol. 2, p. 116.

[6] Bernath, *Habsburgii şi începuturile formǎrii naţiunii române* (1994), pp. 73–89.

acknowledged, but had also clearly stated that Greek rites would not need to be changed.[7]

In Transylvania there were no popular demands for union with Rome, before or during these negotiations, and neither parish clergy nor ordinary lay believers played any significant part in the formal process of uniting the two confessions.[8] Therefore, once the formal process of institutional union was finalized, clear statements were badly needed to explain the agreed doctrine of the new church. A religious union in Transylvania could only take place as ordinary Greek Catholic clergy internalized Catholic doctrine and began to educate their communities in the theology of their new confession. Local communities thus only slowly became aware of their new confessional allegiance and of the changes made to traditional patterns of belief. This process required better levels of education for the lower clergy, and some attempt to raise levels of literacy across Transylvania's Romanian congregations.

One part of this process of implementing the conditions of union, and of developing the institutions of the new Greek Catholic Church, took place through the Transylvanian synod. The Greek Catholic synod, which included secular members alongside the clergy, came to play a very important role in the Transylvanian Church. The synod agreed to sever all institutional links with the Orthodox Church. In 1726 the synod, under bishop Ioan Pataki, forbade priests who had been consecrated outside Transylvania from holding office within the principality. This aimed to prevent any Orthodox infection of the church from Wallachia and Moldavia. The synod also acted to prevent the circulation of books which strayed from accepted doctrine, and discouraged the reception of Orthodox monks in Transylvanian monasteries. However, far from ending Orthodox resistance to union, these decisions may have sparked unrest around Făgăraş (Fogaras/Fogarasch) in southern Transylvania in the late 1720s. The orientation of the Greek Catholic Church towards local Protestants also shifted, and synods decided that children should be educated only in

---

7 'Verum leges disciplinae seu ritum ecclesiastici in variis ecclesiis variae esse possunt, quam haec rituum varietatis fidei unite optime consistat'; *Instructio missionarum Sacra Uniones pangende intentarum; De Orientalis ecclesie ritu inter fideles unitas in sua integritate retinendo* (1669) in N. Nilles, *Symbolae ad illustrandam historiam ecclesiae orientales in terris coronae S. Stephani* (2 vols) (Oeniponte: Rauch, 1885) vol. 1, pp. 111–14.

8 Remus Câmpeanu, 'Aspiraţii spre depăşirea marginalităţii în mediul rural din Transilvania prin unirea religioasă', *Anuarul Institutului de Istorie* 32 (1993), pp. 39–47; Greta Miron, 'Unirea religioasă în mentalul rural transilvănean' in Sorin Mitu, Florin Gogâltan eds, *Viaţă privată, mentalităţi colective şi imaginar social în Transilvania* (Cluj: University Press, 1996), pp. 164–8.

Catholic schools, and not in Transylvania's Reformed schools as had happened during the period of the principality's independence under Calvinist princes.[9]

The Transylvanian synod also defended the distinctiveness of the Greek Catholic Church within the Catholic world. In 1739 the synod agreed that acceptance of key points of Catholic doctrine in the spirit of the Council of Florence had been essential to the success of union with Rome. However, there was also some resistance to introducing elements of Catholic doctrine into liturgy books and other religious literature of the Greek Catholic Church.[10] Although Catholic doctrine was on the whole accepted within Transylvanian Greek Catholicism, the synod was determined that the church remain distinct from Rome in its liturgy and rites of public worship. This had been a sticking-point from the very beginning of the process of ecclesiastical unification, and maintaining eastern rites became the prime means of articulating the particular identity of the Greek Catholic Church. In 1742 the synod demanded that all those Greek Catholic priests who wished to use Latin rites should be prevented from doing so. The importance of not abandoning traditional rites was expressed by bishop Inochentie Micu Klein (1729–51) in terms of maintaining the identity of the Transylvanian Romanian community.[11] Romanians had no representation as a 'nation' in the Transylvanian diet of Hungarian nobles, German urban magistrates and Szeklers, and Klein led a concerted campaign at the Vienna court to have Romanians recognized as a fourth constitutional 'nation' in Transylvania. The results of the 1742 synod suggest that the ecclesiastical elite of the Greek Catholic Church had come to see their church as the most significant means of expressing the interests and identity of the Romanian 'national' community in Transylvania.[12]

The Transylvanian synod also tried to establish higher standards of conduct among Greek Catholic parish clergy as a professional order. In accordance with the principles of reformed Catholicism, new disciplinary and administrative obligations were imposed on local priests. The church hierarchy was determined to increase the levels of

---

[9] Micu Moldovan, *Acte Sinodale* (1872), vol. 2, pp. 108–14.

[10] 'Sacram unionem continentia 4 puncta et irremisibiliter noster v. Clerus observabit et tenebit, ad plura autem nullo sub praetextu adigatur'; Micu Moldovan, *Acte Sinodale* (1872), vol. 2, p. 83.

[11] *Supplex Libellus Valachorum* (1984), pp. 151–98; Francisc Pall, 'Inochentie Micu Klein, deschizător al luptei de emancipare națională a românilor transilvăneni; câteva întrebări și întregiri', *Apulum* 20 (1982), pp. 194–204.

[12] Micu Moldovan, *Acte Sinodale* (1872), vol. 1, p. 150; Dragomir, *Românii din Transilvania* (1963), p. 34.

education of the lower clergy and to improve their pastoral care of local communities. Priests who broke norms of moral behaviour were targeted by the synod and by bishops on regular tours of inspection of parishes. There were repeated resolutions against a range of offences, such as those against inappropriate priestly dress at synods in 1700, 1732 and 1742. Censures were handed down by synods against priests who got drunk or who went to the pub too often in 1700, 1725, 1728 and 1732, against priests who smoked in 1700, against bigamists in 1700 and 1728, and against those who neglected to hold church services in 1725, 1732 and 1742.[13] Ultimately, responsibility for investigating the standards of parish clergy across Transylvania fell to the bishop. The need to set up more effective administrative structures in the church was only slowly dealt with, and a consistory to help the bishop was set up only in the 1820s.[14]

The Transylvanian synod also monitored the practice of religion in local communities, particularly concerned with levels of attendance at church services, and with the effectiveness of parish clergy in educating their parishioners. Crucial to the success of attempts to improve popular understanding of religion and moral discipline in the Greek Catholic Church was some progress in raising the levels of education of parish clergy. Thanks to Klein and Petru Pavel Aron, a theological college and school were founded at the church's episcopal centre at Blaj (Balázsfalva/Blasendorf) in the early 1750s. Aron, who had studied at the College of the Congregation for the Propagation of Faith in Rome, was bishop of Făgăraş between 1752 and 1764. During this period the synod repeatedly stressed the need to raise the educational standards of both clergy and the laity, and the need to create and financially support schools and to develop their syllabus.[15]

Another means of spreading knowledge about the doctrine of the Greek Catholic Church was through catechisms and other religious literature. A synod held during the episcopate of Klein in the 1740s reinforced the need for all the provisions of union to be obeyed throughout the Greek Catholic community. Two early catechisms had circulated within the Transylvanian Greek Catholic Church. *Bread of the Innocents* was published by the Jesuit László Bárányi in 1702, based on the catechism of Peter Canisius, and in 1726 a catechism compiled

---

[13] Micu Moldovan, *Acte Sinodale* (1872), vol. 1, p. 150; vol. 2, pp. 97–8, 102, 110–11, 120–22, 149.

[14] Micu Moldovan, *Acte Sinodale* (1872), vol. 2, p. 72.

[15] Iacob Mârza, *Şcoală şi raţiune. Şcolile Blajului în epoca Renaşterii naţionale* (Cluj: Dacia, 1987); Augustin Bunea, *Episcopii Petru Pavel Aron şi Dionisie Novacovici* (Blaj: Tipografia Seminarului Arhidiecezan, 1902), p. 365.

by the Greek Catholic bishop of Mukačevo (Munkács), Joseph de Camellis, was translated into Romanian.[16] These were not the only early published writings which sought to root Catholic teaching in new Greek Catholic communities. The union with Rome was also defended in polemic works by the Jesuits, Márton Szentiványi and Andreas Freyberger, who was the author of a history of the ecclesiastical union.[17] Catechisms played a significant role in the Transylvanian Church because they presented clergy with the main tenets of faith in a concise and simple form which was also accessible to ordinary lay believers. The Greek Catholic clergy hierarchy believed that the frequent use of catechisms would establish familiarity with basic theological knowledge throughout the church and improve moral standards. Although the effects of this programme of catechizing were very slow to appear in Transylvania, some impact on the quality of lower clergy was made by this basic religious education at least by the second half of the eighteenth century. Core teachings of the new confession were at least conveyed to many rural communities, where literacy rates were beginning to rise by the early nineteenth century.[18]

While the impact of union and reform on rural and popular religion was only felt in the long term among Transylvania's Romanian community, from the middle decades of the eighteenth century a better-educated generation of Greek Catholic clergy emerged in the principality. During the period immediately following the acts of union, locals had made only a limited contribution to explaining the doctrine of the church. However, this changed from the 1740s thanks to clerics from gentry backgrounds such as Gerontie Cotore, Grigorie Maior and Petru Pavel Aron, who were trained at the Jesuit college in Cluj (Kolozsvár/Klausenburg), the Jesuit university in Trnava

---

[16] László Bárányi, *Piinea pruncilor, sau învăţătura credinţii creştineşti strânsa în mica sumă. Care o au scris în mici întrebăciuni şi răspunsuri ungureşti cinstitul pater Boroneai Laslo parohuşul besearicii catoliceşti de la Bălgrad. Şi s-au întors în limba românească de Duma Janăşu din Borbanţi* (Alba Iulia, 1702); *Catechismuş, sau învăţătura creştinească în folosul neamului rusesc din Ţara Ungurească. Dat afara prin osîrdia şi osteneala Mării Sale D: Ioan Iosif Decamilis, ipiscupul Sebastului şi al Muncaciului i proci* (Sâmbata Mare, 1726).

[17] Pompiliu Teodor, 'The Romanians from Transylvania, the Tradition of the Eastern Church, the Counter Reformation and the Catholic Reformation' in Maria Crăciun, Ovidiu Ghitta eds, *Ethnicity and Religion in Central and Eastern Europe* (Cluj: University Press, 1995), pp. 178–81; Martin Szent-Ivány, *Dissertatio Chronologico-Polemica de Ortu, Progressu ac Diminutione Schismatis Orari atque Graeci Ritus Ecclesiae cum Romana Ecclesia sot Votis exoptata reunione* (Tyrnava, 1703); Andreas Freyberger, *Historia Relatio Unionis Wallachicae cum Romana Ecclesia facta a 1701 eorumque, quae in unionis negotio sunbseruta sunt usque ad novembrem anni 1702* (Cluj: Clusium, 1996).

[18] Micu Moldovan, *Acte Sinodale* (1872), vol. 1, p. 148.

(Nagyszombat), and in Vienna and Rome. They returned to Transylvania to write clear explanations of the doctrinal principles and ritual practices of their church in Romanian. The religious literature which they produced was also partly driven by the crisis which faced the Greek Catholic Church in this period. A Serbian Orthodox monk, Visarion Sarai, crossed into Transylvania and instigated an anti-Catholic movement from 1744. Sarai preached on the truths of Orthodoxy and, although he spoke Serbian, Sarai was well-received perhaps because his words sounded similar to the traditional language of church liturgy in Romania, Old Slavonic. Miraculous powers were attributed to Sarai, and many Greek Catholic communities in south-western Transylvania returned to their 'ancestral Greek' faith, and expelled their Greek Catholic priests.[19] Romanian Greek Catholic clergy were intent on regaining the initiative in Transylvania, and the rest of this chapter will examine how they responded to this challenge and defended the confessional identity of the Greek Catholic Church.

Leading Greek Catholic clergy reacted to the success of itinerant Orthodox preachers through printed literature. In 1745 Gerontie Cotore translated the work of Louis Maimbourg, *On the Schism of the Greeks*, into Romanian. Cotore, then a student at Trnava in Hungary, later became the vicar general of the Transylvanian Church between 1754 and 1763. Cotore's history focused on the causes and consequences of the Greek schism for the Christian world and explained the work undertaken by the 1439 Florence Council. This history led up to the negotiations for union in Transylvania and tried to provide historical and theological justifications for the results of these discussions.[20] Cotore also responded to the propaganda of Visarion Sarai by completing a Romanian manuscript which explained the four points of doctrine agreed by the Council of Florence. This manuscript, 'The Articles of Faith', which only partially survives, was the first attempt by a Romanian Greek Catholic priest to write a theological treatise on the doctrine of the Church.[21] Cotore's tract, also written in Trnava, was clearly influenced by the Catholic environment in which he worked. Cotore's tract defended the agreement to recognize the supreme authority of the Pope and acceptance of the idea of purgatory. Cotore also used the work of Kristoph Peiechich, which had addressed

[19] Hitchins, *A Nation Discovered* (1999), pp. 61–84.

[20] Gerontie Cotore, 'Despre schismǎtica grecilor' and 'Articuluşurile cele de price' (1746), in the Romanian Academy Library of Cluj, manuscript no. 86.

[21] Cotore, 'Articuluşurile cele de price' (1746); *Manuscrisele româneşti din Biblioteca Centralǎ de la Blaj*, Nicolae Comşa ed. (Blaj: Tipografia Lumina, 1944), pp. 95–6; Teodor, 'The Romanians from Transylvania' (1995), pp. 181–2.

Romanian Orthodox clergy to defend the legitimacy of the Florentine agenda of union. However, Cotore proved reticent to condemn the lapses of faith of Greek 'schismatics'. Instead, he supported the particular Greek Catholic identity of the Transylvanian Church by quoting the assumed Latin origins of the Romanian people, which, he argued, gave them a common heritage with the Roman Church. While Transylvania's Romanians were thus encouraged to return to their Latin roots, Cotore also argued that they should retain much of Orthodox religious culture, a paradox which was at the heart of the development of Greek Catholic identity.[22]

In the second half of the eighteenth century printed texts were written by various leading clergy at Blaj to defend the union with Rome and to curtail 'schismatic' activity in the Romanian community. Clergy involved included Petru Pavel Aron and Grigorie Maior, based at the Basilian monastery of the Holy Trinity in Blaj which Inochentie Micu Klein had founded. Grigorie Maior had studied in Rome in the 1740s, and was later bishop of the Transylvanian church between 1773 and 1782. These Blaj clergy were responsible for the 1750 publication in Romanian, and later publication in Latin, of *The Flower of Truth, for the peace and love of the community, from the garden of Scripture ... freshly picked to show that the Union is nothing other than the faith and teachings of the Church Fathers*.[23] This text expressed the concern of the ecclesiastical elite at Blaj to defend the position of their church as part of the Catholic world, but also their determination to preserve their eastern ritual and liturgical traditions. The preface to *The Flower of Truth* listed recommended works for readers to consult by the Church Fathers, most of which were printed in Moldavia and Wallachia. This list reflected one of the central themes of the text, to assert that union with Rome did not imply any novelty or innovation in 'Our Holy Church' from the truths of scripture or from the historic Church.[24]

Within this context of consistent respect for the teachings of scripture, the Church Fathers, and the decisions of Church Councils, *The Flower of Truth* insisted on some points of difference between Orthodoxy and Greek Catholicism. The book quoted conciliar acceptance of the apostolic foundations of the Papacy and of the

---

[22] Cotore, 'Articuluşurile cele de price' (1746); Zoltán Tóth, 'Cotore Gerontius és az Erdélyi román nemzetiöntudot', *Hitel* (1944), pp. 84–95.

[23] *Floarea Adevărului pentru pacea şi dragostea de obşte. Din grădinile sfintelor scripturi prin mare strădania cucernicilor între ieromonaşi, în mănăstirea sfintei Troiţe de la Blaj la anul 1750 culeasă* (Blaj, 1750).

[24] *Floarea Adevărului* (1750), preface.

supreme authority of the Pope over the Church.[25] The text also discussed complex arguments over the issue of the Holy Spirit's origins from the Father and the Son ('*filioque*'), supporting points of argument by quotation from scripture and statements from Church Fathers.[26] A further chapter considered the administration of the Eucharist and argued that priests could use either leavened or unleavened bread, as the ancient Church had ordered priests to abide by local custom on this issue.[27] Purgatory was discussed under the title, 'for the souls of the deceased', and defined as 'the place of cleansing', upholding the Florentine resolution that there was no significant difference between the purgatory of the 'Latins' and the 'place to cleanse the soul' of the eastern Church.[28]

The Flower of Truth represented the first attempt in Transylvania to print a work in Romanian which explained and spread understanding of the principles of union with the Roman Church. The Blaj circle of clergy responsible for its production wished to explain the central doctrinal differences between the Greek Catholic and Orthodox Churches in an accessible form. However, the text was not a polemic attack against Orthodoxy, as the common theological roots of the two churches were stressed, and the decision of the Greek Catholic Church to abide by traditional rites was emphasized. *The Flower of Truth* was also published in Latin, attempting to inform non-Romanian Catholics in Transylvania about the Greek Catholic Church, in the wake of debates in the diet about the position of the Church.

In 1752 use of *The Flower of Truth* was prohibited by the Greek Catholic Church authorities, probably because it was perceived to identify too strongly with eastern traditions and had minimized differences between Catholicism and Orthodoxy. Cotore had imagined the universal Church to be like a tree with many branches but with a common trunk, an idea that had been present since the fifteenth century. Aeneas Sylvio Piccolomini, for example, had used the metaphor of the two eyes of Christianity to portray the relationship between Rome and Constantinople.

Later defences of union with Rome in Transylvania followed a much more cautious line on the common heritage of Orthodoxy and Catholicism. In 1755, during the episcopate of Petru Pavel Aron, *Christian teachings through questions and answers, for use in*

25 *Floarea Adevărului* (1750), pp. 6–24.
26 *Floarea Adevărului* (1750), pp. 27–8.
27 *Floarea Adevărului* (1750), pp. 41–2.
28 *Floarea Adevărului* (1750), p. 62.

schools was published in Romanian, and then translated into Latin in 1757.[29] Aron concentrated on the need to get greater conformity in localities to the official doctrines of the church, and worked to end traditional religious practices which he deemed superstitious. Aron's *Christian teachings*, which the bishop decided should be distributed to all priests, insisted that both the western and eastern churches wished for a union of faith in the spirit of the Council of Florence.[30] As with *The Flower of Truth*, Aron's text remained faithful to the principles of union with Rome, but stressed differences in ritual between the Latin Church and the Greek Catholic Church. However, at a time when the union needed to be strengthened through wider familiarity with Greek Catholic theology, the second part of Aron's work particularly stressed shared beliefs with Rome. In addition a dialogue, '*De sacra unione colloquia*', emphasized the ideas behind the union with the Roman Church in very explicit terms. Aron also wrote an open letter, 'The pastor's duty to the Godly flock', and *A Book to teach children how to read and to know Christian teachings*, which clearly defended Catholic understanding of the Holy Spirit, the host and purgatory.[31]

The Greek Catholic Church again faced an anti-union movement between 1758 and 1760, led by the Orthodox monk Sofronie from southern Transylvania. Sofronie proved to be a charismatic preacher, and led communities across southern Transylvania to revolt against the changes made to their religion. Peasants seized Greek Catholic church buildings in a climate of bitterness and violence between the confessional groups. Sofronie's movement led to a decree in July 1759 from Maria Theresa which recognized the Orthodox Church in Transylvania. In April 1761 Dionisie Novacovici was transferred from being Serbian bishop of Buda to become the new Orthodox bishop of Transylvania. The Greek Catholic Church responded again by defending its union with Rome, and canons from the Blaj church published a text in 1760 called *Dogmatic Learning*.[32] The printing press at Blaj also published a series of liturgical books, which were supposed to replace

---

29 Petru Pavel Aron, *Învăţătură creştinească, prin întrebări şi răspunsuri pentru procopseala şcoalelor* (Blaj, 1755); Petru Pavel Aron, *Doctrina Christiana ex probatis authoribus collecta ad usum huis scholasticae juventutis cooptata, cum adjecto de Sacra unione Colloquio* (Vienna, 1757).

30 Aron, *Învăţătură creştinească* (1755).

31 Petru Pavel Aron, 'The pastor's duty to the Godly flock'; Aron, *Despre Credinţa* (Blaj, n. d.); Zenovie Pâclişanu, 'Istoria bisericii române unite', *Perspective* 14–16 (1993), pp. 68–70.

32 *Păstoriceasca poslanie sau dogmatica Învăţătură a bisericii răsăritene către cuvântătoarea turmă* (Blaj, 1760).

Orthodox texts still commonly in use in Greek Catholic communities across Transylvania.[33]

In 1762 a pastoral letter by bishop Aron to Greek Catholics in his diocese was published in Romanian and Latin as *On the Holy Ecumenical Florentine Synod*. This letter again explained the '*exordium*' and points of union as they were decided by the representatives of the two churches.[34] Greek Catholics assumed that the fundamental points of union agreed at Florence were the basis for their own union, an understanding which remained the principal doctrinal focus of Greek Catholic writings throughout the eighteenth century. This letter was addressed to the clergy of Aron's diocese, aiming to regain support for union with Rome, to assist the efforts of those clergy who had remained loyal, and to prevent further losses to the Orthodox Church. During the height of anti-Catholic movements among Romanians in Transylvania, the attitudes of many clergy towards union had appeared ambivalent, and the text tried to legitimize the Greek Catholic Church above all by connecting it with the decisions taken at the Council of Florence. The publication of this letter in Latin suggests that there was also a need to profess the loyalty of the Greek Catholic Church within the structures of the Habsburg state. Aron's letter was even dedicated to Adolf Buccow, the military commander in Transylvania whose forces had restored order and destroyed several Orthodox monasteries in southern Transylvania.

In 1763 bishop Aron published the philosophical and theological works of John of Damascus in Latin, which was then used as a textbook at the school in Blaj.[35] As with other texts published from the 1740s, this book attempted to introduce an eastern element to Catholicism by using Greek writers in the school syllabus. Such efforts to establish the identity of the Greek Catholic Church, by explaining Catholic doctrine but preserving some elements of traditional Orthodox religion, continued during the episcopate of Atanasie Rednic. Rednic recommended that clergy use Aron's *Christian teachings* to explain Greek Catholic doctrine among their communities, and Aron's book became the most significant text used in the instruction of doctrine in Transylvania.[36]

---

[33] Printed liturgical books include *Straşnic* (Blaj, 1753), *Liturghier* (Blaj, 1756/1775), *Psaltire* (Blaj, 1756/1764), *Eulologhion* (Blaj, 1757), *Catavasier* (Blaj, 1762/1768), *Acatist* (Blaj, 1763/1774), *Evangheliar* (Blaj, 1765), *Apostol* (Blaj, 1767), *Penticostar* (Blaj, 1768), *Octoih* (Blaj, 1760/1770) and *Triod* (Blaj, 1771).

[34] Petru Pavel Aron, *Exordium et definitio Sanctae Oecumenicae synodi Florentinae ex antiqua greco latinae editione desumpto* (Blaj, 1762).

[35] *Opera philosophica et teologica Ioannis Damasceni: Dialecticam Phisicam et Hereses; Expositio accurate fidei orthodoxae* (Blaj, 1763); Bianu, Hodoş, *Bibliografia românească veche* (1910), vol. 2, pp. 160–61; vol. 4 (1944), p. 322.

[36] Pâclişanu, 'Istoria bisericii române unite' (1993), pp. 101–102.

During the period immediately following the acts of union between the Catholic Church and clergy from the Transylvanian Orthodox Church, the doctrine and identity of the new Greek Catholic Church was mostly presented by non-Romanian Jesuits. Romanian Greek Catholics only took the lead in defending the position of their Church from the middle decades of the eighteenth century. These defences concentrated above all on explaining the conditions of union in the context of the Council of Florence. Clergy returned again and again to explain the points of Catholic doctrine which had been accepted in discussions at synods, in catechisms and in other forms of religious literature. This continued insistence on spreading understanding of these basic points of union highlights the delicate roots which supported the Greek Catholic Church in Transylvania. These books display an impressive level of theological understanding and familiarity with sacred texts, works by Church Fathers, conciliar decisions, as well as with Latin and especially Orthodox theological literature. Authors were keen to emphasize both their allegiance to Florentine decisions and their adherence to eastern traditions. Aware of the dominant attitudes within Romanian communities, Greek Catholic writers were reticent to introduce changes in the ritual sphere or in the realm of traditional worship. This is probably why they emphasized the common traditions which they suggested existed in the Roman and Orthodox Churches.

Leading clergy who published defences of the Transylvanian Greek Catholic Church had to address a variety of audiences. First, they addressed the Latin Catholic hierarchy in Transylvania and beyond, reassuring them that they had not departed from any of the points of union which would have jeopardized the legal and financial privileges of their clergy. Second, they also had to give leadership to ordinary parish clergy, who had never been involved in the movement towards union, and whose education and social standing linked them firmly to the rural communities which they served. Finally, the Greek Catholic hierarchy also had to address the faithful of their communities, who proved ambivalent about their new Catholic identity when Orthodox movements affected Transylvania. This popular reluctance to accept the Greek Catholic Church in particular focused on the desire to maintain elements of traditional religion.

Confidence in the Greek Catholic Church was also severely weakened by the failed efforts of the Greek Catholic hierarchy to gain political status for the Romanian community within the Transylvanian constitution. The response of the educated clergy elite of the Greek Catholic Church to anti-Catholic movements and the return *en masse* of ordinary parishioners to Orthodoxy was to produce printed literature on the doctrine and history of their church. Educated at Catholic universities, figures like Gerontie Cotore and Petru Pavel Aron produced the first Romanian Greek Catholic printed texts, aiming to secure the loyalty of parish clergy and to spread understanding of Catholic doctrine within local communities. The intellectual clergy elite at Blaj attempted to forge an identity for Transylvanian Greek Catholicism which was based on support for a union of faith with Rome but which maintained traditional church rites. They opposed any further 'Latinization' of their religion and aimed to preserve the distinctiveness of their Greek Catholic Church within the Catholic world. Some printed texts were directed towards the elite, others at ordinary clergy, but all sought to legitimize the position of the church and stressed continued adherence to eastern rites. Through improved standards of education, catechisms and other printed literature, the clergy hierarchy was eventually able to spread awareness of the central points of Greek Catholic faith to the wider Romanian community in Transylvania. However, Greek Catholic identity was first established as an elite religion of intellectuals, which was only slowly able to win acceptance within the conservative rural society of Transylvania's Romanians.

CHAPTER ELEVEN

Attitudes towards the Jews and Catholic identity in eighteenth-century Poland

Judith Kalik

Polemical attacks against Judaism and attitudes towards the Jews have always played a role in shaping the confessional identity of the Catholic Church. In eighteenth-century Poland, home to the largest Jewish population in the world, connections between attitudes towards Jews and the identity of the Polish Catholic Church were especially significant. Attitudes taken by Polish Catholics towards Jews incorporated traditional views taken across the Catholic world but also contained several specifically Polish elements. These offered Polish clergy one means of expressing the particular identity of their Church, as against the general Catholic Church, and even more than this, to define different currents within the Polish Church itself. This chapter will outline some of these expressions of eighteenth-century Polish Catholic identity as reflected in different attitudes towards Jews and Judaism.

Around a half of all Jews lived within the territory of the Polish-Lithuanian commonwealth during the eighteenth century. According to records from 1765, the numbers of Jews in Poland had reached about 750,000 (200,000 in Lithuania and 550,000 in Poland). Although Jews thus constituted only around six per cent of the total population, it would be wrong to simply regard them as an insignificant religious or national minority in Poland. Jews occupied a central position in Polish society for two main reasons. First, they dominated trade in Poland's towns, especially during and after the Northern War which led to the general decline of urban society in Poland. This was despite the fact that Jews were not recognized as part of any existing estate and could not become municipal citizens, join guilds, belong to any profession or hold any public offices. Second, Jews participated in an extensive network of economic connections with Poland's magnates and could lease landowners' economic monopolies, such as the sale of alcohol.

From participation in the Northern War to the partitions of the state, eighteenth-century Poland was characterized by the decentralization and deterioration of the state apparatus and by the growing involvement of foreign powers in Polish affairs. In reaction to this, there were several attempts to reform the state, which was generally regarded as vital to prevent the complete destruction of Poland. The inspiration behind proposed reform measures came from opposing forces of extreme conservatism and revolutionary liberalism. The process of reform culminated in the so-called 'Four Years' Diet' of 1789–92, when Jewish rights of residence in Poland and the freedom of Jews to participate in the economic life of Polish towns were discussed. However, there were no practical results following a 1790 commission, and no changes to the position of Polish Jewry in the famous constitution of 3 May 1791, partly because of determined opposition from municipal representatives in the diet.

Within reform projects in eighteenth-century Poland, there were therefore concerted efforts to change the social position of Jewry. Reflecting general political divisions in Poland, these varied from plans to expel Jews from Poland altogether or to force Jews to work in agriculture, to 'enlightened' ideas of equal rights and equal access to education. The reaction of Jewish society in Poland to these ideas also varied, with enlightened proposals often rejected by Jews because they usually demanded the complete integration of Jews within Polish society and rejection of traditional ways of life. Most of these projects were never realized, but some did profoundly affect Jewish society in eighteenth-century Poland, notably the dissolution in 1764 of the Council of Four Lands (*Vaad Arba Aratzoth*) which was the central insitution of Jewish autonomy in Poland. The upheavals which Poland suffered during this period affected Jews as much as other social groups, resulting in such spiritual movements as Frankism, Khasidism and Hasqalah.[1]

Before the eighteenth century there had been two major strands of anti-Jewish literature in Poland. Considerable differences existed between attitudes expressed towards Jews and Judaism in Catholic Church literature and in material produced by urban elites. Areas of

---

[1] Jacob Goldberg, 'Poles and Jews in the seventeenth and eighteenth centuries: rejection or acceptance?', *Jahrbücher für Geschichte Osteuropas* 22 (1974), pp. 248–82; Jacob Goldberg, 'The Changes in the Attitude of Polish Society towards the Jews in the eighteenth century', *Polin* 1 (1986), pp. 35–48; Artur Eisenbach, *The Emancipation of the Jews in Poland, 1780–1870* (Oxford: Blackwell, 1991); Artur Eisenbach, 'The Four Years' Sejm and the Jews' in Antony Polonsky et al. eds, *The Jews in Old Poland, 1000–1795* (London: Tauris, 1993), pp. 73–89; Gershon David Hundert, *The Jews in a Polish Private Town: the Case of Opatow in the Eighteenth Century* (Baltimore: Johns Hopkins University, 1992); Moshe J. Rosman, *The Lords' Jews. Magnate-Jewish Relations in the Polish-Lithuanian Commonwealth during the eighteenth century* (Cambridge [MA]: Harvard University Press, 1990).

disagreement were so great that one might gain the impression of two distinct strains of Polish Christian thought with completely different perceptions of Jewry. The main focus of ecclesiastical anti-Jewish literature was religious polemic, and especially reflections upon the validity of claims about the Messiah, as well as attacks against Jewish interpretations of the Talmud. Urban burghers' anti-Jewish literature, however, which had its origins in commercial competition with Jews, discussed religion in an entirely different context. This literature was intended to insult Jews and to cause direct harm to their position within local societies. Literature produced by urban groups usually dealt with accusations of the blood libel, and with charges that Jews poisoned Christians, or drew connections between the Jews and the devil, or made other claims of Jewish superstitious and magical activity.[2]

During the eighteenth century considerable changes took place in the approach taken by some Polish clergy towards Jews. This shifted to become more similar to traditional urban attitudes, and thereby deviated from official Church doctrine. For example, until the eighteenth century the Church in Poland was practically uninvolved in accusations against Jews of blood libel which had been current in Polish society from the mid-sixteenth century.[3] The situation changed entirely in the eighteenth century as Polish clergy up to the ranks of the episcopacy became more involved in discussions about blood libel cases. The Church had always opposed such accusations, and indeed the Papacy continued to offer assistance to Jews in some blood libel cases brought by Polish clergy in the eighteenth century.[4] The reasons behind this change in the attitudes of many in the Polish Church towards Jews during the eighteenth century were manifold. The most decisive among them were the general decline of the Polish state and economy and the

---

2 Judith Kalik, 'The Catholic Church and the Jews in Poland' in Israel Bartal, Israel Gutman eds, *The Broken Chain: Polish Jewry through the Ages* (2 vols), (Jerusalem, 1997) vol. 1, pp. 193–208. Blood libel was the accusation that Jews were involved in the ritual murder of Christians, usually children, in order to use their blood for unleavened bread (*matzah*) during Passover. The earliest attested accusations of this kind were made by pagans against Christians, but later they were adapted by Christians and directed against the Jews. See Zenon Guldon, *Procesy o mordy rytualne w Polsce w xvi–xviii w.* (Kielce: DCF, 1995); Hanna Węgrzynek, *Czarna legenda Żydów: Procesy o rzekome mordy rytualne w dawnej Polsce* (Warsaw: Bellona, 1995).

3 Judith Kalik, 'The Catholic Church and the Jews in the Polish-Lithuanian Commonwealth in the seventeenth and eighteenth centuries' (Hebrew University of Jerusalem Ph.D, 1998), pp. 115–29; H. Węgrzynek, 'Ludność Żydowska wobec oskarzeń o popełnianie przestępstw o charakterze rytualnym', *Kwartalnik Historyczny* 4 (1994), pp. 13–27.

4 Majer Bałaban, *Letoldot ha-tnuah ha-franqistit* (2 vols), (Tel Aviv, 1934) vol. 1, pp. 99–100, 127–33, 282–5.

spread of patriotic sentiment in Poland in reaction to the series of wars waged on Polish soil by foreign powers. All of these tendencies found a particular expression in attitudes towards the Jews in Poland. It is also possible that there was some connection with the Polish Church's support for a strong monarchy and opposition to powerful landed magnates, who offered protection to Jews on their estates.[5] However, the most important factor driving changes in the opinions of Polish clergy during the eighteenth century was connected with internal divisions within the Catholic Church over the reception of ideas connected with the Enlightenment. A more enlightened wing of the church was opposed by more traditional and conservative clergy, and both sides in this conflict sharpened their respective positions against each other among other things, if not mainly, by means of their differing attitudes towards Jews and Judaism.[6]

Polish scholars, and most notably Józef Andrzej Gierowski, argue that during the eighteenth century Polish Catholic clergy split into two camps: those who were influenced by, and contributed to, movements related to the Enlightenment, and those who held reactionary views, exemplified over issues such as witch-hunting and the Jewish blood libel. As Gierowski has written, 'the Enlightenment brought an internal split inside the Polish Catholic Church ... A clear division is visible within the Polish clergy between traditionalists and supporters of new spiritual trends connected to the Enlightenment.'[7] However, this split between the Polish clergy, unlike other conflicts inside the Church, never took on an institutionalized form. It is important to stress that Gierowski claims that the Enlightenment began to affect Poland much earlier than the 1760s, the conventional date for some sort of starting-point for a Polish Enlightenment. Gierowski's concept of an 'early Enlightenment' in Poland applies to the period between the 1720s and 1760s, and according to his view the Polish Church already began to split into two camps over the reception of enlightened ideas during this period.[8] Therefore, one wing of the Polish Church was from around 1720 arguably beginning to become influenced by enlightened or pre-enlightened rationalism and by Jansenism. Clergy who were influenced by these movements did not in any way intend to become estranged from the main body of the Church, but rather aspired to use the logic of new intellectual trends to defend the Church's interests. The other

---

5 Józef Andrzej Gierowski, 'Kościół katolicki wobec wczesnego oświecenia w Polsce', *Roczniki Humanistyczne* 25 (1977), pp. 24–5.

6 Kalik, 'The Catholic Church and the Jews' (1997), pp. 25–95.

7 Gierowski, 'Kościół katolicki' (1977), p. 28.

8 Gierowski, 'Kościół katolicki' (1977), pp. 23–9.

conservative or reactionary camp within the Polish Church on the other hand maintained an aggressive stance towards other confessional groups, including making claims about Jewish blood libel.[9]

As these different elements within the Catholic Church turned their attention to Jews, 'pro-Jewish' literature began to appear in Poland during the eighteenth century written by some Catholic clergy. Such compositions conveyed a genuine interest in the nature of Judaism, considerable erudition about Jewish religion, the Talmud, Kabbalah and the Hebrew language, and expressed moderate views about the position of Jews within Polish society. This literary current in Poland was also characterized by the active condemnation of various anti-Jewish libels, and the repudiation of accusations made about connections between the Jews and the devil and about Jews' alleged use of magic. These texts also contained strong opposition to the forced conversion of Jews, especially Jewish children. However, the appearance of this 'pro-Jewish' literature influenced by Enlightenment thought caused a strong counter-reaction in the hardening attitudes of more conservative clergy towards Jews in Poland. New ideas were formulated by reactionary elements within the Polish Church, with a new style of polemical literature directed against enlightened movements. This new fundamentalist Catholic theology replaced the more traditional doctrinal discussions of earlier periods. Such reactionary literature was certainly intended to fight against the influence and threat posed by Jansenism, deism, atheism and naturalism, but much anti-Jewish literature was also produced.[10]

The most important institution which eventually gathered together many of the more enlightened Polish clergy, and gave expression to their desire for some degree of independence for the Polish Church from Rome, was the Commission for National Education (*Komisja Edukacji Narodowej*) established in July 1773. Among other leading members of this institution were the famous publicist and politician, Hugo Kołłątaj, the Polish primate, Michał Poniatowski, and the bishop of Wilna, Ignaci Massalski.[11] Many other members of this Commission, which initiated radical school reforms, were former Jesuits, but even more were drawn from the ranks of Piarists. The Piarists were particularly strongly influenced by Enlightenment thought, although paradoxically some, such as Stanisław Konarski, became well-known as anti-Semites. This Commission for National Education, because of its support for greater

---

9 Andrzej Zakrzewski, *Idee Oświecenia w kazaniach polskich* (Częstochowa, 1986), pp. 31–46.

10 Gierowski, 'Kościół katolicki' (1977), p. 24.

11 Amboise Jobert, *Komisja Edukacji Narodowej w Polsce (1773–1794) jej działo wychowania obywatelskiego* (Wrocław: Zaklad Narodowy, 1979).

independence for the Polish Church, was vehemently opposed by the Papal nuncio, Giuseppe Garampi, who even attempted to gain some assistance from the Russian tsar to support his cause.

Clergy members of the Commission for National Education put forward reform projects for the Jewish population in Poland and expressed positive views about Jews. Many of these prelates also served as high state officials and their programme of reforms, influenced by enlightened ideas, mainly aimed to consolidate the collapsing apparatus of the Polish state.[12] Projects with reforming objectives relating to the life of Jews in Poland were submitted by Kołłątaj to the 'Four Years' Diet'. Similar attempts to broaden religious tolerance, which would have allowed for the practical emancipation of Polish Jewry, were the most radical expression of Enlightenment influence on such leading Catholic clergy.[13] Garampi's successor as Papal nuncio in Poland, Giovanni Andrea Archetti, was particularly enraged by an attempt to reform Cracow Academy, as proposed by Kołłątaj. In his report to Rome, Archetti claimed that Kołłątaj held views 'hostile to Christianity', by which he probably intended to signify some sort of rationalistic, perhaps even deistic or naturalistic influence on his thought.[14]

The stance which this circle of leading Polish clerics took on issues affecting Jews was connected to the responsibility of the Commission for National Education to assume supreme authority over all educational institutions within the Polish state, including all Orthodox and Jewish schools. Mateusz Butrymowicz, head of a commission for Jewish cultural and social reform during the 'Four Years' Diet' proposed to admit Jews into mainstream Catholic schools. However, when Kołłątaj was appointed by the diet to resolve this issue in 1792, he concluded that Jews should have their own schools under the supervision of the Commission. This latter view was also supported by some Jews, such as intellectuals around Moses Mendelson and Mendel Satanower. Despite all these plans and discussions, in the end these educational projects were rejected by the diet.[15]

One of the most important features of the impact of Enlightenment thought within the Catholic Church were attempts to eradicate generally-held prejudices within the Polish Catholic community. This

---

[12] Zakrzewski, *Idee Oświecenia* (1986), p. 32.

[13] Jerzy Michalski, 'Sejmowe projekty reformy położenia ludności żydowskiej w polsce w latach 1789–1792' in Michalski, *Lud żydowski w narodzie polskim* (Warsaw: Instytut Historii Polskiej Akademii Nauk, 1966), pp. 20–44.

[14] Janusz Tazbir, *Historia kościoła katolickiego w Polsce (1460–1795)* (Warsaw: Wiedza Powszechna, 1966), pp. 199–203.

[15] Jobert, *Komisja Edukacji Narodowej* (1979), pp. 204, 248–9.

was directed towards curbing enthusiasm for witch-hunting, questioned ideas of Polish exceptionalism wrapped up in notions of Sarmatia, and challenged views which supported the persecution of Jews. Thus, practically all clergy members of the Commission for National Education opposed the forced conversion of Jews, and particularly any attempts to convert Jewish children. In 1783 the bishop of Wilna, Ignaci Massalski, and in July 1785 the archbishop of Gniezno, the administrator of Cracow, and the primate of Poland and Lithuania, Michał Poniatowski, published pastoral letters prohibiting all clergy and laity from attempting to gain the conversion of Jewish children without parental consent.[16] Polish clergy had generally opposed the forced conversion of Jews since it contradicted official church teaching on the conditions for true faith. Even in the first half of the seventeenth century a priest called Symon Starowolski had explained that the law did not punish Jews for their refusal to accept Christianity, since the Catholic Church did not recognize the conversion of any non-believer by force.[17] Only a very small minority of clergy expressed sympathy with calls for the forced conversion of Jews which mainly came from urban groups, who often demanded that Jews either be compelled to convert or face expulsion from Polish territory.[18] Until the eighteenth century a part of the Polish Catholic clergy maintained that persuasion could bring Jews to true faith. However, many priests, especially during the seventeenth century, argued that no special efforts should be made to convert Jews because they should remain in their religion until the imminently awaited time of final judgement, when it was prophesied that they would voluntarily accept Christianity. This ambiguity within Christian theology on the conversion of Jews was also complicated by the widely held views of aristocratic and urban elites, educated in Jesuit schools. They usually remained great enthusiasts for the conversion of Jews, and in some individual cases became more active than the clergy in this cause.[19]

During the eighteenth century the stance of the great majority of Polish Catholic clergy changed on the issue of converting Jews. The view that more effort should be devoted to converting Jews in order to usher in the salvation of the whole world began to become more popularly held. In 1704, Pope Clement XI confirmed the 1584 bull of Gregory

---

16 Archiwum Główne Akt Dawnych (hereafter AGAD), 'Dokumenty papierowe, 399'.

17 Symon Starowolski, *Prawdziwe obyaśnienie braterskiego napomnienia ad dissidentes in regione przed dwiema laty wydanego* (1646), p. 78.

18 Jacob Goldberg, *Ha-mumarim be-mamlekhet Polin-Lita* (Jerusalem, 1985), pp. 25–31.

19 Goldberg, *Ha-mumarim* (1985), pp. 27–8, 30–31.

XIII, which required the appointment of special preachers and priests to preach in synagogues. These priests were supposed to visit major Jewish centres on a weekly basis, in order to reveal to them the truth of the Christian message primarily using the Old Testament. Instructions emphasized the need to persuade local Jews to convert, and to preach without causing insult to Jewish audiences.[20] This change in Catholic policy affected Poland in particular, and during the eighteenth century Polish clerics began to preach in synagogues. Franciśek Kobelski, bishop of Łuck, with broadly 'pro-Jewish' attitudes, and the more anti-Semitic Dominican priest, Wawrzyniec Obłocimski, were both leading preachers in these campaigns.[21]

In a 1749 report Kobelski wrote that he had preached in synagogues across his diocese in order to try to convert Jews. He related that from the beginning his efforts to encourage conversions were obstructed by the hostility of local magnates, but with God's help he had been permitted to enter synagogues. Hugo Kołłątaj later wrote about Kobelski;

> The bishop of Łuck was a man of great diversity of action, his efforts were directed towards the education of the people: he travelled himself throughout his diocese and preached for the people. This was a man of sweet character, and his special desire was to convert the Jews and to argue with them, and he even preached in their synagogues.[22]

Kobelski's experiences led him to conclude that the Papacy ought to renew again Gregory XIII's bull dealing with the conversion of the Jews.[23] Kobelski published a collection of his sermons written for Jews in Poland,

---

[20] P. Browe, *Die Judenmission im Mittelalter und die Papste* (Rome: SALER, 1942), pp. 13–55; Shlomo Simonson, *Ha-kes ha-qadosh ve-ha-yehudim* (Tel Aviv, 1994); M. Morawski, 'Stanowisko kościoła wobec niebezpieczeństwa żydowskiego w dawnej Polsce' *Ateneum Kapłańskie* 41 (1938), p. 3.

[21] Goldberg, *Ha-mumarim* (1985), pp. 31–3; Bałaban, *Letoldot ha-tnuah ha-franqistit* (1934), pp. 95–100; Jedrzej Kitowicz, *Opis obyczajów za panowania Augusta III* (Wrocław: Zakladu Narodowego, 1951), p. 175; Władysław Smoleński, *Przewrót umysłowy w Polsce wieku xviii* (Warsaw: Panstwowy Instytut, 1949), p. 154; Władysław Smoleński, 'Stan i sprawa Żydów polskich w xviii w.', *Pisma Historyczne* 2 (Cracow, 1901), pp. 223–93; N. M. Gelber, 'Die Taufbewegung unter den polnischen Juden im xviii Jahrhundert', *Monatsschrift für Geschichte und Wissenschaft des Judentums* 32 (1924), p. 227; B. Rok, 'Stosunek polskiego kościoła katolickiego do sprawy żydowskiej w 1 połowie xviii wieku' in Krystyn Matwijowski ed., *Z historii ludności żydowskiej w Polsce i na Śląsku* (Wrocław: Uniwersytetu Wrocławskiego, 1994), pp. 91–2.

[22] Jan Hulewicz ed., *Stan oświecenia w Polsce w ostatnich latach panowania Augusta III (1750–1764)* (Wrocław, 1953), p. 235; Goldberg, *Ha-mumarim*, (1985), p. 32.

[23] Paul Rabikauskas ed., *Relationes Status Diocesium in Magno Ducatu Lituaniae* (2 vols), (Rome: Academiae Lituanae Catholicae Scientiarum, 1971–78), vol. 1, p. 155.

adding as a supplement his discussions with the Jewish community at Brody. In the foreword to this book, Kobelski addressed priests who would preach these sermons and explained to them why a special effort should be made in order to bring Christian knowledge to the Jews. According to Kobelski, Jews should not be held guilty because of their ignorance of Christian doctrine, since they simply required to be enlightened about the truth of the gospel. Kobelski saw this task as an obligation which he shared with all the other priests in his diocese. He argued that if Catholic priests truly loved the body of Christ, which symbolized the unity of the Church, then they should try to bring every sheep into the flock.[24] Kobelski's efforts at converting Jews in his diocese were not his only public intervention on matters relating to Jews. He also defended Jews before the Polish diet in 1748, when a proposal was made to dissolve the Council of Four Lands and to take direct control of the collection of the Jewish poll tax. Kobelski delivered a speech in favour of the contribution of Jews to the economic life of Poland, and argued that the Jewish poll tax should not exceed a tolerable level of burden on the Jewish community.[25]

Kobelski was not alone in his efforts to publish sermons which others might copy when preaching to Jewish audiences in synagogues. A collection of sermons, delivered for the Jewish community at Komarnie by the bishop of Przemyśl in 1797, was also later published by a Carmelite monk, Gabriel Jakubowski.[26] Delivering sermons to Jews in their synagogues became very common in eighteenth-century Poland, and was connected with changing attitudes towards the conversion of Jews within the church across the Continent. It is possible that the revival of the idea of 'return of the Jews' during the eighteenth century might also be connected to some degree to the influence of Jansenism, which also began to affect Poland during this period.[27]

---

24 Francisek Kobelski, *Swiatło na oświecenie narodu niewernego to iest kazania w synagogach żydowskich miane, oraz reflexye y list odpowiadaiący na pyt-ania synagogi brodzkiey* ... (Lwów, 1746).

25 Bałaban, *Letoldot ha-tnuah ha-franqistit* (1934), p. 95; Judith Kalik, *Ha-atzulah ha-polanit vw-ha-yehudim be-mamlekhet Polin-Lita be-rei ha-tkhikah bat ha-zman,* (Jerusalem: Y. L. Magnes, 1997), pp. 25–36.

26 Gabriel Jakubowski, *Analogia między nauką ewangelii i rozsądnym zdaniem siedm kaza-ń przygodnich o błędach Zydow miana do kahału w Komarnie. Dyssertacia v dziełka trzy xiędza Gabriela Jakubowskiego xx. Karmelitów bosych zakonu kapłana, plebana ż-urawickieg* (Przemyśl, 1803).

27 D. Banqir, 'Reayon shivat ha-yehudim be-yansenism ha-tzarfati' in Banqir, *Bein yisrael le-umot* (Jerusalem, 1988), pp. 71–86; Samuel Ettinger, 'Reshit tmurah be-yakhasah shel ha-khevrah ha-eiropit le-yehudim' in Ettinger, *Ha-anti-shemiyut be-et ha-khadashah* (Tel Aviv, 1978), pp. 29–56; Samuel Ettinger, 'Yehudim ve-yahadut be-einei ha-deistim ha-angliim be-meah ha-18', *Zion* 29 (1964), p. 184; Goldberg, *Ha-mumarim* (1985), p. 24.

The attitude of the Church towards other heterodox religious groups, including followers of Jacob Frank, was also linked to ideas about the conversion of Jews.[28] Public disputes were staged between Jews and Frankists under the auspices of the Catholic Church, with at least some Polish Catholic clergy believing that they were realizing an apocalyptic vision of the 'return of the Jews to true faith'. Another aspect of this apocalyptic vision was the idea that Jews would convert other Jews to Christianity. A unique insight into this understanding of Frankism is revealed by a 1759 pastoral letter issued by the bishop of Gniezno and Polish primate, Władysław Aleksander Łubieński. Łubieński urged all clergy within his jurisdiction, and especially in his diocese, to contribute money for those Jews who were willing to try to convert other Jews to Christianity. He wrote that the conversion of the Jews was a sign of the end times, with the fulfilment of prophecy that the remnants of the house of Jacob will convert the Jews, or in other words that Jews themselves would persuade other Jews to accept Christianity. Therefore, according to Łubieński, it was necessary to help such Jews, and he published his letter to collect donations for this work from parish priests and other clergy in his diocese.[29]

Several periodicals which were published by priests largely for a clerical audience also played an important part in debates inside the Catholic Church about Jews and Judaism in Poland during the eighteenth century. Most influential among these periodicals were *Monitor*, published by Franciszek Bohomolec from 1765, *Pastimes Pleasant and Useful (Zabawy przyjemne i pożyteczne)*, published by bishop Adam Naruszewicz from 1769, and *The Historical-Political Memoir (Pamiętnik hystoryczno-polityczny)*, published by Piotr Switkowski from 1782. These periodicals served as the stage for lively discussion between supporters of various currents of thought in the Polish Church. Prominent enlightened clergy used these journals to promote ideas of tolerance towards religious minorities, including Jews. Projects to reform the everday life of Jewish communities were also debated with great enthusiasm in the periodical published by Switkowski.[30] Switkowski attacked anti-Semitic opinions promoted in

---

[28] Frankism was a very important spiritual movement in eighteenth-century Poland. Jacob Frank tried to reform Judaism using Kabbalah, and revived some aspects of the Shabtai Zvi messianic movement of the seventeenth century. Banned by the Jewish establishment, Frank converted to Christianity (and was baptized as Joseph), and later took part in several public disputes with Jews. However, his continuing messianic aspirations led him into confrontations with the Catholic Church. Arrested for heresy, he was eventually released by Russian troops and left Poland.

[29] AGAD, 'Nuncjatura stolicy apostolskej, syg. 006', pp. 160–63.

[30] Irena Dzikowska, *Pamiętnik historyczno-polityczny Piotra Switkowskiego, 1782–1792* (Cracow: Uniwersytetu Jagiellonskiego, 1960), pp. 72–212.

other publications, and defended the Jews against their more radical opponents. Switkowski and other writers with similar opinions were very clearly influenced by western Enlightenment thinkers, and especially by Jean-Jacques Rousseau.[31] Switkowski claimed in his periodical that the poor social condition of Jewish communities across the Continent was caused by the past persecution of the Jews during the 'dark ages'. He also suggested that the abrogation of their constitutional and economic rights had led to their poor record as subjects of the crown, and that if their rights were restored then their contribution to society would surely improve.[32]

A clear division emerged during the eighteenth century between what might be termed 'pro-Jewish' enlightened clergy and reactionary anti-Jewish priests. However, the lines of division were not entirely consistent, and many clergy who were fervent in their anti-Semitism were also among supporters of some enlightened ideas in Poland. For example, some of the anti-Semitic periodicals were published by clergy who were also to some degree influenced by enlightened ideas.[33] One group, influenced by physiocratic ideas about governing society according to a naturally inherent order, demanded the assimilation of Jews into Polish society. They argued that Jews must change their traditional occupations as a condition for acceptance by the rest of Polish society. Mateusz Butrymowicz proposed to withdraw Jewish rights to produce and sell alcohol, and to divert Jews into agricultural and artisanal activity, to conscript Jews for service in the army, and to strip Jewish communities of all their autonomy except over religious affairs.[34]

This other side of Polish Catholic enlightened attitudes towards the Jews above all expected them to become 'like other men'. The bishop of Lifland, Józef Kazimierz Kossakowski, was another among a number of anti-Jewish clergy who engaged with enlightened ideas. This is clear from passages concerning the Jews in his book *For the Parish Priest* published at the end of the eighteenth century. The bishop of Wrocław, Hieronim Sierakowski, who supported new ideas on the church's organization and the duties of the episcopacy, can serve as a further example of the same group of clergy. The Piarist, Stanisław Konarski,

---

31 Bogusław Leśnodorski, 'Idee polityczne Jana Jakuba Rousseau w Polsce' in Lesnodorski, *Wiek xix, prace ofiarowane Stefanowi Kieniewiczowi w 60 rocznic ę urodzin* (Warsaw, 1967), pp. 29–48.

32 Emanuel Ringelblum, 'Żydzi w świetle prasy warszawskiej wieku xviii-go', *Miesięcznik Zydowski* 2 (1932), pp. 489–518.

33 Ringelblum, 'Żydzi w świetle prasy warszawskiej wieku xviii-go' (1932), p. 46.

34 Dzikowska, *Pamiętnik historyczno-polityczny Piotra Switkowskiego* (1960), pp. 72, 208–212.

was another central figure in the reception of enlightened ideas in Poland. Konarski initiated radical reform within the education system, yet remained conservative on questions relating to the position of Polish Jewry. According to his syllabus drawn up for use in Piarist schools, pupils should learn about the need to prohibit Jews from selling wine or to be engaged in any other trade harmful to Catholics. Jews ought to be compelled to undertake hard agricultural labour and to be resettled where necessary. Konarski also suggested that pupils discuss whether or not the Jews should be expelled from Poland altogether.[35] Konarski's writings also made traditional accusations against Jews, typical of urban ideas before the eighteenth century. Konarski accused Jews of offering bribes to ensure that diets dissolved without reaching any decisions, and he prayed that during some future diet 'the Jews will fall asleep'. He also accused the Jews of dominating Polish trade, causing the bankruptcy of Christian merchants, of forging money and of completely ruining Polish towns.[36]

Some laity influenced by enlightened ideas within the social elite, such as the one-time chancellor, Andrzej Zamojski, even reached the conclusion the Jews should be expelled from Poland. Zamojski's law-code proposed that every six years a census of Jews should be made, and that only those with sufficient means to maintain themselves, or whose presence was of benefit to the state, should be allowed to remain. This was intended to exempt only merchants worth more than 1,000 Polish zloty, and various categories of craftsmen and inn-keepers.[37] All other Jews should be forced to leave Poland, and those who stayed were to be given compulsory labour service.[38] Such projects were influenced by the expulsion of Jews from Royal Prussia by Frederick II, but received a mixed reception among Catholic clergy. Opponents sought the support of Pope Benedict XIV, who had explicitly prohibited the expulsion of the Jews in an address to the Polish bishops.[39] Benedict had complained that Jews often lived among Christians in Poland, contrary to canonical requirements for their segregation, and noted that Catholic peasants in many Polish villages were subject to labour duties imposed by Jews who

---

[35] Stanisław Konarski, *Pisma wybrane*, Juliusz Nowak-Długewski ed. (2 vols), (Warsaw: Panstwowy Instytut, 1952), vol. 2, p. 234.

[36] Konarski, *Pisma wybrane* (1952), vol. 2, pp. 126, 183.

[37] Andrzej Zamoyski, *Zbiór praw sądowych przez ... ułożony* (1778), no. 2, art. 32.

[38] Smoleński, *Przewrót umysłowy* (1949), pp. 256–7; Y. Halperin, 'Al sakanat girush le-klal Yisrael be-Polin ve-Lita be-makhtzit ha-sh niya shel ha-meah ha-18', *Zion* 17 (1952), pp. 65–74.

[39] Benedict XIV, *Epistola encyclica ad primatem, archiepiscopos, et episcopos regni Poloniae de his, quae vetita sunt Hebraeis habitantibus in iisdem civitatibus & locis, in quibus habitant Christiani* (Lwów, 1752).

held leased property. However, the main subject of Benedict's address was his strict prohibition against the expulsion of Jews from Poland. Benedict recalled that when the persecution of Jews began in France and Germany during the thirteenth century the church had followed the lead of Saint Bernard and Petrus of Cluny who opposed such measures. He demanded that the Polish Church should follow their historic example, but reiterated his insistence that no church property should be leased to the Jews, as he claimed happened all the time in Poland, and ordered his nuncio to supervise observation of all his rulings on these issues.[40]

The Catholic clergy in Poland was profoundly divided in its reaction to various streams of enlightened thought during the eighteenth century. Attitudes towards the Jews and Judaism served as one of the elements which divided the two camps, while diversity within the reception of different enlightened ideas is also clear in the attitudes of some more enlightened and yet anti-Semitic clergy. That attitudes towards Jews served as such a significant expression of these different wings within the eighteenth-century Polish Catholic Church highlights the significance of Jews within Poland's confessional environment. It is also suggestive of the role which non-Christian communities could play in defining currents of Christian identity in the diverse confessional environment of east-central Europe.

---

[40] Benedict XIV, *Epistola encyclica* (1752).

Bibliography

Bahlcke, Joachim, *Regionalismus und Staatsintegration im Widerstreit: Die Länder der Böhmischen Krone im ersten Jahrhundert der Habsburgerherrschaft (1526–1619)* (Munich: Oldenbourg, 1994).

—— and Arno Strohmeyer eds, *Konfessionalisierung in Ostmitteleuropa: Wirkungen des religiösen Wandels in 16. und 17. Jahrhunderts in Staat, Gesellschaft und Kultur* (Stuttgart: Steiner, 1999).

Bák, János, and Béla Király eds, *From Hunyadi to Rákóczi. War and Society in Late Medieval and Early Modern Hungary* (New York: Brooklyn College Press, 1982).

Balázs, Mihály, and Gizella Keserű eds, *György Enyedi and Central European Unitarianism in the sixteenth and seventeenth centuries* (Budapest: Balassi, 2000).

Bârlea, Octavian, *Ostkirchliche Tradition und westlicher Katholizismus. Die Rumänische Unierte Kirche zwischen 1713–1727* (Munich: Academy of the Socialist Republic of Romania, 1966).

Benz, Ernst, *Wittenberg und Byzanz. Zur Begegnung und Auseinandersetzung der Reformation und der östlich-orthodoxen Kirche* (2nd edn), (Munich: Wilhelm Fink, 1971).

Bérenger, Jean, *A History of the Habsburg Empire, 1700–1918* (Harlow: Longman, 1997).

Binder, Ludwig, *Grundlagen und Formen der Toleranz in Siebenbürgen bis zur Mitte des 17. Jahrhunderts* (Cologne-Vienna: Böhlau, 1976).

Bireley, Robert, *Religion and Politics in the Age of the Counterreformation: Emperor Ferdinand II William Lamormaini, S.J. and the Formation of Imperial Policy* (Chapel Hill [NC]: University of North Carolina Press, 1981).

Brady, Thomas, Heiko Oberman, and James Tracey eds, *Handbook of European History, 1400–1600: Late Middle Ages, Renaissance and Reformation, vol. 2. Visions, Programmes and Outcomes* (Leiden: Brill, 1995).

Bucsay, Mihály, *Der Protestantismus in Ungarn, 1521–1978. Ungarns Reformationskirchen in Geschichte und Gegenwart. 1. Im Zeitalter der Reformation, Gegenreformation und katholischen Reform* (Vienna: Böhlau, 1977).

Caccamo, Domenico, *Eretici Italiani in Moravia, Polonia, Transilvania (1558–1611)*. *Studi e documenti* (Chicago: Newberry Library, 1970).

Crăciun, Maria, and Ovidiu Ghitta eds, *Ethnicity and Religion in Central and Eastern Europe* (Cluj: University Press, 1995).

—— and Ovidiu Ghitta eds, *Church and Society in Central and Eastern Europe* (Cluj: University Press, 1998).

Dán, Róbert, and Antal Pirnát eds, *Antitrinitarianism in the second half of the sixteenth century* (Budapest: Akadémiai kiadó, 1982).

Dillon, Kenneth J., *King and Estates in the Bohemian Lands 1526–1564* (Brussels: Les editions de la Librairie Encyclopédique, 1976).

Eberhard, Winfried, *Konfessionsbildung und Stände in Böhmen 1478–1530* (Munich-Vienna: Oldenbourg, 1981).

—— *Monarchie und Widerstand: Zur ständischen Oppositionsbildung im Herrschaftssytem Ferdinands I in Böhmen* (Munich: Oldenbourg, 1985).

Eisenbach, Artur, *The Emancipation of the Jews in Poland, 1780–1870* (Oxford: Blackwell, 1991).

Evans, Robert J. W., *The Making of the Habsburg Monarchy, 1550–1700: an Interpretation* (Oxford: Clarendon, 1979).

—— and Trevor V. Thomas eds, *Crown, Church and Estates: Central European Politics in the Sixteenth and Seventeenth Centuries* (London: Macmillan, 1991).

Fata, Márta, *Ungarn, das Reich, der Stephanskrone, im Zeitalter der Reformation und Konfessionalisierung. Multiethnizität, Land und Konfession 1500 bis 1700* (Münster: Aschendorff, 2000)

Forster, Marc, *The Counter-Reformation in the Villages. Religion and Reform in the Bishopric of Speyer, 1560–1720* (Ithaca, [NY]: Cornell University Press, 1992).

Fudge, Thomas A., *The Magnificent Ride: The First Reformation in Hussite Bohemia* (Aldershot: Ashgate, 1998).

Gilmont, Jean-François ed., *The Reformation and the book* [tr. Karin Maag] (Aldershot: Ashgate, 1998).

Grell, Ole Peter, and Robert Scribner eds, *Tolerance and Intolerance in the European Reformation* (Cambridge: University Press, 1996).

Gudziak, Borys, *Crisis and Reform. The Kyivan Metropolitanate, the Patriarchate of Constantinople and the Genesis of the Union of Brest* (Cambridge [MA]: Harvard University Press, 1998).

Halecki, Oscar, *From Florence to Brest* (Rome: Sacrum Poloniae Millenium, 1958).

Hitchins, Keith, *A Nation Discovered. Romanian Intellectuals and the Idea of Nation 1700–1848* (Bucharest: Editura Enciclopedică, 1999).

Hsia Po-chia, Ronald, *Social Discipline in the Reformation: Central Europe 1550–1750* (London: Routledge, 1992).

Hutter, Ulrich ed., *Martin Luther und die Reformation in Ostdeutschland und Südost-Europa* (Sigmaringen: Thorbecke, 1991).

Ingrao, Charles ed., *State and Society in Early Modern Austria* (West Lafayette [IN]: Purdue University Press, 1994).

Kann, Robert, *A History of the Habsburg Empire 1526–1918* (Berkeley [CA]: University of California Press, 1977).

—— and Zdeněk David, *The Peoples of the Eastern Habsburg Lands 1526–1918. A History of East Central Europe 6* (Seattle: University of Washington Press, 1984).

Kloczowski, Jerzy, *A History of Polish Christianity* (Cambridge: University Press, 2000).

Köpeczi, Béla ed., *A History of Transylvania* (Budapest: Akadémiai Kiadó, 1994).

Maag, Karin ed., *The Reformation in Eastern and Central Europe* (Aldershot: Scolar, 1997).

Macha, Joseph, *Ecclesiastical Unification. A Theoretical Framework Together With Case Studies From the History of Latin-Byzantine Relations* (Rome: Institutum Orientalium Studiorum, 1974).

Mączak, Antoni, Henryck Samsonowicz, and Peter Burke eds, *East-Central Europe in transition from the fourteenth to the seventeenth centuries* (Cambridge: University Press, 1985).

Murdock, Graeme, *Calvinism on the Frontier, 1600–1660. International Calvinism and the Reformed Church in Hungary and Transylvania* (Oxford: Clarendon, 2000).

Musteikis, Antanas, *The Reformation in Lithuania. Religious fluctuations in the sixteenth century* (New York: Columbia University Press, 1988).

Nischan, Bodo, *Prince, People, and Confession: The Second Reformation in Brandenburg* (Philadelphia [PA]: University of Pennsylvania Press, 1994).

—— *Lutherans and Calvinists in the Age of Confessionalism* (Aldershot: Ashgate, 1999).

Ozment, Steve, *The Reformation in the Cities. The appeal of Protestantism to sixteenth-century Germany and Switzerland* (New Haven [CT]: Yale University Press, 1975).

Pekar, Athanasius, *The History of the Church in Carpathian Rus'* (New York: Columbia University Press, 1992).

Pettegree, Andrew, ed. *The Early Reformation in Europe* (Cambridge: University Press, 1992).

Rady, Martyn, *Nobility, Land and Service in Medieval Hungary* (London: Palgrave, 2000).

Sauzet, Robert ed., *Les frontières religieuses en Europe du 15e au 17e siècle* (Paris: Librairie Philosophique, 1992).

Schilling, Heinz, *Religion, Political Culture and the Emergence of Early Modern Society* (Leiden: Brill, 1992).

Schmidt, Heinrich Richard, *Konfessionalisierung im 16. Jahrhundert* (Munich: Oldenbourg, 1992).

Scribner, Robert and Trevor Johnson eds, *Popular Religion in Germany and Central Europe, 1400–1800* (London: Macmillan, 1996).

Subtelny, Orest, *Domination of Eastern Europe. Native nobilities and foreign absolutism* (Kingston [ONT]: McGill University Press, 1986).

Sugar, Peter, *Southeastern Europe under Ottoman rule, 1354–1804. A History of East Central Europe 5* (Seattle: University of Washington Press, 1977).

Tazbir, Janusz, *A State Without Stakes: Polish religious toleration in the sixteenth and seventeenth centuries* (New York: Kosciuszko Foundation, 1973).

Tóth, István György, *Literacy and written culture in early modern central Europe* (Budapest: CEU Press, 2000).

Wilbur, Earl, *A History of Unitarianism in Transylvania, England and America* (Cambridge [MA]: Harvard University Press, 1952).

Williams, George, *The Radical Reformation* (Philadelphia [PA]: Westminster Press, 1962).

Zach, Krista, *Orthodoxe Kirche und rumänisches Volksbewusstsein im 15. bis 18. Jahrhundert* (Wiesbaden: Harrassowitz, 1977).

Zeman, Jarold, *The Anabaptists and the Czech Brethren in Moravia 1526–1628* (The Hague and Paris: Mouton, 1969).

Index

Wallachia 103, 170, 175
Wallachian 57
Warsaw, Confederation of (1573)
    21
White Mountain, Battle of the (1620)
    15
Wiener Neustadt 153
Wilna 185, 187
witch-hunt 184, 187
Wittenberg 35, 44, 53, 69
Worms, diet of (1521) 31
Wrocław 191
Württemberg 56
Wyclif, John 45

Zagreb (Zágráb/Agram) 154
Zamojski, Andrzej 192
Zápolyai, Isabella 68
Zápolyai, János Zsigmond 64, 65,
    66, 68, 69, 70, 80
Želivský, Jan 31
Žižka, Jan 31, 32
Zoba, Ioan 113, 115
Zorger, Gergely 147
Zurich 50
Zwickau 44
Zwilling, Gabriel 44
Zwingli, Huldrych 44, 50
Zwinglian 11